CAMPUS TO CAREER:

LANDSCAPE AND TRAJECTORY

A Frame Book for engineering Professionals

DR. DINESH NARAIN VYAS

Principal

&

SURAJ KUMAR GUPTA

Faculty

Mechanical Engineering Department

M. L. V. Textile & Engineering College

(A constituent college of Rajasthan Technical University, Kota)

Bhilwara (INDIA)

To

All those from whom we have learnt

and

to all who have learnt from us

Contents

Preface

In 2024, employability among Indian engineering graduates was about 64 percent, an increase from the 57 percent in 2023. The overall employability of the youth in the country was about 52.25 percent in 2024. There has been a significant jump in percentage employability of engineering graduate in 2024 from a consistent rate across last 10 years.

Transitioning from campus to career is a pivotal moment for engineering graduates, full of both opportunities and challenges. **"Campus to Career: Landscape and Trajectory"** is crafted to guide you through this journey, offering practical advice and insights to help you navigate your path from academic life to professional success for both fresh graduate and experienced professional.

This book begins with an **Introduction** to the engineering profession, outlining its scope, trends, and career possibilities. It then explores the **Academic Foundation**, emphasizing the importance of leveraging your education as a stepping stone into the professional world.

Essential Skills are critical for career success, and this section provides strategies to develop both technical and soft skills. Complementing this, **Extra-Curricular Activities and Experience** highlights how involvement in internships, clubs, and volunteer work can enhance your resume and practical experience.

For those considering further education, **Higher Education Opportunities** discusses the benefits of advanced degrees and certifications. **Entrepreneurship and Startups** explores how engineers can leverage their skills to innovate and start their own ventures.

Effective **Resume and Cover Letter Writing** is crucial for job applications, and this section offers tips for creating standout documents. **Interview Preparation** provides strategies for handling interviews confidently, while **Post Offer Considerations** helps you evaluate job offers thoroughly.

Long-term success is built on continuous development, covered in **Long-term Career Development**, which provides guidance on setting and achieving career goals. Finally, the chapter 'Real-Life Stories v/s Case Studies' provides a clear comparison between stories and case studies, highlighting their unique approaches and purposes.

This book aims to equip you with the tools and knowledge needed for a successful transition from campus to career, helping you achieve your professional aspirations with confidence.

– Dinesh Narain Vyas

– Suraj Kumar Gupta

December 2024

Acknowledgements

Writing **"Campus to Career: Landscape and Trajectory"** has been a challenging yet immensely rewarding journey, and we are deeply grateful for the support and contributions of many individuals who made this book possible.

First and foremost, we extend our heartfelt thanks to family and friends for their unwavering encouragement and patience throughout this endeavor. Their belief in our joint vision and their constant support provided us with the strength and motivation needed to complete this project.

We express our deep respect and gratitude to Prof. (Dr.) S. K. Singh, Hon'ble Vice-Chancellor of Rajasthan Technical University, Kota, for his unwavering support and encouragement, which inspired us to push boundaries and create this text for future generations.

We are profoundly grateful to the many professionals and experts who generously shared their insights, experiences, and advice. Your contributions enriched this book with practical knowledge and real-world perspectives that are invaluable to future engineers.

Special thanks go to our colleagues and mentors, whose guidance and constructive feedback helped shape the content and direction of this book. Your expertise and thoughtful critiques were instrumental in refining the material and ensuring its relevance.

We also want to acknowledge the editorial and publishing teams whose hard work and dedication brought this book to life. Your professionalism and commitment ensured that the final product met the highest standards of quality.

Finally, to the engineering students and early professionals who are the intended readers of this book, we hope that the insights and advice provided here will serve as a valuable resource in your journey from campus to career. Your enthusiasm and ambition inspire the work we do, and we are honored to contribute to your professional growth.

Thank you all for your support and encouragement.

– Dinesh Narain Vyas

– Suraj Kumar Gupta

CHAPTER 1

Introduction

Welcome to *Campus to Career: Landscape and Trajectory*. Whether you're stepping into your first engineering course or approaching graduation, this book is your essential companion for navigating the intricate and exciting world of engineering careers.

1.1 The Purpose of This Book

Engineering is a discipline characterized by innovation, problem-solving, and a relentless quest for improvement. As an engineering student, you are preparing to enter a field that not only demands technical expertise but also requires strategic career planning and personal development. This book is designed to equip you with the knowledge and tools to make informed decisions, seize opportunities, and overcome challenges as you shape your professional journey.

Our goal is to provide you with a comprehensive guide that covers all aspects of career development, from understanding the diverse fields within engineering to exploring advanced educational opportunities and entrepreneurial ventures. By offering practical advice, real-world insights, and actionable strategies, we aim to support you in making the most of your engineering education and achieving your career aspirations.

1.2 Why Career Guidance Matters?

There is misconception among graduating guys that career means job. While a job provides immediate employment, a career represents a long-term journey of growth, development, and fulfillment in one's chosen field. Career guidance helps individuals navigate this journey with purpose and direction, rather than just focusing on temporary job opportunities.

Engineering is a rapidly evolving field with new technologies and career opportunities emerging constantly. With such a dynamic landscape, having a clear career strategy is essential. Many students focus intensely on their technical coursework, but equally important are the skills and knowledge that will help you thrive in the job market and advance your career.

Career guidance plays a critical role in helping you:

- **Identify Your Interests and Strengths**: Understanding what excites you and aligns with your skills will help you choose the right career path.

- **Explore Various Career Paths**: Engineering offers a wide range of opportunities, from traditional roles in industry to cutting-edge fields and entrepreneurial ventures.

- **Prepare for the Job Market**: Effective resumes, compelling cover letters, and successful interview techniques are crucial for standing out in a competitive job market.

- **Navigate Career Challenges**: From evaluating job offers to managing long-term career growth, having a strategic approach can help you make informed decisions and adapt to changes.

- **Carve Your Trajectory**: Having chosen the appropriate starting point in engineering and technology it is you who can put in best to carve your own trajectory.

1.3 How to Use This Book?

This book is organized to guide you through the key stages of career development. Here's how to make the most of it:

- **Start with a Foundation**: Begin by understanding the different engineering disciplines and the skills required. This foundational knowledge will help you make informed choices about your career path.

- **Develop Essential Skills**: Learn about both technical and soft skills that are crucial for success in engineering. This section will help you build a strong professional profile.

- **Explore Extracurricular Opportunities**: Discover how internships, projects, and leadership roles can enhance your resume and provide valuable experience.

- **Consider Advanced Education**: If you're contemplating further studies, this book offers guidance on choosing programs, applying, and financing your education.

- **Understand Higher Education Opportunities**: If your intent is to master in the field of interest then you need to be aware of higher education opportunities available across the globe.

- **Delve into Entrepreneurship**: For those interested in starting their own ventures, this section provides insights into building a startup, from ideation to funding and growth.

- **Prepare for the Job Market**: Get practical advice on crafting resumes, writing cover letters, and preparing for interviews.

- **Long-Term Career Planning**: Learn strategies for career advancement, continuous learning, and maintaining work-life balance.

1.4 A Journey of Exploration and Growth

Your career journey will be unique, shaped by your interests, experiences, and aspirations. As you read through each chapter, think of it as an opportunity to explore your potential and refine your career strategy. This book is not just a guide but a resource to inspire you to pursue your goals with clarity and confidence.

Remember, the path to a successful engineering career is not always linear. It involves exploring different opportunities, adapting to changes, and continually learning and growing. By following the advice and strategies outlined in this book, you will be better equipped to navigate this journey and make the most of the exciting opportunities that lie ahead.

1.5 Science, Engineering and Technology

Understanding the distinctions among science, engineering, and technology is crucial for grasping their roles and interrelationships in advancing knowledge and improving society. Here's a breakdown of each:

1.5.1 Science

Science is the study of the natural world through observation, experimentation, and analysis. It aims to understand fundamental principles and uncover truths about the universe and its activities.

Key Characteristics

- **Objective**: To acquire knowledge about natural phenomena and develop theories that explain how things work.
- **Methodology**: Utilizes the scientific method, which involves observation, hypothesis formulation, experimentation, and analysis.

- **Focus**: Investigates the underlying principles and laws of nature. For example, physics studies the laws of motion, chemistry explores the properties of matter, and biology examines living organisms.

- **Outcome**: Produces theories, models, and scientific knowledge that contribute to a deeper understanding of the natural world.

Examples

- Discovering the laws of thermodynamics.

- Understanding the genetic code.

- Exploring the principles of quantum mechanics.

1.5.2 Engineering

Engineering is the systematic application of scientific principles to design, develop, and optimize solutions to practical problems. It involves creating systems, structures, or devices that fulfill specific needs and constraints.

Key Characteristics

- **Objective**: To solve practical problems by applying scientific knowledge to create functional and efficient systems or products that ease human life.

- **Methodology**: Employs engineering design processes, which include defining requirements, brainstorming solutions, designing, prototyping, testing, and refining.

- **Focus**: Concerned with applying scientific principles to develop practical solutions, such as building bridges, designing software, or creating medical devices.

- **Outcome**: Produces tangible solutions and innovations that meet specific needs and improve quality of life.

Examples

- Designing a bridge that can withstand environmental stresses.
- Developing a new type of medical imaging device.
- Creating a software application for data analysis.

1.5.3 Technology

Technology is the output of engineering. It refers to the tools, systems, and methods developed from scientific knowledge and engineering practices to solve problems and perform tasks. It encompasses the practical applications of science and engineering.

Key Characteristics

- **Objective**: To implement and utilize tools, devices, and systems developed through scientific and engineering efforts to address specific practical needs.
- **Methodology**: Focuses on the development and application of tools, techniques, and systems that enhance human capabilities and efficiency.
- **Focus**: Practical application of scientific and engineering knowledge to create products, systems, and processes that improve daily life and solve real-world problems.
- **Outcome**: Results in devices, systems, and processes used in various domains, including communication, transportation, and industry.

Examples

- Smart phones and their operating systems.
- Renewable energy systems like solar panels.
- Automated manufacturing systems.

Interrelationships

- **Science** provides the foundational knowledge and understanding of natural phenomena.

- **Engineering** uses this scientific knowledge to design and build solutions that address specific problems of human society.

- **Technology** represents the practical implementation of engineering solutions, creating tools and systems that are used in everyday life.

In essence:

- **Science** seeks to understand "what" and "why" things happen.

- **Engineering** focuses on "how" to use that understanding to solve problems and create solutions.

- **Technology** involves the "application" of those solutions to improve human activities and resolve practical challenges.

These fields are interconnected, with science informing engineering practices and technology utilizing both scientific discoveries and engineering innovations to advance society.

Frequently Asked Questions

Here are some frequently asked questions (FAQs) for a career in engineering:

1. **What qualifications do I need to become an engineer?**
   - Typically, a bachelor's degree in engineering from a recognized and accredited institution is required. Some fields may require additional certifications or advanced degrees.

2. **What skills are essential for an engineering career?**
   - Key skills include problem-solving, analytical thinking, technical proficiency, teamwork, communication, and project management.

3. **What types of engineering specialties are available?**

   - Engineering fields include civil, mechanical, electrical, chemical, aerospace, computer, and environmental engineering, among others.

4. **How can I gain practical experience while in school?**

   - Participate in internships, co-op programs, engineering projects, and relevant extracurricular activities.

5. **What is the importance of certification in engineering?**

   - Certifications, such as the Professional Engineer (PE) license, can enhance career prospects, demonstrate expertise, and are often required for certain roles.

6. **How can I advance my career in engineering?**

   - Pursue further education, gain specialized skills, take on leadership roles, and seek out challenging projects and responsibilities.

7. **What are common career paths for engineers?**

   - Engineers can work in various roles, including design, project management, research and development, consulting, and teaching.

8. **How do I stay current with technological advancements in my field?**

   - Engage in continuous learning through professional development courses, industry conferences, and relevant publications.

9. **What should I include in my engineering resume?**

   - Highlight relevant education, skills, work experience, projects, and any certifications or achievements.

10. **How important is networking in an engineering career?**

    - Networking is crucial for career development, providing opportunities for mentorship, job leads, and collaboration on projects.

11. **Can I go for civil services?**

    - All the doors are open for an engineer. Not only Civil Services but also Management, Law, Commerce, Arts, CA/CS etc.

Welcome to the start of your career exploration. We are excited to accompany you on this journey and look forward to helping you achieve your professional goals. Let's get started!

CHAPTER 2

Understanding Engineering Profession

Understanding the engineering and technology profession requires delving into both the breadth and depth of the field, recognizing its critical impact on modern society, and appreciating the diverse career opportunities it offers. Engineering is not a monolithic field but rather a wide spectrum of disciplines, each with distinct areas of expertise. For instance, civil engineers design and oversee infrastructure projects such as bridges and roads, while mechanical engineers focus on developing machinery and mechanical systems. Electrical engineers work with electrical systems and circuits, and computer engineers develop software and hardware technologies that drive the digital age.

Beyond the core disciplines, engineering encompasses emerging fields like robotics, artificial intelligence, and bioengineering, each addressing contemporary challenges with innovative solutions. Understanding these specializations helps students identify their areas of interest and how they can contribute to advancements in technology and society. Furthermore, the engineering profession is characterized by its problem-solving nature and emphasis on applying scientific principles to create practical solutions. Engineers are tasked with not only solving technical problems but also considering factors such as cost, safety, and environmental impact.

Moreover, the role of engineers extends beyond technical tasks to include collaboration with multidisciplinary teams, engaging in project management, and communicating complex ideas effectively. This holistic view of engineering highlights the importance of both technical skills and soft skills such as teamwork, leadership, and communication. By gaining a thorough understanding of the engineering profession, students can make informed decisions about their career paths, pursue relevant experiences, and prepare themselves for a rewarding and impactful career in engineering.

2.1 Overview of Engineering Disciplines

Engineering is a diverse and dynamic field that spans numerous disciplines, each with its own unique focus and applications. Here's an overview of the primary engineering disciplines, providing insight into their core functions, areas of specialization, and the roles they play in shaping our world.

Engineering and technology disciplines can be classified into various categories based on their focus areas, applications, and underlying principles. Here is a comprehensive classification that covers a broad range of engineering and technology fields:

2.1.1 Core Engineering Disciplines

- **Aerospace Engineering**
  - *Focus:* Aircraft and spacecraft design, aerodynamics, propulsion.
  - *Specializations:* Aeronautical Engineering, Astronautical Engineering.

- *Overview:* Aerospace engineering is concerned with the design, development, and testing of aircraft and spacecraft. This discipline combines elements of mechanical and electrical engineering to address challenges related to aerodynamics, propulsion, and avionics. Aerospace engineers work on developing innovative solutions for air and space travel, including satellites, rockets, and unmanned aerial vehicles. Specializations include aerodynamics, propulsion systems, and space exploration.

- **Biochemical Engineering**

  - *Focus:* Chemical processes involving biological organisms.

  - *Specializations:* Bioprocess Engineering, Genetic Engineering.

  - *Overview:* **Biochemical Engineering** is a multidisciplinary field that merges principles from chemical engineering with biological sciences to develop and optimize processes that involve biological organisms or their components. This discipline plays a crucial role in various industries, including pharmaceuticals, biotechnology, food and beverage production, and environmental management.

- **Chemical Engineering**

  - *Focus:* Chemical processes, material production.

  - *Specializations:* Process Engineering, Petrochemical Engineering.

  - *Overview:* Chemical engineering combines principles of chemistry, physics, and mathematics to develop processes for converting raw materials into valuable products. Chemical engineers work in industries such as pharmaceuticals, petrochemicals, and food processing. They design and optimize chemical reactors, separation processes, and production systems to ensure efficiency, safety, and environmental sustainability. Specializations include process engineering, materials science, and biotechnological applications.

- **Civil Engineering**
  - *Focus*: Infrastructure design and construction.
  - *Specializations*: Structural Engineering, Geotechnical Engineering, Environmental Engineering.
  - *Overview*: Civil engineering is one of the oldest and broadest branches of engineering, focused on designing, constructing, and maintaining infrastructure projects. This discipline covers a wide range of structures, including bridges, roads, dams, and buildings. Civil engineers work on improving public safety, enhancing transportation networks, and developing sustainable infrastructure solutions. Specializations within civil engineering include structural engineering, environmental engineering, and geotechnical engineering.

- **Computer Engineering**
  - *Focus*: Computer hardware and software systems.
  - *Specializations*: Embedded Systems, VLSI Design, Computer Architecture.
  - *Overview*: Computer engineering integrates electrical engineering and computer science to design and develop computer systems and hardware. This discipline focuses on creating efficient and reliable computer hardware, including processors, memory systems, and embedded systems. Computer engineers also work on developing new technologies in areas like artificial intelligence, cyber security, and software-hardware integration. Specializations include software engineering, hardware design, and network systems.

- **Electrical Engineering**
  - *Focus*: Electrical systems, electronics, and electromagnetics.
  - *Specializations*: Power Systems, Control Systems, Electronics.

- *Overview:* Electrical engineering focuses on the study and application of electrical systems and electronics. This discipline covers a wide range of technologies, including power generation and distribution, circuit design, and telecommunications. Electrical engineers work on developing electrical systems for various applications, from household appliances to complex communication networks. Specializations within this field include power systems, control systems, and electronics.

- **Mechanical Engineering**

  - *Focus:* Mechanical systems and thermodynamics.

  - *Specializations:* Robotics, Automotive Engineering, Thermal Systems.

  - *Overview:* Mechanical engineering deals with the design, analysis, and manufacturing of mechanical systems and devices. It encompasses everything from machinery and engines to thermal systems and robotics. Mechanical engineers apply principles of mechanics, thermodynamics, and materials science to develop and improve mechanical systems. Specializations include aerospace engineering, automotive engineering, and robotics.

- **Materials Science and Engineering**

  - *Focus:* Properties and applications of materials.

  - *Specializations:* Nanotechnology, Ceramics, Metallurgy.

  - *Overview:* **Materials Science & Engineering** is a multidisciplinary field that studies the properties, processing, and applications of materials. It combines principles from physics, chemistry, and engineering to understand and manipulate materials to meet specific needs and solve practical problems. This field is central to advancing technology and innovation in various industries, including aerospace, automotive, electronics, and biotechnology.

- **Industrial Engineering**

  - *Focus*: Optimization of complex systems and processes.

  - *Specializations*: Operations Research, Systems Engineering, Ergonomics.

  - *Overview*: Industrial engineering is centered on optimizing complex systems and processes to improve efficiency, productivity, and quality. Industrial engineers analyze and design workflows, supply chains, and manufacturing processes to enhance performance and reduce waste. They work in various sectors, including manufacturing, logistics, and healthcare. Specializations within industrial engineering include operations research, systems engineering, and ergonomics.

2.1.2 Emerging and Specialized Engineering Disciplines

- **Biomedical Engineering**

  - *Focus*: Medical devices and healthcare technologies.

  - *Specializations*: Medical Imaging, Tissue Engineering, Biomechanics.

  - *Overview*: Biomedical engineering combines engineering principles with medical and biological sciences to develop technologies for healthcare applications. This discipline focuses on creating medical devices, imaging systems, and prosthetics to improve patient care and health outcomes. Biomedical engineers work closely with healthcare professionals to design and implement solutions for medical diagnostics, treatment, and rehabilitation. Specializations include medical device design, tissue engineering, and biomechanics.

- **Environmental Engineering**

  - *Focus*: Environmental protection and resource management.

  - *Specializations*: Water Resources, Air Quality Management, Waste Management.

  - *Overview*: Environmental engineering focuses on developing technologies and solutions to protect and improve the environment. This discipline addresses issues such as water and air quality, waste management, and sustainable practices. Environmental engineers work on designing systems for pollution control, recycling, and resource conservation. Specializations include water resources engineering, air quality management, and environmental health.

- **Food Technology**

  - *Focus*: Food processing, safety, and production.

  - *Specializations*: Food Processing Engineering, Nutritional Technology.

  - *Overview*: Food technology is a specialized field that combines principles of engineering, biology, and chemistry to improve food production, processing, and safety. This discipline focuses on the development and optimization of food products and processes, ensuring that food is nutritious, safe, and of high quality. Food technologists work on a range of activities, including designing and operating food processing systems, developing new food products, and implementing quality control measures. They also address challenges related to food preservation, packaging, and sustainability. Specializations within food technology include food processing, product development, and food safety management.

- **Petroleum Engineering**
  - *Focus*: Oil and gas extraction and production.
  - *Specializations*: Reservoir Engineering, Drilling Engineering, Production Technology.
  - *Overview*: Petroleum engineering focuses on the exploration, extraction, and production of oil and natural gas resources. This discipline involves working with technologies and techniques to locate and efficiently extract hydrocarbons from subsurface reservoirs. Petroleum engineers design and implement drilling and production methods while addressing challenges related to reservoir management and environmental impact. Specializations include reservoir engineering, drilling engineering, and production technology.

- **Textile Technology**
  - *Focus*: Textile production and manufacturing.
  - *Specializations*: Fiber Production, Yarn Manufacturing, Fabric Manufacturing, Garment Technology.
  - *Overview*: Textile technology focuses on the design, development, and manufacturing of textile products, including fibers, yarn, fabrics, and garments. This discipline covers various aspects of textile production, from spinning and weaving to finishing and quality control. Textile technologists work on improving textile production processes, developing new materials, and ensuring product quality. Specializations within this field include fiber production, yarn manufacturing, fabric manufacturing, garment technology, and technical textile product development.

- **Ceramic Engineering**
  - *Focus*: Development and processing of ceramic materials.
  - *Specializations*: Advanced Ceramics, Glass Technology.

- *Overview:* Ceramic engineering focuses on the development and processing of ceramic materials, which are used in a wide range of applications from construction to electronics. This discipline involves working with materials such as clay, glass, and advanced ceramics to create products with specific properties like durability, heat resistance, and electrical conductivity. Ceramic engineers are involved in designing and manufacturing materials for industries including electronics, aerospace, and construction. Specializations include advanced ceramics, glass technology, and traditional ceramics.

- **Automobile Engineering**

  - *Focus:* Design and development of vehicles.

  - *Specializations:* Automotive Systems, Vehicle Dynamics, Electric Vehicles, Non-conventional fuel vehicles.

  - *Overview:* Automobile engineering focuses on the design, development, and manufacturing of vehicles and their components. This discipline involves working on various aspects of automotive systems, including engines, transmission systems, and vehicle dynamics. Automobile engineers strive to improve vehicle performance, safety, and fuel efficiency while incorporating emerging technologies like electric, hydrogen and autonomous vehicles. Specializations within this field include automotive design, vehicle engineering, and automotive electronics.

- **Instrumentation Engineering**

  - *Focus:* Measurement and control systems.

  - *Specializations:* Process Control, Sensors, Automation.

  - *Overview:* Instrumentation engineering focuses on the design, development, and maintenance of instruments and control systems used for measuring and controlling physical variables like temperature, pressure, and flow. This discipline is crucial in industries such as manufacturing, aerospace, and process control, where precise measurement and control are essential. Instrumentation engineers work on developing sensors, controllers, and data acquisition systems. Specializations include process instrumentation, control systems engineering, and automation.

2.1.3 Information and Communication Technologies

- **Information Technology (IT)**

  - *Focus:* Computing systems, data management, and information processing.

  - *Specializations:* Software Development, Network Management, Cyber Security.

  - *Overview:* Information technology (IT) encompasses the use and management of computer systems and software to handle and process information. This discipline covers a broad range of technologies and practices related to computing, including software development, network management, database systems, and cyber security. IT professionals work on designing, implementing, and maintaining systems that manage and secure information for organizations and individuals. The field of IT is critical in various sectors, including business, healthcare, and education, where effective information management is essential. Specializations within IT include software engineering, network administration, and data analysis.

- **Electronics & Communication Engineering**

  - *Focus:* Electronic systems and communication networks.

- *Specializations*: Telecommunications, Signal Processing, Embedded Systems.

- *Overview*: Electronics & communication engineering deal with the design, development, and application of electronic devices and communication systems. This discipline encompasses a wide range of technologies, including signal processing, telecommunications, and electronic circuit design. Engineers in this field work on developing and improving devices such as smart phones, satellite systems, and communication networks. Specializations include wireless communication, embedded systems, and digital signal processing.

- **Computer Science**

  - *Focus*: Theoretical and practical aspects of computing.

  - *Specializations*: Algorithms, Artificial Intelligence, Data Science.

  - *Overview*: **Computer Science** is the study of algorithms, data structures, programming languages, and the theoretical foundations of computing. It encompasses both the theoretical aspects of computation and the practical aspects of designing and implementing software and hardware systems. Computer science plays a crucial role in virtually every aspect of modern life, from basic utilities to complex systems that drive advancements in technology and industry.

2.1.4 Applied Technology Disciplines

- **Agricultural Engineering**

  - *Focus*: Machinery and systems for agriculture.

  - *Specializations*: Farm Equipment Design, Soil and Water Engineering.

- *Overview.* Agricultural engineering combines principles of engineering with agricultural sciences to enhance the efficiency and sustainability of farming practices. This discipline focuses on designing and improving machinery, equipment, and systems for agricultural production. Agricultural engineers work on developing technologies for irrigation, soil management, crop harvesting, and livestock management. They also address challenges related to environmental impact and resource management. Specializations include farm machinery design, irrigation systems, and bio-energy.

- **Biotechnology**

  - *Focus.* Application of biological processes in various industries.

  - *Specializations.* Industrial Biotechnology, Bioinformatics.

  - *Overview.* Biotechnology merges biological sciences with engineering principles to develop technologies and products that improve health, agriculture, and industry. This interdisciplinary field involves the use of living organisms or their systems to create innovative solutions, such as pharmaceuticals, bio-fuels, and agricultural products. Biotechnologists work on genetic engineering, cell culture, and bio-processing to address issues in healthcare, environmental management, and food production. Specializations include genetic engineering, bioinformatics, and industrial biotechnology.

- **Metallurgical Engineering**

  - *Focus.* Metals and alloys processing.

  - *Specializations.* Extractive Metallurgy, Physical Metallurgy.

  - *Overview.* Metallurgical engineering involves the study and application of metals and alloys to develop materials with specific properties for various applications. This discipline covers the extraction of metals from ores, their processing, and the development of metal products. Metallurgical engineers work on improving the strength, durability, and performance of metal components used in industries like aerospace, automotive, and construction. Specializations include extractive metallurgy, materials processing, and physical metallurgy.

- **Textile Chemistry**
  - *Focus*: Chemical finishing processes in textile production.
  - *Specializations*: Dyeing Technology, Textile Coatings.
  - *Overview*: Textile chemistry combines principles of chemistry with textile science to develop and improve textile materials and processes. This discipline involves working on the chemical processes used in dyeing, finishing, and treating textiles to achieve desired properties such as color fastness, durability, and functionality. Textile chemists work on developing new materials, enhancing existing products, and ensuring quality in textile production. Specializations include dyeing technology, textile coatings, and fiber chemistry.

2.1.5 Interdisciplinary and Emerging Fields

- **Robotics Engineering**
  - *Focus*: Design and development of robotic systems.
  - *Specializations*: Autonomous Systems, Human-Robot Interaction.
  - *Overview*: **Robotic Engineering** focuses on the design, construction, operation, and application of robots. This interdisciplinary field integrates principles from mechanical engineering, electrical engineering, and computer science to

create robots and automated systems that can perform tasks autonomously or semi-autonomously.

- **Renewable Energy Engineering**
  - *Focus:* Sustainable energy solutions.
  - *Specializations:* Solar Energy, Wind Energy, Bio-energy.
  - *Overview:* **Renewable Energy Engineering** is dedicated to the development, implementation, and optimization of technologies that generate energy from renewable sources. This field aims to provide sustainable and environmentally friendly energy solutions to meet global energy demands.

- **Smart Systems Engineering**
  - *Focus:* Integration of smart technologies into systems.
  - *Specializations:* IoT (Internet of Things), Smart Grid Systems.
  - *Overview:* **Smart Systems Engineering** focuses on creating advanced systems that integrate sensors, data processing, and automation to enhance functionality and intelligence. This field combines elements of systems engineering, computer science, and electronics to develop systems that can adapt to changing conditions and make intelligent decisions.

Each of these engineering disciplines offers unique challenges and opportunities, contributing to advancements in technology, industry, and society. By understanding these fields, students can better align their interests and skills with their career aspirations and explore a wide range of possibilities within the engineering profession.

2.2 Role of Engineers in Society

Engineers play a crucial role in shaping modern society by solving complex problems, improving quality of life, and driving technological and economic advancements. Their contributions are diverse and impactful, spanning across various sectors and influencing almost every aspect of daily life. Here's an overview of the significant roles engineers play in society:

2.2.1 Solving Complex Problems

- **Innovative Solutions**: Engineers tackle intricate problems by developing creative and practical solutions. From designing bridges and skyscrapers to creating advanced medical devices and software, they address challenges that require a deep understanding of science and technology.

- **Optimization and Efficiency**: Engineers improve processes and systems to enhance efficiency, reduce waste, and lower costs. For example, industrial engineers optimize manufacturing processes, while software engineers streamline code to improve application performance.

2.2.2 Enhancing Quality of Life

- **Infrastructure Development**: Civil engineers design and construct essential infrastructure, such as roads, bridges, and water supply systems, which are fundamental to modern living and economic development.

- **Healthcare Innovations**: Biomedical engineers develop medical technologies, such as diagnostic imaging systems and prosthetic limbs, which improve patient care and enhance the quality of life for individuals with health challenges.

- **Environmental Protection**: Environmental engineers work on projects that address pollution control, waste management, and sustainable practices, contributing to a healthier and more sustainable environment.

2.2.3 Driving Technological Advancement

- **Research and Development**: Engineers are at the forefront of technological innovation, conducting research and developing new technologies that drive progress in various fields, including information technology, aerospace, and renewable energy.

- **Product Development**: Engineers design and develop new products, from consumer electronics to advanced machinery. Their work leads to the creation of innovative solutions that meet the evolving needs of society.

2.2.4 Supporting Economic Growth

- **Industry and Manufacturing**: Engineers play a critical role in industrial and manufacturing sectors by designing production systems, improving product quality, and increasing efficiency. Their work supports economic growth and job creation.

- **Entrepreneurship and Startups**: Many engineers contribute to the economy by starting their own businesses or working in startups, driving innovation and creating new markets.

2.2.5 Ensuring Safety and Security

- **Structural Integrity**: Engineers ensure the safety and reliability of structures and systems, including buildings, bridges, and transportation networks. They use rigorous standards and testing to prevent failures and ensure public safety.

- **Cyber Security**: Engineers specializing in cyber security protect sensitive data and systems from cyber threats, ensuring the security and integrity of digital information and infrastructure.

2.2.6 Addressing Global Challenges

- **Sustainable Development**: Engineers work on projects that promote sustainability, such as developing renewable energy sources, improving energy efficiency, and addressing climate change. Their efforts contribute to a more sustainable future for the planet.

- **Disaster Relief and Recovery**: Engineers are involved in disaster response and recovery efforts, designing solutions for rebuilding infrastructure and providing essential services after natural or man-made disasters.

2.2.7 Enhancing Education and Knowledge

- **Education and Mentorship**: Engineers contribute to education by teaching and mentoring the next generation of engineers, sharing their expertise, and inspiring students to pursue careers in engineering.

- **Public Awareness**: Engineers help raise public awareness about technological issues, safety concerns, and the benefits of engineering innovations, fostering a better understanding of their work and its impact.

2.2.8 Improving Daily Life

- **Consumer Products**: Engineers design and improve everyday consumer products, such as smart phones, appliances, and transportation vehicles, making daily tasks easier and more convenient.

- **Urban Development**: Engineers contribute to urban planning and development, creating smart cities with advanced infrastructure, transportation systems, and amenities that enhance the quality of urban living.

Conclusion

Engineers are vital to societal progress, playing multifaceted roles that extend beyond technical expertise. Their work impacts various aspects of life, from infrastructure development and healthcare to technology and environmental sustainability. By solving problems, driving innovation, and ensuring safety, engineers contribute significantly to enhancing quality of life, supporting economic growth, and addressing global challenges. Their contributions shape the present and future of society, demonstrating the profound and far-reaching influence of engineering on the world.

CHAPTER 3

Academic Foundation

The academic foundation of engineering education is crucial as it establishes the bedrock upon which future professional skills and expertise are built. It encompasses a broad range of fundamental subjects that are essential for understanding complex engineering concepts and applications. This foundation typically includes core courses in mathematics, physics, and chemistry, which provide the quantitative and analytical skills necessary for problem-solving. Additionally, foundational courses in engineering mechanics, thermodynamics, and circuit theory introduce students to the principles of various engineering disciplines.

A strong academic foundation not only ensures that students have a deep comprehension of theoretical concepts but also equips them with critical thinking and analytical abilities. These foundational skills are vital for tackling advanced topics, engaging in research, and applying engineering principles in real-world scenarios. Thus, a solid academic base is indispensable for any aspiring engineer, as it fosters the intellectual rigor and technical proficiency needed to excel in the profession and adapt to evolving technological advancements.

3.1 Choosing the Right Engineering Discipline

Selecting the right engineering discipline is a pivotal decision that can significantly influence a person's career trajectory and overall job satisfaction. The process involves a careful evaluation of personal interests, strengths, and long-term goals, as well as understanding the unique aspects and opportunities within different engineering fields. Here are key factors to consider when choosing the right engineering discipline:

3.1.1 Personal Interests and Passion

- **Self-Assessment**: Reflect on what subjects or activities you enjoy the most. Do you have a keen interest in designing structures, developing software, or working with environmental issues? Aligning your career with your interests can lead to greater motivation and fulfillment.

- **Exploration**: Engage in internships, projects, or extracurricular activities related to various engineering fields. This hands-on experience can provide valuable insights into what a specific discipline entails and help clarify your preferences.

3.1.2 Strengths and Skills

- **Academic Strengths**: Evaluate your strengths in core subjects such as mathematics, physics, and computer science. Different engineering disciplines require varying levels of expertise in these areas. For example, Aerospace Engineering demands a strong grasp of physics and mathematics, while Software Engineering relies heavily on programming skills.

- **Technical Skills**: Consider the technical skills you excel in. Are you better at analytical problem-solving, creative design, or practical application? Choose a discipline that leverages your strongest skills.

3.1.3 Career Goals and Opportunities

- **Job Market**: Research the job market for different engineering disciplines. Some fields may offer more job opportunities, higher salaries, or growth prospects than others. Understanding industry trends and demand can help you make an informed decision.

- **Professional Goals**: Reflect on your long-term career goals. Do you aspire to work in research and development, management, or entrepreneurship? Different disciplines offer various career paths, such as working on cutting-edge technologies in Biomedical Engineering or leading large projects in Civil Engineering.

3.1.4 Educational Requirements

- **Curriculum**: Review the curriculum for different engineering programs. Assess whether the coursework aligns with your interests and strengths. Some disciplines may have a heavier focus on theoretical concepts, while others may emphasize practical applications and hands-on projects.

- **Specializations**: Consider the availability of specializations within the discipline. Many engineering fields allow for further specialization in areas such as robotics, renewable energy, or structural engineering, which can align with your specific interests.

3.1.5 Industry and Work Environment

- **Work Settings**: Different engineering disciplines often have unique work environments. For example, Mechanical Engineers may work in manufacturing plants or research labs, while Environmental Engineers might work in field-based roles or consulting firms. Consider where you see yourself thriving and contributing effectively.

- **Impact and Contribution**: Think about the kind of impact you want to make through your work. Some fields focus on solving global challenges, such as climate change in Environmental Engineering, while others may concentrate on technological advancements and innovations.

3.1.6 Advice and Guidance

- **Mentorship**: Seek advice from mentors, professors, or professionals in the engineering fields you are considering. Their experiences and insights can provide a realistic view of what to expect and help guide your decision.

- **Networking**: Connect with professionals and alumni from various engineering disciplines. Attend industry events and career fairs to learn more about different fields and network with individuals who can share their experiences.

Conclusion

Choosing the right engineering discipline is a decision that requires careful consideration of your interests, strengths, career goals, and the opportunities within each field. By evaluating these factors and seeking guidance, you can make an informed choice that aligns with your passions and aspirations, ultimately leading to a rewarding and fulfilling career in engineering.

3.2 Dos and Don'ts While Choosing the Right Engineering Discipline

Choosing the right engineering discipline is a significant decision that can shape your career and future opportunities. Here are some essential dos and don'ts to guide you through the process:

Dos

1. **Do Self-Reflect on Your Interests and Strengths**

   - **Identify Passions**: Reflect on subjects and activities that genuinely excite you. For instance, if you have a passion for renewable energy and environmental sustainability, consider disciplines like Environmental Engineering or Renewable Energy Engineering.

   - **Assess Skills**: Evaluate your strengths in core subjects such as mathematics, physics, or computer science. Choose a discipline that aligns with your natural abilities and academic strengths.

2. **Do Research Different Engineering Disciplines**

   - **Explore Fields**: Investigate various engineering disciplines to understand their core principles, typical job roles, and industry applications. Read about what professionals in those fields do on a day-to-day basis.

   - **Check Industry Trends**: Stay updated on emerging trends and future demands in different engineering sectors. This can help you choose a field with strong growth potential and job stability.

3. **Do Seek Advice from Professionals and Mentors**

   - **Talk to Experts**: Reach out to professionals and academics in engineering disciplines of interest. Their insights can provide valuable perspectives on career prospects and work environments.

   - **Get Mentorship**: Find mentors or advisors who can guide you based on their experiences and help you navigate your decision-making process.

4. **Do Consider Long-Term Career Goals**

   - **Define Objectives:** Clarify your long-term career goals, such as whether you aspire to work in research, management, or entrepreneurship. Choose a discipline that aligns with these aspirations.

   - **Explore Specializations:** Investigate potential specializations within disciplines that could align with your interests and career goals.

5. **Do Gain Practical Experience**

   - **Internships and Projects:** Engage in internships, co-op programs, or personal projects related to different engineering fields. This hands-on experience can help you understand the practical aspects of each discipline.

   - **Participate in Extra-curricular Activities:** Join engineering clubs or societies to explore various fields and network with peers who share similar interests.

Don'ts

1. **Don't Choose Based on Trends Alone**

   - **Avoid Fads:** Don't select a discipline solely based on current trends or high salaries without considering your personal interests and strengths. Trends can change, and job satisfaction often depends on aligning your passion with your career.

2. **Don't Rush the Decision**

   - **Take Your Time:** Avoid making a hasty decision. Take the time to research, reflect, and explore different options before committing to a particular discipline.

   - **Don't Succumb to Pressure:** Resist external pressures from family, friends, or societal expectations. Choose a discipline based on what suits you best, not what others expect.

3. **Don't Overlook the Curriculum**

   - **Review Courses**: Don't ignore the specifics of the curriculum for each discipline. Ensure that the courses and content align with your interests and career goals.

   - **Assess Workload**: Be aware of the academic rigor and workload associated with each discipline to ensure you can handle the demands.

4. **Don't Ignore Your Work Environment Preferences**

   - **Consider Work Settings**: Don't disregard the type of work environment you prefer. Some disciplines may require fieldwork, while others may be office-based or lab-oriented.

   - **Think About Impact**: Consider the kind of impact you want to make through your work. Choose a field that aligns with your values and desired contributions to society.

5. **Don't Neglect Future Learning and Growth**

   - **Plan for Continuing Education**: Don't assume your learning ends with your degree. Consider how each discipline supports continuing education and professional development opportunities.

   - **Adaptability**: Choose a field that allows for growth and adaptation, as technology and industry needs evolve over time.

3.3 Core Engineering Subjects and Skills

In engineering education, a set of core subjects and skills forms the foundation upon which advanced concepts and specialized knowledge are built. These core areas are crucial for developing a comprehensive understanding of engineering principles and practices. Here's an overview of these essential subjects and skills:

3.3.1 Core Engineering Subjects

1. **Mathematics**

   - **Calculus**: Fundamental for understanding changes, motion, and various engineering processes. Topics include differentiation, integration, and differential equations.

   - **Linear Algebra**: Essential for dealing with vectors, matrices, and linear systems, which are widely used in various engineering applications such as computer graphics and control systems.

   - **Probability and Statistics**: Important for data analysis, quality control, and risk assessment. Engineers use statistical methods to analyze data and make informed decisions.

2. **Physics**

   - **Mechanics**: Covers the principles of forces, motion, and energy. Topics include dynamics, statics, and fluid mechanics, which are fundamental to understanding how forces affect physical systems.

   - **Electromagnetism**: Focuses on electric and magnetic fields, and their interactions. This knowledge is crucial for electrical and electronics engineering.

   - **Thermodynamics**: Deals with heat, work, and energy transfer. Understanding thermodynamic principles is vital for fields such as mechanical and chemical engineering.

3. **Chemistry**

   - **General Chemistry**: Provides foundational knowledge about chemical reactions, bonding, and properties of materials. This is essential for disciplines like chemical and materials engineering.

   - **Organic and Inorganic Chemistry**: Focuses on the chemistry of organic compounds and inorganic substances, respectively, which are important for understanding material properties and processes.

4. **Engineering Mechanics**

   - **Statics**: Study of forces in equilibrium, critical for designing stable structures and systems.

   - **Dynamics**: Analyzes forces and motion in systems, which is important for understanding mechanical systems and vehicle dynamics.

5. **Electrical Circuits**

   - **Circuit Theory**: Involves the analysis and design of electrical circuits. Topics include Ohm's Law, Kirchhoff's Laws, and circuit components.

   - **Electronics**: Focuses on semiconductor devices, analog and digital circuits, and signal processing.

6. **Thermodynamics and Fluid Mechanics**

   - **Thermodynamics**: Study of energy transformations and heat transfer. Key concepts include the laws of thermodynamics and cycle analysis.

   - **Fluid Mechanics**: Involves the study of fluid behavior and its interaction with solid boundaries, crucial for designing systems involving fluids, such as pipelines and airfoils.

7. **Materials Science**

   - **Properties of Materials**: Understanding the mechanical, thermal, and electrical properties of materials. This is crucial for selecting appropriate materials for engineering applications.

   - **Material Testing and Failure Analysis**: Techniques for testing material properties and analyzing failure modes to ensure reliability and safety.

8. **Control Systems**

   - **Systems Dynamics**: Study of system behavior and feedback control. Topics include stability, control theory, and system modeling.

   - **Automation and Control**: Focuses on the design and implementation of control systems for automated processes.

9. **Computer Programming and Software Engineering**

   - **Programming Fundamentals**: Knowledge of programming languages (e.g., Python, C++) and software development principles. This is essential for simulation, modeling, and automation tasks.

   - **Software Development**: Involves understanding algorithms, data structures, and software design principles.

3.3.2 Core Engineering Skills

1. **Analytical Thinking**

   - **Problem Solving**: Ability to analyze complex problems, identify root causes, and develop effective solutions.

   - **Critical Thinking**: Assessing situations logically and making decisions based on sound reasoning and evidence.

2. **Technical Proficiency**

   - **Mathematical Modeling**: Using mathematical techniques to model real-world systems and predict their behavior.

   - **Engineering Design**: Applying principles to design and optimize systems, components, or processes.

3. **Practical Skills**

   - **Lab Work**: Hands-on experience with laboratory equipment and experimental techniques for testing and analysis.

- **Prototyping and Testing**: Developing prototypes and conducting tests to validate design concepts and ensure functionality.

4. **Communication**

   - **Technical Writing**: Ability to document and communicate technical information clearly and effectively through reports, papers, and documentation.

   - **Presentation Skills**: Presenting technical concepts and project results to diverse audiences, including peers, stakeholders, and non-experts.

5. **Project Management**

   - **Planning and Organization**: Skills in managing projects, including budgeting, scheduling, and resource allocation.

   - **Team Collaboration**: Working effectively with interdisciplinary teams to achieve project goals and address challenges.

6. **Ethical and Professional Responsibility**

   - **Ethical Decision Making**: Understanding and applying ethical principles in engineering practice, ensuring public safety and environmental stewardship.

   - **Professionalism**: Adhering to industry standards, codes of conduct, and continuing professional development.

7. **Adaptability and Lifelong Learning**

   - **Staying Updated**: Keeping up with technological advancements and industry trends to remain relevant and effective in the field.

   - **Learning New Skills**: Continuously developing new skills and knowledge to address emerging challenges and opportunities in engineering.

3.3.3 *Program Outcomes (POs)*

POs are statements that describe what students are expected to know and be able to do upon graduating from the program. These relate to the skills, knowledge, analytical ability attitude and behavior that students acquire through the program. The POs essentially indicate what the students can do from subject-wise knowledge acquired by them during the program. As such, POs define the professional profile of an engineering graduate. Here're celebrated program outcomes defined by the National Board of Accreditation:

i.   **Engineering Knowledge:** Apply the knowledge of mathematics, science, engineering fundamentals, and an engineering specialization to the solution of complex engineering problems.

ii. **Problem Analysis:** Identify, formulate, review research literature, and analyze complex engineering problems reaching substantiated conclusions using first principles of mathematics, natural sciences and engineering sciences.

iii. **Design/Development of Solutions:** Design solutions for complex engineering problems and design system components or processes that meet the specified needs with appropriate consideration for the public health and safety, and the cultural, societal, and environmental considerations.

iv. **Conduct Investigations of Complex Problems:** Use research-based knowledge and research methods including design of experiments, analysis and interpretation of data, and synthesis of the information to provide valid conclusions for complex problems:

v.   **Modern Tool Usage:** Create, select, and apply appropriate techniques, resources, and modern engineering and IT tools including prediction and modeling to complex engineering activities with an understanding of the limitations.

vi. **The Engineer and Society:** Apply reasoning informed by the contextual knowledge to assess societal, health, safety, legal and cultural issues and the consequent responsibilities relevant to the professional engineering practice.

vii. **Environment and Sustainability:** Understand the impact of the professional engineering solutions in societal and environmental contexts, and demonstrate the knowledge of, and need for sustainable development.

viii.**Ethics:** Apply ethical principles and commit to professional ethics and responsibilities and norms of the engineering practice.

ix. **Individual and Team Work:** Function effectively as an individual, and as a member or leader in diverse teams, and in multidisciplinary settings.

x. **Communication:** Communicate effectively on complex engineering activities with the engineering community and with society at large, such as, being able to comprehend and write effective reports and design documentation, make effective presentations, and give and receive clear instructions.

xi. **Project Management and Finance:** Demonstrate knowledge and understanding of the engineering and management principles and apply these to one's own work, as a member and leader in a team, to manage projects and in multidisciplinary environments.

xii. **Life-long Learning:** Recognize the need for, and have the preparation and ability to engage in independent and lifelong learning in the broadest context of technological change.

3.3.4 Program Specific Outcomes (PSOs):

Program Specific Outcomes means what the graduate students of a specific degree program should be able to do and Course Outcomes are the resultant knowledge skills that the students acquire at the end of the course.

Conclusion

Core engineering subjects and skills form the foundation of engineering education and practice in the frame work of program outcomes and program specific outcomes. A solid grasp of these areas enables engineers to tackle complex problems, innovate for solutions, and contribute effectively to their fields. Mastery of these subjects and skills prepares engineers for a successful career and equips them to adapt to evolving technological and industry demands.

3.4 Importance of Academic Performance in Engineering

Academic performance plays a crucial role in an engineering student's journey, influencing their immediate educational outcomes and long-term career prospects. Here's a detailed look at why academic performance is vital in the field of engineering:

3.4.1 Foundation for Advanced Learning

- **Concept Mastery**: Strong academic performance ensures a solid understanding of fundamental engineering concepts. Mastery of core subjects like mathematics, physics, and engineering principles is essential for grasping advanced topics and specialized courses.

- **Prerequisite Knowledge**: Many engineering courses build upon previous knowledge. A solid academic record helps students smoothly transition to more complex subjects, as they are better prepared to handle advanced material.

3.4.2 Career Opportunities and Professional Growth

- **Job Prospects**: Academic performance is a key factor in securing internships, co-op positions, and entry-level jobs. Many employers use academic achievements as a benchmark for evaluating candidates' skills and potential.

- **Graduate Programs**: For those pursuing further education, such as master's or doctoral degrees, academic performance is critical. Admissions committees often look at academic records to assess a candidate's readiness for advanced study and research.

3.4.3 Skill Development

- **Analytical and Problem-Solving Skills**: Consistent academic performance reflects strong analytical and problem-solving abilities, which are fundamental to engineering practice. Success in coursework often indicates a student's capability to apply these skills in practical scenarios.

- **Discipline and Time Management**: Academic success requires effective time management, organization, and discipline. These skills are transferable to professional environments, where project management and meeting deadlines are crucial.

3.4.4 Professional Reputation and Opportunities

- **Industry Recognition**: High academic performance can enhance a student's reputation among peers, faculty, and industry professionals. It can lead to networking opportunities, mentorships, and recommendations from respected individuals in the field.

- **Scholarships and Honors**: Achieving high grades can qualify students for scholarships, awards, and honors that not only provide financial support but also add prestige to their academic and professional profiles.

3.4.5 Personal Development and Confidence

- **Self-Efficacy**: Achieving academic success boosts self-confidence and reinforces a student's belief in their ability to tackle challenging tasks. This confidence can positively impact their approach to problem-solving and innovation in engineering projects.

- **Motivation and Engagement**: Strong academic performance can increase motivation and engagement in studies. It encourages students to set and achieve higher goals, fostering a growth mindset that is essential for lifelong learning and career advancement.

3.4.6 Understanding and Innovation

- **Research and Development**: In engineering fields, where innovation is key, a solid academic foundation allows students to engage in research and development. Understanding complex theories and principles enables them to contribute effectively to cutting-edge projects and advancements.

- **Technical Proficiency**: High academic performance often correlates with a deep understanding of technical subjects, which is crucial for designing, analyzing, and improving engineering systems and solutions.

3.4.7 Ethical and Professional Standards

- **Academic Integrity**: Maintaining strong academic performance requires adherence to ethical standards and academic integrity. These principles are essential for professional practice, where ethical behavior and honesty are paramount in engineering responsibilities.

- Academic integrity is a cornerstone of the educational process, reflecting the ethical and moral principles that underpin scholarly work and learning. It involves maintaining honesty and fairness in all academic endeavors, from conducting research to completing assignments and examinations. Here's a comprehensive overview of academic integrity:

1. **Definition and Principles**

   - **Honesty**: Academic integrity is fundamentally about being truthful and transparent in all aspects of academic work. This includes presenting one's own ideas and research accurately and giving proper credit to others for their contributions.

   - **Fairness**: It ensures that all students are evaluated based on their own work and abilities. This principle helps to maintain a level playing field and prevents unfair advantages or disadvantages in academic assessments.

   - **Trust**: Upholding academic integrity fosters a culture of trust among students, faculty, and institutions. It assures that academic qualifications and achievements are based on genuine efforts and merit.

   - **Respect**: Respect for others' intellectual property and work is integral to academic integrity. This involves acknowledging sources, avoiding plagiarism, and upholding the ethical standards of research and scholarship.

2. **Importance in Education**

   - **Credibility**: Academic integrity enhances the credibility of educational institutions and their degrees. It ensures that qualifications awarded reflect genuine knowledge and skills, which is crucial for maintaining the value of academic credentials.

   - **Learning and Growth**: Upholding academic integrity promotes authentic learning experiences. It encourages students to engage in independent thinking, problem-solving, and the development of their own ideas, rather than relying on dishonesty.

- **Ethical Development**: Practicing academic integrity helps students develop ethical habits that are essential for their future professional lives. It prepares them to face ethical challenges with integrity and responsibility in their careers.

3. **Common Violations**

- **Plagiarism**: Presenting someone else's work, ideas, or words as one's own without proper citation. Plagiarism undermines the originality and credibility of academic work.

- **Cheating**: Using unauthorized resources or methods during exams or assignments, such as copying from another student or using prohibited materials.

- **Fabrication**: Falsifying data, information, or results in research or assignments. This can include inventing sources or altering data to misrepresent findings.

- **Facilitation of Academic Dishonesty**: Helping others to cheat or plagiarize, such as providing pre-written papers or sharing answers during an exam.

4. **Promoting Academic Integrity**

- **Education and Awareness**: Institutions should educate students and faculty about the principles and importance of academic integrity. This includes providing clear guidelines on what constitutes academic dishonesty and the consequences of violating these standards.

- **Clear Policies**: Establishing and enforcing clear academic integrity policies is essential. These policies should outline acceptable behaviors, the procedures for addressing violations, and the penalties for dishonesty.

- **Support Systems**: Offering resources and support, such as writing centers or academic advisors, can help students understand proper citation practices, avoid unintentional plagiarism, and seek guidance on academic integrity issues.

- **Fostering a Culture of Integrity**: Encouraging an environment where integrity is valued and upheld can help deter dishonest behavior. This includes modeling ethical behavior, recognizing and rewarding honest efforts, and creating a supportive academic community.

5. **Addressing Violations**

   - **Investigation and Resolution**: When academic integrity violations are suspected, institutions should conduct thorough investigations to determine the nature and extent of the dishonesty. The resolution process should be fair and consistent, respecting the rights of all parties involved.

   - **Consequences**: Consequences for academic dishonesty may vary depending on the severity of the violation. They can range from a warning or educational intervention to more serious penalties such as failing the assignment, course, or facing disciplinary action.

   - **Rehabilitation**: Providing opportunities for students to learn from their mistakes and understand the importance of integrity can help them rectify their behavior and make amends.

Conclusion

Academic performance in engineering is not merely a measure of grades but a reflection of a student's understanding, skills, and readiness for professional challenges. It lays the groundwork for advanced learning, influences career opportunities, and fosters personal and professional growth. By prioritizing academic excellence, engineering students can build a robust foundation for their future careers, contributing effectively to their fields and the broader engineering community.

3.5 Building a Strong Foundation in STEM

Establishing a robust foundation in STEM (Science, Technology, Engineering, and Mathematics) is crucial for students aiming to excel in these fields and pursue successful careers. A strong STEM foundation not only equips students with essential knowledge and skills but also fosters critical thinking, problem-solving, and innovation. Here's a guide to building a solid STEM foundation:

3.5.1 Emphasize Core Subjects

- **Mathematics**: Mathematics is the bedrock of STEM. Focus on mastering fundamental areas such as algebra, geometry, calculus, and statistics. These topics are integral for problem-solving and analytical thinking in all STEM disciplines.

- **Science**: Develop a strong grasp of basic scientific principles through subjects like physics, chemistry, and biology. Understanding these core sciences provides the groundwork for more specialized studies in areas such as environmental science or biochemistry.

- **Technology**: Gain proficiency in using technology tools and software relevant to STEM fields. Familiarize yourself with programming languages, data analysis tools, and engineering software to enhance your technical capabilities.

- **Engineering**: Explore fundamental engineering concepts such as mechanics, thermodynamics, and electrical circuits. Hands-on experience with engineering principles through labs and projects is essential for applying theoretical knowledge.

3.5.2 Foster Critical Thinking and Problem-Solving

- **Analytical Skills**: Cultivate the ability to analyze complex problems and devise effective solutions. Engage in activities that challenge your critical thinking, such as solving mathematical problems, conducting scientific experiments, or tackling engineering design challenges.

- **Project-Based Learning**: Participate in project-based learning opportunities that involve real-world problem-solving. This approach helps apply theoretical knowledge to practical scenarios, enhancing understanding and creativity.

3.5.3 Develop Practical Skills

- **Hands-On Experience**: Engage in laboratory work, coding projects, and engineering design projects. Practical experience helps solidify theoretical concepts and develop skills in experimental techniques, data analysis, and technical writing.

- **Extracurricular Activities**: Join STEM clubs, competitions, or organizations that provide opportunities for hands-on learning and collaboration. Activities like robotics clubs, science fairs, or coding HACKATHONS can be valuable for applying and expanding your knowledge.

3.5.4 Encourage Curiosity and Continuous Learning

- **Stay Informed**: Keep up with advancements in STEM fields by reading scientific journals, technology blogs, and industry news. Staying informed about the latest developments and breakthroughs helps maintain a strong understanding of current trends and future directions.

- **Pursue Additional Learning**: Take advantage of online courses, workshops, and seminars to further your knowledge. Continuous learning through additional resources can provide insights into specialized topics and emerging technologies.

3.5.5 Build Strong Problem-Solving Skills

- **Practice Problem-Solving**: Regularly tackle challenging problems in mathematics, science, and engineering. Practice through exercises, simulations, and real-world scenarios enhance your ability to approach and solve complex issues.

- **Learn from Mistakes**: Analyze errors and setbacks to understand what went wrong and how to improve. This reflective practice is crucial for developing resilience and refining problem-solving strategies.

3.5.6 Emphasize Collaboration and Communication

- **Teamwork**: Work collaboratively on STEM projects and research. Collaboration with peers fosters diverse perspectives and enhances problem-solving capabilities. It also mirrors real-world scenarios where teamwork is often essential.

- **Effective Communication**: Develop strong communication skills to convey complex ideas clearly and effectively. Practice writing technical reports, presenting findings, and explaining concepts to different audiences.

3.5.7 Seek Mentorship and Guidance

- **Find Mentors**: Seek guidance from teachers, professors, or professionals in STEM fields. Mentors can provide valuable insights, career advice, and support for academic and professional development.

- **Networking**: Build connections with individuals and organizations in STEM fields. Networking can open doors to internships, research opportunities, and career advancement.

3.5.8 *Engage in Interdisciplinary Learning*

- **Integrate Knowledge**: Explore how different STEM disciplines intersect and complement each other. For example, understanding the interplay between mathematics and engineering or the relationship between biology and technology can provide a more holistic view of STEM fields.

- **Innovative Thinking**: Encourage creative thinking by exploring interdisciplinary projects or problems that require integrating knowledge from multiple STEM areas. This approach fosters innovation and a deeper understanding of complex issues.

Conclusion

Building a strong foundation in STEM involves a combination of mastering core subjects, developing practical skills, and fostering a mindset of curiosity and continuous learning.

CHAPTER 4

Developing Essential Skills

Developing essential skills in engineering students involves a balanced approach to honing both technical and soft skills. Technical skills, such as proficiency in mathematics, engineering principles, and software tools, are foundational for solving complex problems and executing precise designs. Simultaneously, cultivating soft skills like communication, teamwork, and critical thinking enhances the ability to collaborate effectively and navigate the interdisciplinary nature of modern engineering projects. Engineering students must engage in hands-on experiences, such as internships and group projects, to apply theoretical knowledge practically and refine these skills. By integrating rigorous technical training with a focus on interpersonal and organizational competencies, students prepare themselves to tackle real-world challenges and thrive in dynamic professional environments.

4.1 Technical Skills

Technical skills are the specialized knowledge and abilities required to perform specific tasks and solve problems in a particular field. In engineering, these skills encompass proficiency in mathematics, understanding of engineering principles, and the use of specialized software and tools such as CAD programs or simulation software. Technical skills also include programming capabilities, data analysis, and familiarity with laboratory techniques. Mastery of these skills enables engineers to design, analyze, and implement solutions effectively, making them crucial for success in technical roles and projects.

1. **Mathematics and Analysis**: Proficiency in calculus, linear algebra, differential equations, and other mathematical tools essential for engineering problem-solving.

2. **Engineering Principles**: Understanding of core concepts specific to the engineering discipline, such as thermodynamics for mechanical engineers or circuit analysis for electrical engineers.

3. **Computer-Aided Design (CAD)**: Ability to use CAD software to create and modify designs. This is crucial for designing components, systems, or structures.

4. **Programming**: Knowledge of programming languages like Python, C++, or MATLAB, which are used for simulations, automations, and developing algorithms.

5. **Data Analysis**: Skills in analyzing data through statistical methods or software tools like Excel, R, or specialized engineering software.

6. **Technical Communication**: The ability to create technical documentation, reports, and presentations that clearly convey complex engineering information.

7. **Systems Design and Analysis**: Understanding how to design and analyze systems, including the integration of various components and understanding their interactions.

8. **Laboratory Skills**: Hands-on experience with lab equipment and experimental techniques relevant to the engineering discipline.

9. **Project Management Tools**: Familiarity with tools like Gantt charts or project management software for planning and managing engineering projects.

4.1.1 Methods of Acquiring Technical Skills

Acquiring technical skills involves a combination of formal education, hands-on practice, and continuous learning. Here are some effective methods:

1. **Formal Education**: Enroll in degree programs or specialized courses at universities or technical schools that provide foundational knowledge and advanced training in specific engineering and technology disciplines.

2. **Online Courses and Certifications**: Utilize online platforms like National Portal for Technological Enabled Learning (NPTEL) through Study Webs for Active Young Aspiring Minds (SWAYAM), COURSERA, edX, UDACITY, MIT-OCW etc. to take specialized courses and earn certifications in areas such as programming, data analysis, or CAD.

3. **Hands-On Projects**: Engage in practical projects, either through coursework, personal initiatives, or internships, to apply theoretical knowledge and gain real-world experience.

4. **Workshops and Seminars**: Attend industry workshops, seminars, and conferences to learn about the latest technologies, tools, and methodologies from experts in the field.

5. **Internships and Co-op Programs**: Gain valuable experience and technical skills through internships or cooperative education programs that provide on-the-job training and exposure to professional practices.

6. **Mentorship**: Seek guidance from experienced professionals who can offer insights, advice, and practical knowledge that complement formal learning.

7. **Self-Study and Practice**: Utilize textbooks, online tutorials, and practice exercises to deepen understanding and refine skills independently.

8. **Industry Certifications**: Obtain certifications from industry-recognized organizations to validate expertise in specific tools or technologies and enhance employability.

Nut Shell: By integrating these methods, individuals can effectively build and enhance their technical skill set, staying current with industry developments and advancing their professional capabilities.

4.2 Soft Skills

Soft skills are essential interpersonal and cognitive abilities that facilitate effective interaction and problem-solving in various settings. In engineering, these skills include communication, which ensures clear and efficient exchange of ideas; teamwork, which fosters collaboration in multidisciplinary projects; and critical thinking, which aids in evaluating complex issues and devising innovative solutions. Additionally, skills such as time management, adaptability, and emotional intelligence contribute to navigating the challenges of the engineering profession and enhancing overall performance. Developing strong soft skills complements technical expertise and is vital for thriving in dynamic and collaborative work environments.

1. **Communication**: The ability to clearly and effectively communicate ideas, both verbally and in writing, to various audiences, including technical and non-technical stakeholders.

2. **Teamwork**: Collaborating effectively with others, often in multidisciplinary teams, to achieve common goals.

3. **Problem-Solving**: The capacity to approach complex problems systematically and creatively, using both analytical and intuitive methods.

4. **Time Management**: Managing one's time efficiently to balance coursework, projects, and extracurricular activities.

5. **Adaptability**: Being flexible and open to new methods, technologies, and changes in project requirements or work environments.

6. **Leadership**: Skills in leading a team, guiding projects, and taking initiative to drive projects to successful completion.

7. **Critical Thinking**: The ability to evaluate information critically, make reasoned judgments, and approach problems from different angles.

8. **Emotional Intelligence**: Understanding and managing one's emotions and those of others to facilitate better teamwork and communication.

9. **Conflict Resolution**: Handling disagreements or conflicts constructively and finding solutions that are acceptable to all parties involved.

In summary, technical skills are specific to engineering and involve the knowledge and abilities required to perform engineering tasks. Soft skills, on the other hand, are more about how you interact with others, manage your time, and approach problems. Both types of skills are crucial for a successful career in engineering.

4.2.1 Methods of Acquiring Soft Skills

Acquiring soft skills involves actively engaging in activities and practices that enhance interpersonal and cognitive abilities. Here are some effective methods:

1. **Communication Workshops**: Participate in workshops or seminars focused on improving verbal and written communication skills, including presentation techniques and effective listening.

2. **Team Projects and Group Activities**: Engage in team-based projects, group assignments, or collaborative activities to practice teamwork, conflict resolution, and leadership.

3. **Public Speaking and Debate**: Join public speaking clubs available in your locality or participate in debate forums to develop confidence, persuasion skills, and articulate expression.

4. **Mentorship and Coaching**: Seek guidance from mentors or coaches who can provide feedback, support, and practical advice on developing specific soft skills.

5. **Volunteering**: Get involved in volunteer work or community service, which can enhance skills like empathy, adaptability, and teamwork through real-world experiences.

6. **Networking Events**: Attend professional networking events to practice and refine your ability to build relationships, engage in conversations, and navigate professional settings.

7. **Self-Reflection and Feedback**: Regularly assess your own skills and seek constructive feedback from peers, colleagues, or supervisors to identify areas for improvement and growth.

8. **Online Courses and Training**: Take online courses focused on soft skills such as emotional intelligence, time management, or negotiation to gain theoretical knowledge and practical techniques.

By actively participating in these activities, individuals can develop and strengthen their soft skills, enhancing their ability to interact effectively, manage challenges, and succeed in various professional environments.

4.3 Problem Solving and Analytical Thinking

Problem-solving and analytical thinking are fundamental skills essential for navigating complex challenges and making informed decisions.

Problem-solving involves identifying issues, generating potential solutions, and implementing strategies to address problems effectively. It requires creativity and practical execution to overcome obstacles and achieve desired outcomes.

Analytical thinking, on the other hand, focuses on breaking down complex information into manageable components to understand underlying causes and patterns. By employing logical reasoning and systematic analysis, individuals can derive insights and make data-driven decisions. Together, these skills enable individuals to tackle difficulties with a structured approach and make well-considered choices in both professional and personal contexts.

4.3.1 Problem Solving

Problem Solving is a multifaceted process crucial for overcoming challenges and achieving objectives. It can be broken down into several detailed stages:

1. **Problem Identification**:

   - **Recognizing Symptoms**: Identifying indicators that something is wrong or not working as intended.

   - **Defining the Problem**: Clearly articulating what the problem is, its boundaries, and its impact. This involves distinguishing between the symptoms and the root cause.

2. **Gathering Information**:

   - **Data Collection**: Accumulating relevant facts, figures, and insights from various sources. This may include quantitative data, qualitative observations, and stakeholder input.

   - **Contextual Understanding**: Understanding the context in which the problem exists, including environmental, organizational, or situational factors.

3. **Generating Solutions**:

    - **Brainstorming**: Creatively generating a wide range of potential solutions without immediately judging their feasibility.

    - **Innovative Thinking**: Using creative techniques to think outside the box and consider unconventional solutions.

4. **Evaluating Alternatives**:

    - **Criteria Development**: Establishing criteria to assess potential solutions, such as effectiveness, cost, time, and resources required.

    - **Comparative Analysis**: Weighing the pros and cons of each alternative solution and predicting their potential outcomes.

5. **Implementing a Solution**:

    - **Action Plan**: Developing a step-by-step plan for implementing the chosen solution, including resource allocation, timelines, and responsibilities.

    - **Execution**: Putting the plan into action while ensuring adherence to the planned procedures and making necessary adjustments.

6. **Monitoring and Reviewing**:

    - **Performance Measurement**: Assessing how well the implemented solution is addressing the problem by monitoring outcomes and collecting feedback.

    - **Feedback Loop**: Reviewing the results, identifying any new issues, and making iterative improvements if needed.

Nut Shell: Effective problem solving requires both structured methodologies and adaptability to changing circumstances. It combines logical reasoning with creativity and practical execution.

4.3.2 Analytical Thinking

Analytical Thinking is about systematically examining information to understand complex issues and derive well-informed conclusions. Here's a detailed look at its components:

1. **Data Analysis**:

    - **Quantitative Analysis**: Using statistical methods and mathematical techniques to analyze numerical data. This might include regression analysis, statistical tests, or data visualization.

    - **Qualitative Analysis**: Interpreting non-numerical data, such as text or interviews, to identify themes, patterns, or insights.

2. **Logical Reasoning**:

    - **Deductive Reasoning**: Drawing specific conclusions from general principles or premises. For example, if all engineers are problem solvers and John is an engineer, then John is a problem solver.

    - **Inductive Reasoning**: Making generalizations based on specific observations. For instance, observing that a particular software consistently improves project efficiency and concluding that it may be beneficial in other contexts.

3. **Critical Evaluation**:

    - **Validity and Reliability**: Assessing the accuracy and trustworthiness of information sources and data.

    - **Bias Identification**: Recognizing and mitigating personal or external biases that could affect the analysis.

4. **Systematic Approach**:

    - **Structured Analysis**: Using frameworks or models to break down complex problems into manageable parts. Techniques such as SWOT analysis, root cause analysis, or flowcharting can be employed.

- **Process Mapping**: Creating visual representations of processes or systems to understand their components and interactions.

5. **Detail Orientation**:

- **Precision**: Ensuring that every detail is accurately considered and documented, which is essential for high-stakes analysis.

- **Thoroughness**: Avoiding oversights by thoroughly examining all aspects of the problem or data set.

Analytical thinking helps in breaking down complex problems, understanding underlying factors, and making data-driven decisions. It's crucial for tasks that require a deep understanding of how different elements interact and impact each other.

Nut Shell: Both Problem Solving and Analytical Thinking are integral to navigating challenges effectively and are widely applicable across various domains, from engineering to business management.

4.4 Communication and Teamwork

Communication and teamwork are essential skills that drive successful collaboration and productivity in any professional setting. Communication involves the clear and effective exchange of ideas, information, and feedback, ensuring that all parties understand and are aligned with objectives and expectations. It encompasses both verbal and written forms and is crucial for preventing misunderstandings and fostering strong relationships.

Teamwork, on the other hand, focuses on working cohesively with others towards a common goal, leveraging each team member's strengths and skills. It requires coordination, mutual respect, and collective problem-solving to achieve shared objectives efficiently. Mastery of both communication and teamwork enhances overall performance and contributes to a harmonious and productive work environment.

4.4.1 Communication

Communication is the process of exchanging information, ideas, and feelings between individuals or groups to achieve mutual understanding and collaboration. Effective communication is fundamental in both personal and professional contexts, and it involves several key aspects:

1. **Verbal Communication**

   - **Clarity**: Speaking clearly and articulately to ensure that the message is easily understood. This includes using appropriate language, tone, and pace.

   - **Active Listening**: Paying close attention to the speaker, acknowledging their message, and responding thoughtfully. Active listening helps in understanding the speaker's perspective and ensures that responses are relevant and constructive.

2. **Written Communication**

   - **Precision**: Writing clearly and concisely to convey the intended message without ambiguity. This includes proper grammar, spelling, and formatting.

   - **Documentation**: Creating and maintaining records, reports, and emails that are organized and easy to reference. Good written communication helps in ensuring that information is preserved and accessible.

3. **Non-Verbal Communication**

   - **Body Language**: Using gestures, facial expressions, and posture to complement and reinforce verbal messages.

Non-verbal cues can provide additional context and emotional tone.

- **Eye Contact**: Maintaining appropriate eye contact to show engagement and confidence, and to build trust.

4. **Feedback**

- **Constructive Criticism**: Providing and receiving feedback in a way that is helpful and aimed at improvement. Constructive feedback focuses on specific behaviors or outcomes rather than personal attributes.

- **Open Dialogue**: Encouraging open and honest discussions where feedback is welcomed and considered as driving force for improvement or refinement.

Effective communication fosters collaboration, resolves conflicts, and ensures that goals and expectations are clearly understood by all parties involved. It is a cornerstone of productive relationships and successful teamwork.

4.4.2 Teamwork

Teamwork is the collaborative effort of a group of individuals working together towards a common goal. Successful teamwork involves several key elements:

1. **Collaboration**

- **Role Definition**: Clearly defining and assigning roles, responsibilities and well defined protocols to ensure that each team member knows their tasks and how they contribute to the overall objective.

- **Shared Goals**: Aligning team members around common objectives and ensuring that everyone understands how their contributions support these goals.

2. **Coordination**

   - **Task Management**: Organizing and scheduling tasks to ensure that work is completed efficiently and deadlines are met. Effective coordination involves managing dependencies and ensuring that team members are synchronized in their efforts.

   - **Resource Allocation**: Utilizing resources such as time, tools, and skills effectively to support team activities and achieve desired outcomes.

3. **Communication within the Team**

   - **Information Sharing**: Ensuring that relevant information is shared among team members to keep everyone informed and involved in decision-making.

   - **Problem-Solving**: Collaborating to address challenges and find solutions collectively, drawing on diverse perspectives and expertise.

4. **Trust and Respect**

   - **Building Relationships**: Fostering a positive team dynamics by showing respect, valuing each other's contributions, and supporting one another.

   - **Conflict Resolution**: Addressing and resolving conflicts constructively, focusing on finding solutions rather than assigning blame.

5. **Motivation and Support**

   - **Encouragement**: Providing motivation and encouragement to team members, recognizing their achievements and contributions.

   - **Feedback and Recognition**: Offering regular feedback and acknowledging individual and team successes to maintain morale and commitment.

Effective teamwork enhances productivity, leverages diverse skills, and leads to more innovative and acceptable solutions. It requires continuous effort, mutual respect, and a commitment to working collaboratively towards shared goals.

4.5 Time Allocation and Productivity: Engineer's Perspective

In the fast-paced world of engineering, effective time allocation and productivity are crucial for managing complex projects and meeting tight deadlines. Engineers often juggle multiple tasks, from intricate problem-solving and design work to collaborative team efforts and client interactions. Mastering time management not only enhances individual efficiency but also ensures that projects progress smoothly and meet quality standards.

From prioritizing tasks and setting realistic goals to leveraging productivity tools and techniques, understanding how to allocate time effectively is essential for engineers aiming to excel in their roles and contribute meaningfully to their projects and teams. This perspective on time allocation and productivity will explore strategies and best practices that help engineers optimize their workflow, balance competing demands, and ultimately drive successful outcomes in their professional endeavors.

4.5.1 Time Allocation

Time Allocation is the practice of planning and exercising conscious control over the amount of time spent on specific activities. It is crucial for achieving goals, meeting deadlines, and reducing stress. Effective time management involves several key components:

1. **Prioritization**:

   - **Identifying Priorities**: Assessing tasks based on their importance and urgency. Techniques such as the Eisenhower Matrix or ABC prioritization can help in distinguishing between high-priority and low-priority tasks.

   - **Setting Goals**: Establishing clear, measurable, and achievable goals to focus efforts and measure progress. Goals should be SMART (Specific, Measurable, Achievable, Relevant, Time-bound).

2. **Planning and Scheduling**:

   - **Creating To-Do Lists**: Compiling a list of tasks to be completed, which helps in organizing and tracking progress. Lists should be regularly updated and reviewed.

   - **Using Calendars and Planners**: Scheduling tasks and appointments in a calendar or planner to visualize deadlines and allocate time effectively. Tools such as digital calendars (Google Calendar, Outlook) can assist in setting reminders and managing schedules.

3. **Time Blocking**:

   - **Allocating Time Blocks**: Setting aside specific periods for focused work on particular tasks. Time blocking helps in minimizing interruptions and enhancing concentration.

   - **Avoiding Multitasking**: Focusing on one task at a time to improve efficiency and quality of work. Multitasking can lead to reduced productivity and increased errors.

4. **Managing Distractions**:

   - **Creating a Conducive Work Environment**: Minimizing environmental distractions by setting up a dedicated workspace and using tools to block digital interruptions.

   - **Implementing Techniques**: Using methods like the Pomodoro Technique (working in intervals with breaks) to maintain focus and productivity.

5. **Review and Adjustment**:

   - **Regular Evaluation**: Reviewing time management practices to identify what works and what doesn't. Making adjustments based on this feedback helps in refining time management strategies.

   - **Reflecting on Efficiency**: Assessing the effectiveness of time use and making necessary changes to improve overall productivity.

4.5.2 Productivity

Productivity refers to the ability to achieve significant outputs with the efficient use of time, resources, and energy. It involves several key elements:

1. **Efficiency**:

   - **Optimal Resource Utilization**: Using tools, skills, and resources in the most effective manner to maximize output. This includes leveraging technology and automation where appropriate.

   - **Streamlining Processes**: Identifying and eliminating inefficiencies in workflows to enhance productivity. Techniques like process mapping and workflow analysis can help in optimizing processes.

2. **Goal Setting**:

   - **Defining Clear Objectives**: Setting specific, achievable goals that guide efforts and measure success. Clear objectives provide direction and motivation.

   - **Breaking-up Goals**: Dividing larger goals into smaller, manageable tasks to make progress more attainable and less overwhelming.

3. **Focus and Concentration**:

   - **Minimizing Interruptions**: Creating an environment that reduces distractions and fosters concentration. Techniques such as noise-canceling headphones or designated quiet times can enhance focus.

   - **Using Productivity Techniques**: Implementing methods like time blocking, the Two-Minute Rule (completing tasks that take less than two minutes immediately), and task batching to improve concentration and output.

4. **Motivation and Discipline**:

   - **Maintaining Motivation**: Using incentives, rewards, and positive reinforcement to stay motivated. Setting personal milestones and celebrating achievements can boost morale.

   - **Developing Discipline**: Cultivating habits and routines that support consistent productivity. Discipline involves adhering to schedules, resisting procrastination, and managing time effectively.

5. **Work-Life Balance**:

   - **Avoiding Overwork**: Ensuring that work demands do not negatively impact personal life and well-being. Balancing work with relaxation and personal activities helps maintain overall productivity and health.

- **Regular Breaks**: Taking scheduled breaks to rest and recharge, which helps in maintaining high levels of productivity and preventing burnout.

Nut Shell: Effective time management and productivity are interlinked, as managing time well leads to improved productivity, and being productive often involves efficient time use.

4.6 Time Allocation and Productivity: Student's Perspective

For engineering students, effective time allocation and productivity are crucial to navigating the rigorous demands of their academic and personal lives. Time allocation involves organizing and planning how to allocate study time, project work, and extracurricular activities to meet deadlines and achieve academic goals.

Productivity focuses on maximizing efficiency and output during study sessions and project work, ensuring that each task is completed to a high standard. Mastering these skills helps students balance their coursework, enhance their learning experiences, and maintain overall well-being, ultimately contributing to their success in a challenging and dynamic field. Here's how these skills can be applied effectively:

4.6.1 Time Allocation

1. **Prioritization of Tasks**

   - **Identify Key Responsibilities**: Determine the most critical tasks such as assignments, lab work, and exam preparation. Use prioritization techniques like the Eisenhower Matrix to focus on urgent and important tasks.

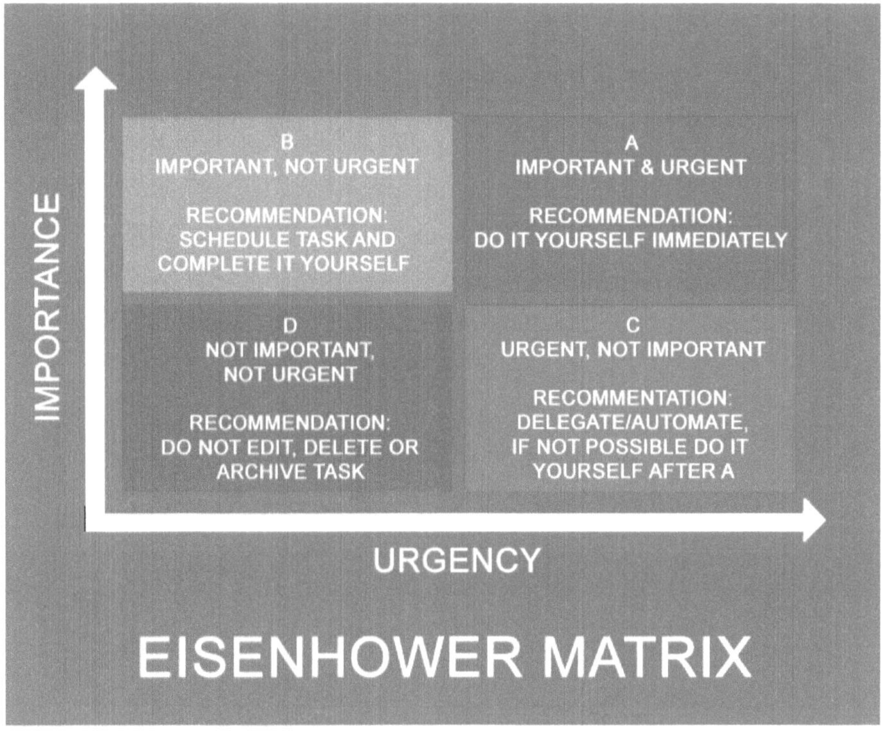

- **Set Academic Goals**: Establish clear, achievable goals for each semester or course. For example, aiming to complete a specific number of practice problems or mastering a particular concept by a set date.

2. **Planning and Scheduling**

   - **Create a Semester Plan**: Outline important dates, including exam schedules, project deadlines, and assignment due dates. Use a calendar or planner to keep track of these dates and plan your study sessions accordingly.

   - **Weekly and Daily Schedules**: Break down your semester plan into weekly and daily tasks. Allocate specific times for studying, attending classes, working on projects, and personal activities. Tools like Google Calendar or scheduling apps can be helpful.

3. **Time Blocking and Task Management**

   - **Block Study Time**: Allocate dedicated blocks of time for studying each subject, working on lab reports, or preparing for exams. This focused approach helps in deepening understanding and improving retention.

   - **Avoid Procrastination**: Use techniques such as the Pomodoro Technique (25-minute work intervals with 5-minute breaks) to maintain focus and productivity.

A productive 5-minute break can be a great way to refresh your mind and boost your productivity. Here are a few ideas for making the most of a short break:

   a. **Stretching**: Do a quick stretch or a series of simple stretches to release tension and improve circulation. Focus on areas that might be tense from sitting, such as your neck, shoulders, and back.

   b. **Mindfulness or Deep Breathing**: Practice mindfulness or deep breathing exercises to calm your mind and reduce stress. Spend a few minutes focusing on your breath or a calming visualization.

c. **Quick Walk**: Take a brisk walk around your study area or outside if possible. A short walk can increase your energy levels and help clear your mind.

d. **Hydrate and Snack**: Drink a glass of water and have a healthy snack, like fruit or nuts. Staying hydrated and nourished can enhance your focus and energy.

e. **Micro-Reflection**: Spend a few minutes reflecting on what you've accomplished so far and what your next steps will be. This helps in resetting your goals and prioritizing tasks.

4. **Managing Distractions**

   - **Create a Study Environment**: Set up a distraction-free study area. This includes minimizing digital distractions by using apps or tools that block social media or notifications during study periods.

   - **Set Boundaries**: Communicate with roommates or family members about your study schedule to minimize interruptions.

5. **Review and Adjust**

   - **Regular Check-ins**: Assess your progress weekly to ensure you're on track with your goals and deadlines. Adjust your schedule or priorities if necessary based on workload and upcoming deadlines.

4.6.2 Productivity

1. **Efficient Study Techniques**

   - **Active Learning**: Engage in active study methods such as summarizing information, teaching concepts to others, and solving practice problems. Active learning enhances understanding and retention.

   - **Use Study Aids**: Employ tools like flashcards, diagrams, and mind maps to reinforce learning and aid in memorization.

2. **Goal Setting and Milestones**

   - **Set Specific Objectives**: Define clear objectives for each study session, such as completing a certain number of practice problems or understanding a specific topic. Breaking goals into smaller milestones makes them more manageable.

   - **Track Progress**: Monitor your progress towards academic goals and adjust your strategies based on performance and feedback.

3. **Focus and Discipline**

   - **Maintain Focus**: Apply techniques like single-tasking and time blocking to stay focused on one task at a time. Avoid multitasking, which can reduce the quality of work and efficiency.

   - **Develop Routines**: Establish productive routines, such as regular study sessions, consistent sleep schedules, and scheduled breaks, to maintain high levels of productivity and well-being.

4. **Utilizing Resources**

   - **Leverage Campus Resources**: Take advantage of resources such as study groups, tutoring services, and academic advisors. Engaging with these resources can enhance understanding and provide additional support.

   - **Seek Help When Needed**: Don't hesitate to ask professors, peers, or mentors for help with challenging topics or project difficulties. Collaborative learning can enhance productivity and problem-solving.

5. **Balancing Work and Life**

   - **Maintain Balance**: Ensure a healthy balance between academic responsibilities and personal life. Include time for relaxation, exercise, and social activities to prevent burnout and maintain overall productivity.

- **Regular Breaks**: Incorporate short breaks into your study routine to rest and recharge. This helps in maintaining focus and preventing fatigue.

Nut Shell: Applying effective time allocation and productivity strategies, engineering students can better handle the rigorous demands of their studies, optimize their learning experiences, and achieve academic success while maintaining a balanced lifestyle.

4.6.3 Habits and Productivity

An engineering student's productivity can be significantly influenced by various individual habits. Here's a look at habits that can impact productivity, both positively and negatively:

A. Habits That Enhance Productivity

1. **Consistent Study Routine**: Establishing a regular study schedule helps in building discipline and maintaining a steady workflow. Consistency aids in better time management and reduces the likelihood of last-minute cramming.

2. **Effective Goal Setting**: Setting clear, achievable goals for each study session or project phase helps maintain focus and motivation. Breaking down larger goals into smaller, manageable tasks can make progress more tangible.

3. **Active Learning Techniques**: Using active learning strategies such as summarizing information, teaching concepts to peers, and solving practice problems can deepen understanding and improve retention.

4. **Regular Review Sessions**: Regularly reviewing and revisiting material helps reinforce learning and keep information fresh. Scheduled review sessions can prevent forgetting and aid long-term retention.

5. **Healthy Lifestyle Choices**: Maintaining a balanced diet, regular exercise, and adequate sleep supports overall cognitive function and energy levels, enhancing productivity.

B. Habits That Hinder Productivity

1. **Procrastination**: Delaying tasks and assignments can lead to last-minute stress and reduced quality of work. Procrastination often results from poor time management and a lack of motivation.

2. **Multitasking**: Attempting to juggle multiple tasks at once can reduce overall efficiency and increase the likelihood of errors and omissions. Focus on one task at a time to achieve better results.

3. **Disorganization**: A cluttered study environment and disorganized materials can waste time and hinder productivity. Keeping a tidy workspace and using organizational tools can improve focus and efficiency.

4. **Poor Time Allocation**: Ineffective scheduling and lack of prioritization can lead to missed deadlines and increased stress. It's essential to plan and allocate time effectively for various tasks and activities.

5. **Overuse of Technology**: Excessive time spent on social media, gaming, or other distractions can divert attention away from academic responsibilities. Implementing strategies to manage screen time and minimize distractions is crucial.

6. **Neglecting Breaks**: Skipping breaks and overworking can lead to burnout and reduced productivity. Regular breaks are important for maintaining focus and mental well-being.

Nut Shell: Developing positive habits and addressing negative ones can significantly impact an engineering student's productivity. By adopting effective study practices, managing time well, and maintaining a healthy lifestyle, students can enhance their academic performance and overall efficiency.

CHAPTER 5

Extra-curricular Activities & Experience

Extra-curricular activities and experiences play a crucial role in shaping a successful engineering career, extending well beyond the technical skills acquired through formal education. These activities, ranging from participation in engineering clubs and competitions to internships and volunteer work, provide invaluable opportunities for personal growth, leadership development, and practical application of theoretical knowledge. Engaging in diverse projects and initiatives allows aspiring engineers to build a well-rounded skill set, enhance problem-solving abilities, and cultivate teamwork and communication skills. By leveraging these experiences, individuals can not only stand out in a competitive job market but also pave the way for continuous professional development and career advancement in the ever-evolving engineering field.

Outcomes:

- **Skill Development**: Acquired both technical and interpersonal skills.

- **Practical Experience**: Gained hands-on experience complementing academic knowledge.

- **Networking**: Expanded professional connections and mentorship opportunities.

- **Leadership and Teamwork**: Developed leadership and collaborative abilities.

- **Career Advancement**: Strengthened resume and improved job prospects.

- **Confidence Boost**: Increased self-confidence through achievements.

- **Broadened Perspectives**: Gained diverse viewpoints and cultural insights.

- **Community Impact**: Contributed to societal and community development.

Pre-requisites

Here are the pre-requisites for engaging in extra-curricular activities and gaining relevant experience:

- **Time Management Skills**: Ability to balance academic, personal, and extra-curricular commitments effectively.

- **Interest and Passion**: Genuine enthusiasm and interest in the chosen activity or field.

- **Commitment**: Willingness to dedicate time and effort consistently.

- **Basic Knowledge**: Fundamental understanding or background related to the activity.

- **Communication Skills**: Ability to interact and collaborate effectively with others.

- **Organizational Skills**: Capability to plan, organize, and execute tasks and projects.

- **Openness to Learning**: Willingness to learn new skills and adapt to different roles.

- **Teamwork Ability**: Willingness and skill to work collaboratively in group settings.

- **Professional Attitude**: Demonstration of reliability, responsibility, and professionalism.

- **Networking Readiness**: Ability to engage and build relationships with peers, mentors, and professionals.

5.1 Internship and Co-op Programs

Internship and co-op programs are integral components of career development in many fields, particularly in engineering. Both provide practical, hands-on experience that complements academic learning, but they differ in structure and scope.

5.1.1 Internships

Internships are typically short-term work experiences, often lasting between 10 to 12 weeks, and are usually undertaken during academic breaks such as summer. Interns work on specific projects or tasks within a company or organization, gaining exposure to the industry, company culture, and the day-to-day responsibilities of their field. Internships can be paid or unpaid and are designed to give students a glimpse into the professional world, allowing them to apply classroom knowledge in real-world settings.

Importance of Internships

1. **Practical Experience**: Internships provide hands-on experience that allows students to apply theoretical knowledge gained in the classroom to real-world scenarios. This practical application helps solidify understanding and enhances technical skills, making students more competent, confident and future readiness.

2. **Industry Insight**: Through internships, students gain a valuable perspective on the engineering industry, including its trends, challenges, and standards. This insight helps them understand industry-specific practices and prepares them for future roles.

3. **Skill Development**: Internships offer opportunities to develop both technical and soft skills. Technical skills include proficiency with industry-specific tools and technologies, while soft skills such as communication, teamwork, and problem-solving are also honed in a professional setting.

4. **Networking Opportunities**: Internships provide access to a network of professionals, mentors, and peers in the industry. Building relationships during an internship can lead to valuable connections, references, and potential job offers.

5. **Career Exploration**: Network is the net worth in one's professional career. For many students, internships are a chance to explore variety of areas of engineering and determine which specialization aligns best with their interests and career goals. This exploration helps in making informed decisions about future career paths.

6. **Enhanced Employability**: Completing an internship often makes candidates more attractive to potential employers. It demonstrates practical experience, a proactive attitude, and a commitment to the profession, which can be a differentiator in a competitive job market.

The Way Forward

1. **Identify Relevant Opportunities**: Students should actively seek internships that align with their career interests and goals. This involves researching companies, networking with professionals, and utilizing career services and job boards at their educational institutions.

2. **Prepare for the Application Process**: Crafting a strong resume, writing a tailored cover letter, and preparing for interviews are crucial steps in securing an internship. Students should highlight relevant coursework, projects, and any previous experience that showcases their skills and enthusiasm.

3. **Set Clear Goals**: Before starting an internship, students should define their learning objectives and career goals. This helps in making the most of the experience, focusing on areas of interest, and seeking out opportunities to contribute to meaningful projects.

4. **Seek Feedback and Reflect**: Regularly seeking feedback from supervisors and peers during the internship is essential for personal and professional growth. Reflecting on experiences and lessons learned helps in evaluating progress and identifying areas for improvement.

5. **Leverage the Experience**: After completing an internship, students should leverage their experience by updating their resumes, LinkedIn profiles, and portfolios. Additionally, maintaining contact with mentors and colleagues can provide ongoing support and opportunities in the future.

6. **Stay Adaptable**: The landscape of internships is evolving, with increasing opportunities for remote and virtual internships. Staying adaptable and open to various formats can provide additional avenues for gaining experience and skills.

Nut Shell: **By embracing the full potential of internships, engineering students can significantly enhance their educational experience, build a robust professional foundation, and advance their careers in a competitive field.**

5.1.2 Co-op programs

Co-op Programs (short for cooperative education) are more extensive, often spanning several semesters, and involve alternating periods of full-time work and academic study. Co-op students are typically employed part-time or full-time for a semester or more, and their work experience is directly integrated into their academic curriculum. This structure allows students to gain in-depth experience and build stronger professional networks, as they spend a significant amount of time with their employer. Co-op programs are generally paid and offer a more immersive experience, often resulting in a deeper understanding of the industry and potentially leading to job offers upon graduation.

Importance of Co-op Programs

1. **Extended Work Experience**: Co-op programs typically involve multiple work terms over a longer duration compared to internships. This extended exposure allows students to engage in more complex projects and gain a deeper understanding of the engineering field.

2. **Academic Integration**: Co-op programs are integrated into the academic curriculum, meaning that students alternate between full-time work and academic study. This integration ensures that the work experience complements academic learning, enhancing overall educational outcomes.

3. **Enhanced Professional Skills**: Through extended, hands-on work experience, students develop a wide range of professional skills, including technical competencies, project management, and problem-solving abilities. The immersive nature of co-op programs fosters significant growth in both hard and soft skills.

4. **Career Readiness**: By working in a real-world setting, co-op students become familiar with industry standards, practices, and expectations. This familiarity enhances their readiness for full-time employment and helps them adapt more quickly to professional roles after graduation.

5. **Networking and Mentorship**: Co-op programs facilitate extensive networking opportunities with industry professionals, mentors, and peers. Building these relationships can lead to valuable advice, job referrals, and potential employment opportunities in the future.

6. **Informed Career Decisions**: The opportunity to work in various roles or companies through co-op programs allows students to explore different engineering specializations and industries. This exploration aids in making informed decisions about career paths and areas of specialization.

7. **Potential for Full-Time Employment**: Many companies view co-op students as potential future employees. Performing well during co-op terms can lead to job offers upon graduation, providing a smooth transition from academic life to a professional career.

The Way Forward

1. **Identify and Apply to Co-op Programs**: Students should research and apply to co-op programs that align with their career goals and interests. This involves checking with their university's co-op office, attending career fairs, and applying to companies that offer co-op opportunities.

2. **Prepare for the Selection Process**: Crafting a strong resume, writing tailored cover letters, and preparing for interviews are critical steps in the co-op application process. Students should highlight relevant coursework, projects, and any previous work experience.

3. **Set Clear Objectives**: Before starting a co-op placement, students should establish clear learning objectives and career goals. This clarity helps in selecting projects and tasks that align with their professional aspirations and makes the most of the co-op experience.

4. **Actively Engage and Contribute**: During the co-op term, students should actively participate in projects, seek out additional responsibilities, and demonstrate initiative. Engaging fully with the team and contributing to meaningful work enhances the learning experience and professional development.

5. **Seek Feedback and Reflect**: Regularly seeking feedback from supervisors and peers is essential for continuous improvement. Reflecting on experiences, challenges, and achievements helps in personal and professional growth and prepares students for future roles.

6. **Maintain Professional Relationships**: Building and maintaining relationships with colleagues, mentors, and supervisors can provide ongoing support and career opportunities. Staying connected after the co-op term can be beneficial for future job searches and professional networking.

7. **Leverage Co-op Experience**: After completing a co-op program, students should update their resumes, LinkedIn profiles, and portfolios to reflect their new skills and experiences. Additionally, using the co-op experience to explore career options and make informed decisions about future job opportunities is crucial.

8. **Stay Flexible and Open-Minded**: The co-op landscape is evolving, with opportunities for remote and virtual placements becoming more common. Staying flexible and open to various formats can expand the range of opportunities available and provide diverse experiences.

Nut Shell: By fully engaging with co-op programs, engineering students can gain valuable experience, build a strong professional foundation, and enhance their career prospects, setting the stage for long-term success in the engineering field.

5.2 Engineering Projects and Competitions

Engineering projects and competitions are pivotal in shaping a successful engineering career, bridging the gap between theoretical knowledge and practical application. Engaging in these activities provides a platform for students and professionals to tackle real-world problems, innovate, and experiment with creative solutions. Projects often involve designing, building, and testing prototypes or systems, offering valuable hands-on experience and a deeper understanding of engineering principles. Competitions, on the other hand, challenge participants to solve complex problems under time constraints, fostering critical thinking and teamwork. These experiences not only enhance technical skills but also build a robust portfolio that highlights an individual's ability to apply their knowledge in dynamic and competitive environments.

By actively participating in projects and competitions, aspiring engineers can demonstrate their initiative, creativity, and commitment to the field, which are crucial traits sought by employers. Moreover, these activities provide opportunities for networking with industry professionals, gaining mentorship, and potentially securing job offers or internships. As the engineering profession continues to evolve, staying engaged in projects and competitions can significantly contribute to career development, offering both personal fulfillment and professional advancement.

5.2.1 Engineering Projects

Engineering projects are fundamental to translating theoretical knowledge into practical applications, offering students and professionals the opportunity to tackle real-world challenges and innovate solutions. These projects encompass a wide range of activities, from designing and constructing new systems and technologies to improving existing processes and solving complex problems. Engaging in engineering projects fosters critical thinking, enhances technical skills, and provides hands-on experience with industry-standard tools and methodologies.

Additionally, they develop project management and teamwork abilities, as many projects require coordination, resource management, and collaboration with others. Successfully completing engineering projects not only builds a robust portfolio that demonstrates technical proficiency and creativity but also prepares individuals for the dynamic demands of the engineering profession, making them more competitive and effective in their careers.

Importance of Engineering Projects

1. **Practical Application of Theory**: Engineering projects provide a hands-on opportunity to apply theoretical knowledge gained in the classroom to real-world problems. This practical experience helps solidify understanding of complex concepts and demonstrates how they function in practice.

2. **Problem-Solving Skills**: Projects often require engineers to tackle open-ended problems, encouraging critical thinking and innovative solutions. This process develops problem-solving skills and the ability to approach challenges from multiple perspectives.

3. **Technical Proficiency**: Working on engineering projects enhances technical skills by involving the use of tools, technologies, and methodologies relevant to the field. This includes everything from design software to experimental techniques and manufacturing processes.

4. **Project Management Experience**: Engineering projects often require planning, budgeting, scheduling, and coordination of resources. Managing these aspects fosters project management

skills, such as time management, resource allocation, and team collaboration.

5. **Teamwork and Collaboration**: Many engineering projects are team-based, requiring effective communication and collaboration. Working with others on projects helps develop interpersonal skills, team dynamics understanding, and the ability to function in diverse teams.

6. **Portfolio Development**: Successful engineering projects contribute to a portfolio that showcases a candidate's skills, creativity, and accomplishments. A well-documented portfolio can be a powerful tool in job applications, interviews, and career advancement.

7. **Industry Exposure**: Projects often involve working with industry-standard practices and technologies. This exposure helps bridge the gap between academic learning and industry expectations, providing a more comprehensive understanding of the field.

8. **Career Advancement**: Demonstrating involvement in significant engineering projects can enhance employability by showing potential employers that candidates have practical experience, initiative, and a proven track record of problem-solving and innovation.

The Way Forward

1. **Select Relevant Projects**: Choose projects that align with your interests and career goals. Whether working on academic projects, research initiatives, or personal endeavors, selecting projects that match your professional aspirations ensures more meaningful and targeted experience.

2. **Set Clear Objectives**: Define specific goals and outcomes for each project. Setting clear objectives helps in focusing efforts, measuring progress, and evaluating the success of the project. Objectives should be realistic and aligned with both personal learning and project requirements.

3. **Develop a Plan**: Create a detailed project plan that includes timelines, milestones, resources, and responsibilities. A well-organized plan helps manage the project efficiently, ensuring that tasks are completed on schedule and within budget.

4. **Leverage Resources**: Utilize available resources, such as mentors, industry contacts, and educational materials, to enhance the project's success. Seeking guidance and feedback from experienced professionals can provide valuable insights and improve the project outcome.

5. **Document Progress**: Keep detailed records of the project's progress, including design iterations, testing results, and final outcomes. Thorough documentation not only helps in troubleshooting and refining the project but also serves as a valuable component of your portfolio.

6. **Seek Feedback**: Regularly seek feedback from peers, mentors, and supervisors. Constructive feedback helps identify areas for improvement, refine skills, and ensure that the project meets its objectives.

7. **Reflect and Learn**: After completing a project, take time to reflect on what worked well and what could be improved. Analyzing the project's successes and challenges provides insights into your strengths and areas for growth, contributing to ongoing professional development.

8. **Showcase Achievements**: Highlight completed projects in your resume, LinkedIn profile, and professional portfolio. Emphasize key achievements, technical skills, and contributions to demonstrate your capabilities and value to potential employers.

9. **Stay Updated**: Engineering practices and technologies are constantly evolving. Stay informed about industry trends, new tools, and

emerging technologies to ensure that your projects remain relevant and incorporate the latest advancements.

Nut Shell: By actively engaging in engineering projects and following these strategies, individuals can enhance their technical expertise, develop valuable skills, and build a strong foundation for a successful engineering career.

5.2.2 Competitions

Engineering competitions serve as a dynamic platform for students and professionals to showcase their ingenuity, problem-solving skills, and technical expertise in a competitive environment. These contests often present complex challenges that require innovative solutions, pushing participants to apply their knowledge in novel ways and under time constraints. Competitions foster creativity, collaboration, and perseverance, as teams work together to develop and refine their ideas, prototype solutions, and present their results.

Beyond the immediate challenge, participating in engineering competitions offers valuable exposure to industry trends, networking opportunities with peers and professionals, and potential pathways to career advancement. Success in these competitions can enhance one's resume, demonstrate practical skills and a proactive mindset to employers, and provide a significant boost to professional development and recognition in the engineering field.

Importance of Engineering Competitions

1. **Encourages Innovation**: Competitions often present unique and challenging problems that require creative and novel solutions. This environment stimulates innovative thinking and encourages participants to push the boundaries of conventional engineering practices.

2. **Hands-On Experience**: Competitions provide practical, hands-on experience that complements academic learning. Participants work on real-world problems, develop prototypes, and test their solutions, which helps translate theoretical knowledge into practical application.

3. **Skill Development**: Engaging in competitions helps develop a wide range of skills, including technical proficiency, project management, teamwork, and problem-solving. Participants learn to work under pressure, manage time effectively, and navigate the complexities of real-world engineering tasks.

4. **Networking Opportunities**: Competitions bring together individuals from diverse backgrounds and industries, offering valuable networking opportunities. Participants can connect with industry experts, potential employers, and fellow competitors, expanding their professional network and opening doors to future opportunities.

5. **Career Advancement**: Success in engineering competitions can significantly enhance a participant's resume and professional profile. It demonstrates to employers a high level of competence, creativity, and the ability to tackle challenging problems, making candidates more attractive for internships and job positions.

6. **Recognition and Rewards**: Many competitions offer awards, scholarships, and other forms of recognition. Achievements in these contests can lead to public recognition, increased visibility in the engineering community, and even financial incentives that support further education or projects.

7. **Teamwork and Collaboration**: Competitions often require participants to work in teams, which fosters collaboration and improves interpersonal skills. Learning to work effectively with

others, share responsibilities, and resolve conflicts are crucial skills in both academic and professional settings.

The Way Forward

1. **Identify Relevant Competitions**: Research and select competitions that align with your interests, skills, and career goals. Whether local, national, or international, choosing contests that resonate with your professional aspirations ensure a more focused and meaningful experience.

2. **Prepare Strategically**: Start preparing well in advance by studying past competition problems, understanding the judging criteria, and assembling a skilled team if applicable. Effective preparation involves both technical skill development and strategic planning.

3. **Leverage Resources**: Utilize available resources such as mentorship from experienced professionals, academic advisors, and industry contacts. These resources can provide guidance, technical support, and insights that enhance your competitive edge.

4. **Document and Reflect**: Keep detailed records of your competition experience, including project development, challenges faced, and solutions implemented. Reflecting on these experiences helps in understanding your strengths, areas for improvement, and overall growth.

5. **Engage Actively**: Participate actively in the competition process, from brainstorming and prototyping to presenting and evaluating results. Full engagement maximizes learning opportunities and demonstrates commitment and enthusiasm to judges and peers.

6. **Network and Follow Up**: Use the competition as a platform to network with industry professionals, judges, and fellow participants. Follow up with these connections to build relationships, seek advice, and explore potential career opportunities.

7. **Showcase Achievements**: Highlight your competition successes on your resume, LinkedIn profile, and professional portfolio. Emphasize specific accomplishments, technical skills, and lessons learned to enhance your professional profile and appeal to employers.

8. **Stay Informed**: Keep up with trends and advancements in your field by participating in ongoing competitions and staying engaged with industry developments. Continued involvement in competitions can provide a continuous learning experience and maintain relevance in a rapidly evolving field.

Nut Shell: By embracing engineering competitions and following these strategies, individuals can enhance their skills, gain valuable experience, and advance their careers while making a meaningful impact in the engineering field.

5.3 Volunteering and Leadership Role

Volunteering and leadership roles are integral to developing a comprehensive engineering career, offering opportunities that extend well beyond technical proficiency. Volunteering allows engineers to apply their skills to address real-world problems, support community initiatives, and contribute to causes they are passionate about. This engagement fosters a sense of social responsibility and provides practical experience in diverse settings.

Meanwhile, assuming leadership roles within these volunteer activities or in professional environments helps build crucial management skills, such as strategic thinking, team coordination, and effective communication. These experiences not only enhance personal growth but also demonstrate to potential employers a candidate's ability to take initiative, lead teams, and drive projects to success. By combining technical expertise with strong leadership and a commitment to community service, engineers can create a well-rounded professional profile that stands out in a competitive job market, paving the way for career advancement and long-term success.

5.3.1 Volunteering Role

Volunteering roles offer engineers a unique platform to apply their skills and knowledge in meaningful ways outside of traditional work settings. By participating in volunteer activities, engineers can address community needs, contribute to social causes, and support initiatives that leverage their technical expertise. These roles often involve working on projects such as building infrastructure for underserved areas, providing educational workshops, or developing technology solutions for non-profit organizations.

Engaging in such activities not only enhances personal satisfaction and a sense of purpose but also broadens professional horizons by offering exposure to diverse challenges and perspectives. Volunteering helps engineers develop soft skills like leadership, communication, and teamwork while demonstrating their commitment to social responsibility. Moreover, these experiences enrich their resumes, showcasing their ability to apply engineering skills in real-world, impactful ways and fostering connections with like-minded professionals and community leaders.

Importance of Volunteering

1. **Skill Application and Enhancement**: Volunteering provides engineers with the opportunity to apply their technical skills in diverse and often unconventional settings. This practical application helps reinforce and expand their expertise, while also allowing them to develop new skills that might not be covered in their formal education.

2. **Broader Impact**: Through volunteering, engineers can contribute to meaningful social and community initiatives, from building infrastructure in underserved areas to developing technology for non-profits. This involvement can make a significant difference in addressing societal challenges and improving quality of life for various communities.

3. **Personal Growth**: Volunteering fosters personal growth by challenging engineers to step outside their comfort zones, take on new responsibilities, and work with individuals from different backgrounds. This experience can enhance emotional intelligence, adaptability, and resilience.

4. **Networking Opportunities**: Engaging in volunteer work exposes engineers to a network of professionals, community leaders, and organizations. These connections can lead to valuable mentorship opportunities, collaborations, and potential career advancements.

5. **Leadership Development**: Many volunteer roles involve taking on leadership responsibilities, such as managing teams, coordinating projects, or spearheading initiatives. These experiences help engineers develop essential leadership skills, including strategic thinking, team management, and effective communication.

6. **Career Enhancement**: Volunteering can enrich an engineer's resume by showcasing their commitment to social responsibility and their ability to handle diverse challenges. This can make them more attractive to potential employers who value candidates with a well-rounded skill set and a strong sense of community engagement.

The Way Forward

1. **Identify Interests and Goals**: To make the most of volunteering, engineers should identify causes and projects that align with their interests and career goals. Whether it's mentoring students in STEM

fields, working on sustainable development projects, or supporting local non-profits, choosing the right fit ensures that the volunteer experience is both meaningful and enjoyable.

2. **Seek Relevant Opportunities**: Look for volunteer opportunities that leverage your engineering skills and offer the chance to tackle real-world problems. This can include partnering with non-profit organizations, participating in community-based projects, or joining engineering-focused volunteer groups.

3. **Set Clear Objectives**: Before starting a volunteer role, define what you hope to achieve. Setting clear goals helps in focusing efforts and measuring the impact of your contributions. Objectives could include developing specific skills, expanding your professional network, or making a tangible difference in a community.

4. **Commit Time and Resources**: Effective volunteering requires a commitment of time and effort. Ensure that you can balance your volunteer work with professional and personal responsibilities. Being reliable and dedicated to your volunteer role maximizes its impact and effectiveness.

5. **Develop and Document Skills**: Actively seek opportunities to develop new skills and take on leadership roles within your volunteer activities. Document your experiences and accomplishments to highlight in your resume and professional portfolio, showcasing your contributions and growth.

6. **Reflect and Adapt**: After completing a volunteer role, take time to reflect on the experience. Evaluate what you learned, the challenges you faced, and the skills you developed. Use these insights to adapt your future volunteering efforts and continue building on your personal and professional growth.

7. **Leverage Connections**: Build and maintain relationships with fellow volunteers, community leaders, and organizations. These

connections can provide ongoing support, advice, and potential career opportunities. Engage with your network to stay informed about new volunteer opportunities and industry trends.

8. **Promote Volunteering Culture**: Advocate for and promote the value of volunteering within your professional circles. Encourage colleagues and peers to get involved in community service, creating a culture of giving back and contributing to societal betterment.

Nut Shell: By actively engaging in volunteering and following these strategies, engineers can significantly enhance their personal and professional development, create a positive impact in their communities, and build a well-rounded and fulfilling career.

5.3.2 Leadership Role

Leadership roles are crucial in shaping the direction and success of teams and organizations, requiring a blend of strategic vision, effective communication, and team management. A leader's ability to set clear goals, inspire and motivate team members, and make informed decisions drives both individual and collective achievements. Beyond directing day-to-day operations, leaders play a pivotal role in fostering a positive work environment, encouraging innovation, and addressing challenges proactively. They influence organizational culture and contribute to personal and professional growth within their teams.

By demonstrating integrity, resilience, and a commitment to continuous improvement, leaders not only advance their own careers but also drive their teams and organizations toward long-term success.

Importance of Leadership Roles

1. **Strategic Vision and Direction**: Leaders provide a vision for the future and set strategic goals that align with organizational objectives. Effective leadership involves charting a clear path forward, making

informed decisions, and ensuring that all team members are aligned with the overarching goals.

2. **Team Management and Development**: Leadership roles require the ability to manage and motivate a team. This includes delegating tasks, providing feedback, and fostering a positive work environment. Strong leaders help team members develop their skills, promote collaboration, and address conflicts constructively.

3. **Innovation and Problem Solving**: Leaders play a key role in driving innovation and solving complex problems. They are responsible for encouraging creative thinking, exploring new approaches, and implementing solutions that advance projects and improve processes.

4. **Effective Communication**: Communication is a cornerstone of effective leadership. Leaders must be able to clearly articulate goals, expectations, and feedback, as well as listen to and address concerns from team members. Strong communication helps build trust and ensures that everyone is on the same page.

5. **Responsibility and Accountability**: Leaders are accountable for the success and performance of their teams and projects. This involves taking responsibility for outcomes, addressing challenges, and making decisions that drive results. Accountability helps ensure that goals are met and standards are upheld.

6. **Career Advancement**: Demonstrating leadership skills can significantly impact career progression. Effective leaders are often recognized for their contributions and may be considered for higher-level positions and more complex projects, leading to greater professional opportunities and advancement.

7. **Organizational Culture**: Leaders influence the culture and values of an organization. By modeling desired behaviors and fostering a positive work environment, leaders contribute to a culture of excellence, collaboration, and integrity.

The Way Forward

1. **Develop Leadership Skills**: To excel in leadership roles, focus on developing key skills such as strategic thinking, emotional intelligence, communication, and conflict resolution. Pursue leadership training, workshops, and mentorship opportunities to enhance these skills.

2. **Seek Leadership Opportunities**: Proactively seek out and volunteer for leadership roles within your current organization, professional associations, or community projects. Taking on responsibilities such as project management, team leadership, or committee roles provides valuable experience and demonstrates your readiness for higher-level positions.

3. **Set Clear Goals**: Define clear and achievable goals for your leadership role. This includes setting objectives for team performance, project outcomes, and personal development. Regularly review and adjust these goals to ensure alignment with organizational priorities and evolving challenges.

4. **Foster Team Collaboration**: Focus on building strong, collaborative teams by encouraging open communication, recognizing contributions, and providing support. Promote an environment where team members feel valued and motivated to contribute their best work.

5. **Lead by Example**: Model the behaviors and values you expect from your team. Demonstrate integrity, accountability, and a strong work ethic. Leading by example helps establish credibility and fosters a culture of trust and respect.

6. **Seek Feedback and Adapt**: Regularly seek feedback from team members, peers, and mentors. Use this feedback to identify areas for improvement and adapt your leadership approach as needed. Being open to constructive criticism helps you grow as a leader and better support your team.

7. **Build Relationships and Network**: Develop strong relationships with colleagues, stakeholders, and industry professionals. Networking provides insights into best practices, trends, and opportunities for collaboration, and can support your leadership development and career growth.

8. **Continuously Learn and Innovate**: Stay informed about industry trends, emerging technologies, and new leadership strategies. Continuously learning and adapting ensures that you remain effective in your role and can guide your team through evolving challenges and opportunities.

Nut Shell: Embracing leadership roles and following these strategies, individuals can effectively guide teams, drive organizational success, and advance their careers while making a positive impact on their professional environment.

5.4 Networking and Professional Associations

Networking and professional associations are fundamental to the career trajectory of engineering graduates, serving as essential tools for transitioning from academic settings to the professional world. For recent graduates, these platforms offer critical opportunities to build connections with seasoned professionals, explore career paths, and gain practical insights that complement their technical education. By joining engineering societies and attending industry events, graduates can engage in discussions about current challenges and innovations, access exclusive job boards, and benefit from tailored career resources.

Moreover, involvement in these associations often provides avenues for continuing education, certifications, and leadership roles, which are vital for career advancement. Through active participation, engineering graduates not only enhance their knowledge and skills but also increase their visibility in the field, paving the way for successful and fulfilling careers.

5.4.1 Networking

Networking is the art of building and maintaining professional relationships that can support career growth and development. For engineering graduates, it involves connecting with peers, mentors, and industry professionals to exchange knowledge, explore job opportunities, and gain insights into emerging trends. Effective networking requires active participation in industry events, joining relevant associations, and fostering genuine connections through meaningful interactions. By cultivating a robust network, graduates can enhance their professional visibility, access valuable resources, and navigate their career paths more effectively.

1. **The Importance of Strategic Networking**: Effective networking for engineering graduates means moving beyond surface-level interactions and fostering genuine, long-term relationships. This involves being proactive in seeking out and connecting with individuals who can provide mentorship, career advice, or introductions to other key professionals. By participating in professional associations such as the IEEE (Institute of Electrical and Electronics Engineers), ASME (American Society of Mechanical Engineers), or other specialized engineering organizations, graduates can access a wealth of resources, from industry publications and professional development workshops to networking events and certification programs.

2. **Building and Nurturing Relationships**: Building a robust professional network requires intentional effort. Graduates should focus on identifying and reaching out to individuals who align with their career goals and interests. This includes engaging in conversations at industry events, joining relevant online

groups, and actively participating in discussions and projects. Maintaining these relationships is equally important—regular follow-ups, sharing relevant information, and offering support to others in the network can help sustain these connections over time.

3. **Leveraging Networking for Career Growth**: Networking can significantly impact career development by providing access to job opportunities, industry insights, and professional advice. For example, connections made through networking can lead to job referrals, collaborations on projects, or even invitations to speak at conferences. Furthermore, staying engaged with a network of industry professionals helps graduates stay informed about the latest trends, technologies, and best practices in their field, which is crucial for career advancement.

4. **Embracing Continuous Learning and Adaptability**: The engineering field is continuously evolving, with new technologies and methodologies emerging rapidly. To stay relevant, graduates must embrace a mindset of continuous learning and adaptability. Networking provides a channel to remain updated on these advancements, as professionals in the field often share insights and experiences that can be invaluable. Participating in ongoing education, obtaining certifications, and engaging in industry-related discussions can help graduates adapt to changes and enhance their expertise.

5. **The Long-Term Benefits of Effective Networking**: In the long run, effective networking can lead to numerous career benefits, including leadership opportunities, collaborative projects, and professional recognition. Building a solid network helps establish a support system that can provide guidance, encouragement,

and opportunities throughout one's career. By staying actively engaged and contributing to their professional community, engineering graduates can achieve sustained career success and growth.

Nut Shell: Networking is a critical component of career development for engineering graduates. By adopting a strategic approach, actively building and maintaining relationships, and staying informed about industry trends, graduates can leverage their networks to enhance their professional journey and achieve their career aspirations.

5.4.2 Professional Associations

Professional associations are organizations dedicated to advancing the interests of individuals within a specific field, providing resources, support, and opportunities for professional growth. For engineering graduates, these associations offer a range of benefits, from networking opportunities and industry insights to professional development and certification programs. Examples include the American Society of Civil Engineers (ASCE), the Institute of Electrical and Electronics Engineers (IEEE), the Society of Mechanical Engineers (ASME) and Textile Association of India (TAI). These organizations serve as a hub for knowledge sharing, career advancement, and peer support.

1. **Engaging with Professional Associations**: Active participation in professional associations allows engineering graduates to stay abreast of industry trends, access continuing education, and engage in collaborative projects. Membership often provides access to exclusive industry publications, technical journals, and professional conferences where members can present their work, learn from experts, and network with peers. Additionally, many

associations offer mentorship programs, career services, and job boards that can be instrumental in finding employment and advancing one's career.

2. **Professional Development and Certification**: One of the key advantages of joining a professional association is the access to professional development resources. Many associations offer certification programs, workshops, and training courses that help members enhance their skills and stay competitive in the rapidly evolving engineering field. These credentials not only boost a graduate's qualifications but also demonstrate a commitment to ongoing learning and excellence in their profession.

3. **The Way Forward**: Looking ahead, engineering graduates should consider leveraging professional associations as a strategic component of their career development plan. Engaging actively in these organizations can lead to numerous opportunities, including leadership roles, collaborative projects, and involvement in cutting-edge research. Graduates should seek out associations relevant to their specific engineering discipline, participate in their activities, and utilize the resources they offer to further their professional growth. By doing so, you can build a strong professional network, stay informed about industry advancements, and position themselves for long-term career success.

Nut Shell: Professional associations are invaluable for engineering graduates, offering a platform for continuous learning, career advancement, and professional networking. By embracing these opportunities and remaining actively involved, graduates can effectively navigate their careers and achieve their professional goals.

5.4.3 Challenges before engaging with professional associations

Engaging with professional associations offers numerous benefits, but it also comes with its own set of challenges. For engineering graduates, these challenges can impact their ability to fully leverage the resources and opportunities that associations provide. Key challenges include:

1. **Time Constraints**: Balancing the demands of a new job with active participation in professional associations can be difficult. Graduates may struggle to find time for association meetings, events, and activities amidst their professional responsibilities and personal commitments.

2. **Financial Costs**: Membership fees, conference registrations, and certification programs can be costly. For recent graduates, managing these expenses while starting their careers can be a significant hurdle. Some associations offer discounted rates for students or early-career professionals, but costs can still be a barrier.

3. **Understanding the Value**: New graduates may have difficulty seeing the immediate value of joining a professional association, especially if they lack experience in the field. It can be challenging to understand how participation will translate into tangible career benefits without a clear understanding of the association's offerings.

4. **Networking Skills**: Effective networking requires strong interpersonal skills and confidence. Graduates who are new to the industry or introverted may find it challenging to build relationships and engage with established professionals, which can limit the effectiveness of their networking efforts.

5. **Overcoming Initial Inertia**: Getting started with professional associations can be daunting. Graduates may feel overwhelmed by the process of joining, participating in events, and making the most of available resources. Overcoming this initial inertia requires motivation and a proactive approach.

6. **Relevance of the Association**: Not all associations may align perfectly with a graduate's specific career goals or interests. Finding the right association that offers relevant resources and opportunities can be a challenge, especially if there are multiple options to choose from.

7. **Staying Updated**: Keeping up with association activities, newsletters, and changes in membership benefits requires consistent engagement. Graduates may struggle to stay informed about new opportunities or developments due to a lack of time or attention.

To address these challenges, engineering graduates can take several proactive steps. They can start by researching and selecting associations that closely align with their career goals, seeking out student or early-career memberships to reduce costs, and setting manageable goals for their involvement. Additionally, improving networking skills through practice and **seeking mentorship within the association** can enhance their experience and effectiveness. By navigating these challenges thoughtfully, graduates can maximize the benefits of professional associations and support their long-term career development.

And may more…

CHAPTER 6

Higher Education Opportunities

Higher education opportunities for engineering graduates offer a pathway to deepen expertise, enhance career prospects, and drive innovation within the field. As technology and engineering practices evolve rapidly, advanced degrees and specialized certifications become increasingly valuable. Engineering graduates can pursue master's and doctoral programs to gain advanced knowledge in their specific areas of interest, engage in cutting-edge research, and develop leadership skills.

Additionally, professional certifications and executive education programs provide targeted learning that complements practical experience. These opportunities not only broaden technical competencies but also open doors to higher-level positions, interdisciplinary roles, and academic or research-focused careers. By leveraging these educational advancements, engineering graduates can position themselves at the forefront of their profession and contribute to shaping the future of engineering.

Outcomes

- **Advanced Expertise:** Deepen knowledge and specialized skills in engineering.

- **Career Advancement:** Access higher-level positions and leadership roles.

- **Research Opportunities:** Contribute to innovative research and advancements.

- **Interdisciplinary Skills:** Work across various engineering disciplines.

- **Professional Certification:** Obtain advanced certifications for career competitiveness.

- **Leadership Development:** Enhance management and leadership abilities.

- **Networking:** Build professional connections for collaborations and opportunities.

- **Academic Careers:** Pursue teaching and research roles in academia.

- **Increased Earning Potential:** Boost earning potential with advanced qualifications.

- **Global Opportunities:** Expand career prospects in the international job market.

Pre-requisites

Relevant Undergraduate Degree:

- Engineering: A bachelor's degree in engineering or a closely related field.

- Management: A bachelor's degree in business, management, or a related field; sometimes degrees in other fields are also acceptable.

Strong Academic Record:

- Engineering: A solid foundation in mathematics, science, and engineering principles.

- Management: A good academic performance in business-related courses and quantitative subjects.

Standardized Test Scores (if required):

- Engineering: GATE or GRE etc. scores may be required for certain graduate programs.

- Management: GMAT or GRE scores are often required for MBA programs.

Relevant Work Experience:

- Engineering: Industry experience or internships can be beneficial but may not always be required.

- Management: Professional experience, especially in managerial or leadership roles, is often required or preferred.

Letters of Recommendation:

- Engineering: Recommendations from professors or professionals who can attest to academic and technical abilities.

- Management: Recommendations from supervisors or colleagues who can speak to leadership, work ethic, and managerial potential.

Statement of Purpose:

- Engineering: A clear explanation of research interests, career goals, and motivation for pursuing advanced studies.

- Management: An articulation of career aspirations, leadership experiences, and reasons for pursuing an MBA or management degree.

Resume/Curriculum Vitae:

- Engineering: A detailed resume highlighting academic achievements, research experience, and technical skills.

- Management: A CV showcasing professional achievements, managerial experience, and leadership roles.

Prerequisite Coursework (if applicable):

- Engineering: Completion of specific undergraduate courses or coursework relevant to the chosen specialization.

- Management: Completion of foundational business courses or prerequisites depending on the program.

Interview (if required):

- Engineering: Some programs may require an interview to assess fit and research interests.

- Management: Many MBA programs conduct interviews to evaluate candidates' fit and potential.

English Language Proficiency (if applicable):

- For non-native speakers, proof of proficiency through tests such as TOEFL or IELTS may be required.

6.1 Graduate Studies: Masters and PhDs

Pursuing a Master's or PhD in engineering represents a significant step toward deepening technical expertise, engaging in advanced research, and expanding career opportunities. A Master's degree typically provides specialized knowledge and skills in a particular engineering discipline, preparing graduates for advanced roles in industry or further academic pursuits. In contrast, a PhD program focuses on developing high-level research capabilities, contributing original knowledge to the field, and preparing individuals for careers in academia, research institutions, or specialized industry roles. Both advanced degrees offer a pathway to enhance one's professional credentials, drive innovation, and address complex engineering challenges, thus positioning graduates at the forefront of technological advancement and leadership within their field.

6.1.1 Opportunities

1. **Advanced Knowledge and Specialization:**

   - **Master's:** Gain in-depth understanding and specialized skills in a specific area of engineering, enhancing expertise and technical competence.

   - **PhD:** Conduct pioneering research and contribute original knowledge, establishing you as an expert in a niche area of engineering.

2. **Career Advancement:**

   - **Master's:** Open doors to higher-level positions, management roles, and specialized technical jobs within industry.

   - **PhD:** Access academic positions, research roles, and high-level consultancy opportunities, often with greater influence and responsibility.

3. **Research and Innovation:**

   - **Master's:** Participate in advanced projects and research initiatives, contributing to innovative solutions and technological advancements.

   - **PhD:** Lead cutting-edge research, drive technological breakthroughs, and influence the future direction of the field.

4. **Professional Networking:**

   - **Master's:** Build connections with industry professionals, professors, and peers, which can lead to job opportunities and collaborative projects.

- **PhD:** Develop a network of academic and research professionals, potentially collaborating on high-impact research and gaining access to exclusive conferences and journals.

5. **Teaching and Academic Careers:**

   - **Master's:** Opportunities to teach part-time or as a guest lecturer at educational institutions, enhancing teaching skills and academic experience.

   - **PhD:** Pursue a full-time academic career, including roles as a professor, researcher, or academic advisor, shaping the next generation of engineers.

6. **Enhanced Earning Potential:**

   - **Master's:** Achieve higher earning potential compared to a bachelor's degree, with access to advanced roles and specialized positions.

   - **PhD:** Command high salaries in specialized research and academic roles, often coupled with significant opportunities for grants and funding.

6.1.2 Challenges

1. **Time Commitment:**

   - **Master's:** Requires a substantial commitment of time and effort, balancing coursework, projects, and potentially work responsibilities.

   - **PhD:** Involves a long-term commitment, often taking several years to complete, with rigorous demands for research and dissertation work.

2. **Financial Implications:**

   - **Master's:** Can be expensive, with costs including tuition, books, and other expenses, which may require significant financial planning or taking on student loans.

- **PhD:** Often involves even higher costs, though some programs offer stipends or funding. Balancing financial demands with research responsibilities can be challenging.

3. **Work-Life Balance:**

   - **Master's:** Balancing academic workload with personal life and possibly professional responsibilities can be demanding.

   - **PhD:** The intense focus on research can lead to long hours and potential stress, impacting work-life balance and personal well-being.

4. **Academic Pressure:**

   - **Master's:** High expectations for academic performance and project outcomes can be stressful, especially in competitive programs.

   - **PhD:** Significant pressure to produce original research, meet publication requirements, and defend a dissertation can be overwhelming.

5. **Uncertainty in Career Path:**

   - **Master's:** While it opens up advanced roles, the specific career trajectory may still be uncertain, requiring strategic planning and job search efforts.

   - **PhD:** Academic and research careers can be highly competitive, with a need to secure postdoctoral positions or tenure-track roles, which may involve uncertainty and high competition.

6. **Specialization Limiting Flexibility:**

   - **Master's:** Specializing in a particular area can limit career flexibility if interests or industry demands shift.

   - **PhD:** Highly specialized research may narrow career options, making transitions to different fields or industries more challenging.

Nut Shell: Overall, while advanced degrees in engineering offer significant opportunities for career growth, research, and specialization, they also present challenges that require careful consideration and preparation. Balancing these opportunities and challenges is key to making the most of a Master's or PhD program.

6.2 Specializations and Advanced Degrees

Specialization and advanced degrees are pivotal in shaping the trajectory of an engineering career, providing the expertise and credentials needed to excel in complex and evolving fields. Specialization allows professionals to focus on a particular area of interest, such as robotics in mechanical engineering or cyber security in computer engineering, honing their skills and knowledge to address specific challenges and drive innovation.

Advanced degrees, such as a Master's or PhD, further enhance this specialization by offering in-depth study and research opportunities, leading to greater career advancement, leadership roles, and contributions to cutting-edge developments. Together, specialization and advanced degrees equip engineers with the advanced competencies and credentials necessary to tackle intricate problems, lead impactful projects, and remain at the forefront of their disciplines.

1. **Mechanical Engineering:**

- **Specializations:**
  - Thermodynamics and Heat Transfer
  - Robotics and Automation
  - Aerospace Engineering
  - Manufacturing and Production Systems
  - Mechanics of Materials

- **Advanced Degrees:**
  - **Master's:** M.S./M.E./M. Tech in Mechanical Engineering with a focus on specific areas like robotics, thermodynamics, or manufacturing.
  - **PhD:** Ph.D. in Mechanical Engineering, often focusing on advanced research in robotics, energy systems, or materials science.

2. **Electrical Engineering:**

- **Specializations:**
  - Power Systems and Energy
  - Electronics and Circuits
  - Control Systems
  - Communication Systems
  - Signal Processing

- **Advanced Degrees:**
  - **Master's:** M.S./M.E./M.Tech in Electrical Engineering with concentrations in power systems, electronics, or communications.
  - **PhD:** Ph.D. in Electrical Engineering, focusing on advanced topics such as renewable energy, integrated circuits, or machine learning applications.

3. **Civil Engineering:**

- **Specializations:**
  - Structural Engineering
  - Environmental Engineering
  - Geotechnical Engineering
  - Transportation Engineering
  - Water Resources Engineering

- **Advanced Degrees:**
  - **Master's:** M.S./M.E./M. Tech in Civil Engineering with specializations in structural, environmental, or transportation engineering.
  - **PhD:** Ph.D. in Civil Engineering, often focusing on advanced research in structural analysis, environmental impact, or geotechnical methods.

4. **Chemical Engineering:**

- **Specializations:**
  - Process Engineering
  - Biochemical Engineering
  - Materials Science
  - Catalysis and Reaction Engineering
  - Environmental Chemical Engineering

- **Advanced Degrees:**
  - **Master's:** M.S./M.E./M. Tech in Chemical Engineering with a focus on process design, biochemical processes, or environmental engineering.
  - **PhD:** Ph.D. in Chemical Engineering, focusing on advanced topics such as reaction kinetics, biochemical systems, or nano-materials.

5. **Computer Engineering:**

- **Specializations:**
  - Embedded Systems
  - Software Engineering
  - Computer Networks
  - Cyber security
  - Artificial Intelligence and Machine Learning

- **Advanced Degrees:**
  - **Master's:** M.S./M.E./M.Tech in Computer Engineering with specializations in embedded systems, cyber security, or software development.
  - **PhD:** Ph.D. in Computer Engineering, focusing on cutting-edge research in AI, ML, cyber security, or advanced computational systems.

6. **Aerospace Engineering:**

- **Specializations:**
  - Aerodynamics
  - Propulsion Systems
  - Structural Analysis
  - Space Systems
  - Avionics

- **Advanced Degrees:**
  - **Master's:** M.S./M.E./M. Tech in Aerospace Engineering with a focus on aerodynamics, propulsion, or space systems.
  - **PhD:** Ph.D. in Aerospace Engineering, concentrating on advanced research in aerodynamics, spacecraft design, or propulsion technologies.

7. **Biomedical Engineering:**

- **Specializations:**
  - Biomaterials
  - Medical Devices
  - Biomechanics
  - Tissue Engineering
  - Medical Imaging

- **Advanced Degrees:**
  - **Master's:** M.S./M.E./M.Tech in Biomedical Engineering with specializations in medical devices, biomechanics, or tissue engineering.
  - **PhD:** Ph.D. in Biomedical Engineering, focusing on research in biomaterials, medical imaging, or innovative medical technologies.

8. **Environmental Engineering:**

- **Specializations:**
  - Water and Wastewater Treatment
  - Air Quality Management
  - Environmental Health
  - Sustainable Development
  - Climate Change Mitigation

- **Advanced Degrees:**
  - **Master's:** M.S./M.E./M.Tech in Environmental Engineering with concentrations in water treatment, air quality, or sustainable practices.
  - **PhD:** Ph.D. in Environmental Engineering, focusing on advanced research in environmental systems, climate change, or pollution control technologies.

9. **Industrial Engineering:**

- **Specializations:**
  - Operations Research
  - Supply Chain Management
  - Human Factors Engineering

- Systems Engineering
- Quality Engineering
- **Advanced Degrees:**
  - **Master's:** M.S./M.E./M.Tech in Industrial Engineering with focuses on operations research, supply chain management, or systems engineering.
  - **PhD:** Ph.D. in Industrial Engineering, concentrating on advanced topics such as optimization, system design, or quality control.

10. **Materials Science and Engineering:**

- **Specializations:**
  - Nano-materials
  - Polymers
  - Ceramics
  - Metals and Alloys
  - Biomaterials
- **Advanced Degrees:**
  - **Master's:** M.S./M.E./M. Tech in Materials Science and Engineering with specializations in nano-materials, polymers, or biomaterials.
  - **PhD:** Ph.D. in Materials Science and Engineering, focusing on advanced research in material properties, nanotechnology, or composite materials.

Each branch of engineering offers a variety of specializations and advanced degrees tailored to specific interests and career goals, enabling graduates to pursue careers in cutting-edge areas of their field.Top of Form

6.3 Choosing the Right Program and Institution

Choosing the right program and institution for advanced studies is a crucial decision that significantly impacts your academic and professional future. Whether you're pursuing a specialization in engineering or transitioning to a new field like management, selecting a program that aligns with your career goals, interests, and values is essential. The right institution should offer a curriculum that matches your desired focus, access to esteemed faculty, and opportunities for hands-on experience and networking.

Factors such as the program's reputation, resources, location, and financial considerations also play a vital role in this decision. By carefully evaluating these aspects, you can ensure that your choice will provide the knowledge, skills, and opportunities necessary to achieve your long-term career aspirations and personal growth.

Challenges:

1. **Program Fit and Specialization:**
   - **Challenge:** Identifying a program that aligns perfectly with your career goals and interests can be difficult, especially when programs offer varying specializations and focuses.
   - **Possible Solution:** Research program curriculums thoroughly and consult with academic advisors or industry professionals. Attend informational sessions and connect with current students or alumni to gain insights into how well the program matches your career objectives.

2. **Institution Reputation and Quality:**
   - **Challenge:** Assessing the reputation and quality of institutions can be challenging, as rankings and reviews may not always

reflect the specific strengths or weaknesses relevant to your chosen field.

- **Possible Solution:** Look for accreditation status and program-specific rankings, and consider institutions known for strong faculty and research in your area of interest. Seek out testimonials and reviews from graduates and industry professionals.

3. **Cost and Financial Aid:**

   - **Challenge:** Evaluating the cost of programs and the availability of financial aid can be complex, particularly if you are considering multiple institutions with varying tuition fees and funding options.

   - **Possible Solution:** Compare tuition costs and explore scholarship opportunities, assistantships, and financial aid options. Reach out to financial aid offices at prospective institutions to understand the full range of available support.

4. **Location and Logistics:**

   - **Challenge:** Deciding on a program's location involves considering factors such as geographic preference, cost of living, and proximity to potential job markets or family.

   - **Possible Solution:** Weigh the benefits of location, including proximity to industry hubs, lifestyle preferences, and available resources. If possible, visit campuses to get a feel for the environment and logistical aspects.

5. **Program Duration and Flexibility:**

   - **Challenge:** Determining how long a program will take to complete and how flexible it is regarding part-time options, online formats, or course scheduling can impact your decision, especially if you are balancing work or personal commitments.

   - **Possible Solution:** Review program structures and course formats. Consider whether the program offers flexible scheduling, part-time options, or online courses to accommodate your personal and professional life.

6. **Admission Requirements:**

   - **Challenge:** Understanding and meeting admission requirements, including prerequisites, standardized tests, and application materials, can be daunting and time-consuming.

   - **Possible Solution:** Carefully review admission criteria for each program and create a checklist of required materials. Contact admissions offices for clarification and assistance if needed.

7. **Career Services and Outcomes:**

   - **Challenge:** Evaluating the effectiveness of career services and the program's impact on employment outcomes can be challenging, as outcomes can vary widely across institutions.

   - **Possible Solution:** Investigate the career support services offered by the program and review employment statistics and job placement rates for graduates. Look for information on internships, industry connections, and alumni career achievements.

Way Out

- **Conduct Thorough Research:** Utilize online resources, program websites, and academic reviews to gather detailed information about each program. Attend open houses, webinars, and networking events to gain a deeper understanding of the offerings and culture of prospective institutions.

- **Seek Advice:** Engage with academic advisors, mentors, and professionals in your field to get personalized recommendations and insights. Their experiences and advice can provide valuable perspective on making an informed decision.

- **Evaluate Personal Goals:** Reflect on your long-term career goals, personal preferences, and financial situation. Align your program choice with these factors to ensure that it supports your aspirations and lifestyle.

- **Visit Campuses and Talk to Alumni:** Whenever possible, visit campuses to experience the environment and interact with current students and alumni. Their firsthand experiences can offer a clearer picture of what to expect from the program and institution.

- **Plan Financially:** Develop a comprehensive budget and explore all available financial aid options. Plan ahead to manage costs effectively and ensure that you can afford your chosen program without undue financial strain.

Nut Shell: By addressing these challenges with careful research and strategic planning, you can make a well-informed decision about the right program and institution that best suits your academic and professional goals.

6.4 Application Processes and Funding Options

The application process for higher education typically involves several key steps to ensure a thorough evaluation of your qualifications and fit for the program. It begins with researching programs and institutions to identify those that align with your academic and career goals. Next, you'll need to prepare and submit essential documents, including transcripts, standardized test scores, letters of recommendation, and a statement of purpose (*in case you wish to opt for higher education from Universities or institutions other than your own country*).

Each program may have specific requirements, so careful attention to deadlines and application instructions are crucial. Additionally, some programs may require interviews or portfolio submissions. By meticulously following application guidelines and showcasing your strengths and aspirations, you can enhance your chances of admission to your desired higher education program.

6.4.1 Steps in Application Process

In India

1. **Research and Selection:**

   - **Identify Programs and Institutions:** Research various universities and colleges to find programs that match your academic interests and career goals.

   - **Check Eligibility:** Verify the eligibility criteria for each program, including academic qualifications, entrance exams, and any specific requirements.

2. **Entrance Exams:**

   - **Prepare and Register:** Many programs require entrance exams (e.g., JEE, GATE, CAT). Register for the relevant exams and prepare accordingly.

   - **Take the Exam:** Complete the entrance exams as per the scheduled dates.

3. **Application Form:**

   - **Fill Out Forms:** Obtain and complete the application forms for the chosen institutions. This can often be done online through the institution's application portal.

- **Submit Documents:** Provide necessary documents such as academic transcripts, test scores, proof of identity, and photographs.

4. **Statement of Purpose (SOP) and Essays:**

   - **Prepare SOP/Essays:** Write and submit a Statement of Purpose or personal essays as required, detailing your academic background, career goals, and reasons for choosing the program.

5. **Letters of Recommendation (LOR):**

   - **Obtain Recommendations:** Request letters of recommendation from professors, employers, or professionals who can attest to your academic and professional abilities.

6. **Interview (if required):**

   - **Prepare and Attend:** Some programs may require an interview as part of the selection process. Prepare for and attend the interview if applicable.

7. **Application Fee:**

   - **Pay Fee:** Pay the application fee as required by the institution, which can usually be done online or via bank transfer.

8. **Submit Application:**

   - **Review and Submit:** Review your application thoroughly before submitting it through the institution's application portal or via post, as required.

9. **Follow-Up:**

   - **Track Application Status:** Monitor the status of your application through the institution's online portal or via email. Respond promptly to any additional requests or information.

10. Admission Offer and Enrollment:

- **Accept Offer:** If accepted, confirm your admission by following the institutions instructions, which may include paying an initial deposit and completing enrollment paperwork.

Abroad (Foreign Country)

1. Research and Selection:

- **Identify Programs and Institutions:** Explore universities and programs globally that align with your academic interests and career goals.

- **Check Requirements:** Review specific admission requirements for each program, including standardized tests, prerequisites, and application deadlines.

2. Standardized Tests:

- **Prepare and Register:** Register and prepare for standardized tests such as the GRE, GMAT, SAT, or TOEFL/IELTS for English proficiency.

- **Take the Test:** Complete the required tests and ensure scores are sent to the relevant institutions.

3. Application Form:

- **Complete Forms:** Fill out the application forms for each institution, typically done through their online application systems or Common Application platforms.

- **Submit Documents:** Include required documents such as academic transcripts, standardized test scores, proof of English proficiency, and other necessary documents.

4. Statement of Purpose (SOP) and Essays:

- **Draft and Submit:** Write and submit a Statement of Purpose and any required essays that highlight your academic background, experiences, and goals.

5. **Letters of Recommendation (LOR):**

   - **Request and Submit:** Obtain and submit letters of recommendation from professors, employers, or supervisors who can provide strong endorsements of your qualifications.

6. **Interview (if required):**

   - **Prepare and Participate:** Some programs may conduct interviews as part of the selection process. Prepare for and attend any interviews if required.

7. **Application Fee:**

   - **Pay Fee:** Pay the application fees for each institution as required, which can usually be done online through the application portal.

8. **Submit Application:**

   - **Review and Submit:** Double-check all parts of your application before submission to ensure accuracy and completeness. Submit applications according to each institution's deadlines.

9. **Follow-Up:**

   - **Track Status:** Monitor the status of your application through the institution's portal or email. Provide any additional information or documentation as requested.

10. **Admission Offer and Enrollment:**

    - **Accept Offer:** If offered admission, follow the instructions provided by the institution to accept the offer, which may include paying a deposit and completing visa procedures.

6.4.2 Funding Options

1. **Scholarships and Fellowships:**
   - **India:**
     - **Government Scholarships:** Look for scholarships offered by the Indian government, such as the National Scholarship

Scheme, INSPIRE Scholarship, and scholarships for SC/ST/OBC students.

- **Institutional Scholarships:** Many Indian universities offer merit-based or need-based scholarships. Check with the specific institution you are applying to for details.

- **Private and Corporate Scholarships:** Companies and private organizations, like the Tata Trusts and Reliance Foundation, offer scholarships to support higher education.

- **Abroad:**

  - **University Scholarships:** Many universities offer scholarships to international students based on merit, need, or specific criteria. Research the scholarship opportunities at the universities you are interested in.

  - **Government Scholarships:** Programs like the Fulbright Program (USA), Chevening Scholarships (UK), and Erasmus Mundus (EU) etc. offer financial aid for international students.

  - **Private and Non-Profit Organizations:** Organizations like the Gates Foundation, Infosys Foundation, Ajim Premji Foundation and the Rotary Foundation etc. provide scholarships and fellowships for international study.

2. **Grants:**

- **India:**

  - **Government Grants:** Apply for grants from government bodies such as the University Grants Commission (UGC) or the All India Council for Technical Education (AICTE) for specific research or academic programs.

  - **Institutional Grants:** Check if your institution offers research or project grants for higher studies.

- **Abroad:**
    - **Research Grants:** Many universities and research institutions offer grants for research-based programs or projects. Look into grants provided by entities like the National Science Foundation (NSF) in the US or similar bodies in other countries.
    - **Study Abroad Grants:** Some countries and institutions offer grants specifically for students studying abroad. Investigate options available through international study programs.

3. **Assistantships and Fellowships:**
    - **India:**
        - **Teaching and Research Assistantships:** Many Indian universities offer assistantships that provide a stipend in exchange for teaching or research work. Check with the departments of interest for available positions.
        - **Research Fellowships:** Apply for fellowships that support research projects or PhD studies, often offered by research institutions or academic bodies.
    - **Abroad:**
        - **Graduate Assistantships:** Universities in countries like the US and Canada often offer teaching or research assistantships that cover tuition and provide a stipend.
        - **Research Fellowships:** Look for fellowships from research institutions like DAAD (Germany), Endeavour Postgraduate Award (Australia) etc. or academic societies that provide funding for advanced research projects.

4. **Student Loans:**
    - **India:**
        - **Government-Backed Loans:** Consider loans from government schemes like the Vidyalakshmi Education Loan

Scheme, which offers subsidized interest rates and flexible repayment options.

- **Private Banks:** Explore education loan options from banks like SBI, HDFC, and ICICI, which offer loans for higher education with various repayment plans.

- **Abroad:**

  - **Federal Student Loans:** In countries like the US, federal student loans such as Direct Subsidized Loans and Perkins Loans are available for eligible students.

  - **Private Loans:** Private lenders and banks offer student loans for studying abroad. Research lenders who specialize in international student loans and compare interest rates and terms.

5. **Crowd funding and Sponsorships:**

- **India:**

  - **Crowd funding Platforms:** Use suitable platforms like to raise funds for education expenses from friends, alumni association, family, and the public.

  - **Corporate Sponsorships:** Approach companies for sponsorships or educational sponsorship programs that support higher education.

- **Abroad:**

  - **Crowd funding:** Appropriate international platforms can be used to raise funds for educational expenses from a global audience.

  - **Corporate Sponsorships:** Some multinational companies offer sponsorships or partnerships for students pursuing higher education abroad.

6. **Financial Planning and Budgeting:**

   - **India and Abroad:**

     - **Create a Budget:** Plan a detailed budget covering tuition, living expenses, travel, and other costs. Include potential sources of income and financial aid.

     - **Save in Advance:** Start saving early for education expenses. Consider setting up a dedicated savings account or investment plan.

Nut Shell: By exploring these financial aid options and planning strategies, you can effectively manage the costs of higher education, whether studying in India or abroad. Research thoroughly, apply for multiple sources of financial support, and create a robust financial plan to ensure a smooth and affordable educational journey.

6.5 Migration from Engineering to Management

Migrating from engineering to management can be a highly rewarding career move, depending on your personal goals, interests, and skills. Here are some considerations to help determine if this transition is right for you:

Advantages:

1. **Broader Impact:** Management roles often involve overseeing projects, teams, and organizational strategies, allowing you to influence broader aspects of the business and drive significant change.

2. **Career Growth:** Transitioning to management can open doors to higher-level positions, including executive roles, which typically offer increased responsibilities and higher compensation.

3. **Diverse Skill Set:** Managing projects and teams requires a range of skills beyond technical expertise, such as leadership, communication, and strategic thinking. This transition can enhance your overall skill set and professional development.

4. **Leadership Opportunities:** If you enjoy guiding teams, making strategic decisions, and leading initiatives, a management role allows you to leverage these interests and capabilities.

5. **Interdisciplinary Experience:** Management roles often require collaboration across various departments and disciplines, offering a chance to gain experience and insights outside of engineering.

Challenges:

1. **Skill Gap:** Management roles require different skills compared to technical engineering roles, such as budgeting, team dynamics, and strategic planning. Bridging this gap may require additional training or education.

2. **Change in Focus:** Shifting from a technical role to a management role means moving away from hands-on engineering tasks to a focus on people, processes, and organizational goals. This change in focus might not suit everyone.

3. **Increased Responsibility:** Management positions come with increased responsibilities and pressures, including handling team conflicts, meeting organizational goals, and managing budgets, which can be stressful.

4. **Learning Curve:** Adapting to management practices, understanding organizational behavior, and mastering business strategy may require significant learning and adjustment.

5. **Potential for Reduced Technical Work:** In a management role, you might have less opportunity to engage in technical problem-solving

and engineering tasks, which could be a downside if you enjoy the technical aspects of engineering.

Conclusion

If you have a passion for leadership, strategic planning, and influencing organizational outcomes, migrating from engineering to management can be a fulfilling and beneficial career move. It's important to assess your long-term career goals, interest in managerial responsibilities, and willingness to acquire new skills. Gaining management experience through roles, projects, or additional education can help facilitate a smooth transition and enhance your effectiveness in a management position.

Most preferred higher technical education institutions in India

Here's a branch-wise list of the most preferred higher technical education institutions (Institutions of National Importance) in India, known for their strong programs and research facilities:

1. **Mechanical Engineering:**
   - Indian Institute of Technology (IIT) Bombay
   - Indian Institute of Technology (IIT) Madras
   - Indian Institute of Technology (IIT) Kanpur
   - Indian Institute of Technology (IIT) Kharagpur
   - Indian Institute of Technology (IIT) Delhi
   - National Institute of Technology (NIT) Tiruchirappalli
   - Indian Institute of Technology (IIT) Hyderabad

2. **Electrical Engineering:**
   - Indian Institute of Technology (IIT) Bombay
   - Indian Institute of Technology (IIT) Delhi
   - Indian Institute of Technology (IIT) Kanpur

- Indian Institute of Technology (IIT) Madras
- Indian Institute of Technology (IIT) Kharagpur
- National Institute of Technology (NIT) Warangal
- Indian Institute of Technology (IIT) Ropar

3. **Civil Engineering:**

- Indian Institute of Technology (IIT) Bombay
- Indian Institute of Technology (IIT) Kharagpur
- Indian Institute of Technology (IIT) Delhi
- Indian Institute of Technology (IIT) Madras
- Indian Institute of Technology (IIT) Roorkee
- National Institute of Technology (NIT) Calicut
- Indian Institute of Technology (IIT) Gandhinagar

4. **Chemical Engineering:**

- Indian Institute of Technology (IIT) Bombay
- Indian Institute of Technology (IIT) Kharagpur
- Indian Institute of Technology (IIT) Madras
- Indian Institute of Technology (IIT) Delhi
- Indian Institute of Technology (IIT) Roorkee
- National Institute of Technology (NIT) Rourkela
- Institute of Chemical Technology (ICT) Mumbai

5. **Computer Engineering:**

- Indian Institute of Technology (IIT) Bombay
- Indian Institute of Technology (IIT) Delhi
- Indian Institute of Technology (IIT) Kanpur
- Indian Institute of Technology (IIT) Madras
- Indian Institute of Technology (IIT) Hyderabad

- National Institute of Technology (NIT) Warangal
- International Institute of Information Technology (IIIT) Hyderabad

6. **Aerospace Engineering:**
   - Indian Institute of Technology (IIT) Bombay
   - Indian Institute of Technology (IIT) Kharagpur
   - Indian Institute of Technology (IIT) Kanpur
   - Indian Institute of Technology (IIT) Madras
   - Indian Institute of Technology (IIT) Hyderabad
   - National Institute of Technology (NIT) Trichy
   - Indian Institute of Space Science and Technology (IIST) Thiruvananthapuram

7. **Biomedical Engineering:**
   - Indian Institute of Technology (IIT) Kharagpur
   - Indian Institute of Technology (IIT) Delhi
   - Indian Institute of Technology (IIT) Bombay
   - Indian Institute of Technology (IIT) Madras
   - National Institute of Technology (NIT) Rourkela
   - Jawaharlal Nehru Technological University (JNTU) Hyderabad
   - Indian Institute of Technology (IIT) Jodhpur

8. **Environmental Engineering:**
   - Indian Institute of Technology (IIT) Bombay
   - Indian Institute of Technology (IIT) Kharagpur
   - Indian Institute of Technology (IIT) Delhi
   - Indian Institute of Technology (IIT) Madras

- Indian Institute of Technology (IIT) Roorkee
- National Institute of Technology (NIT) Warangal
- Jawaharlal Nehru University (JNU), New Delhi

9. **Industrial Engineering:**

- Indian Institute of Technology (IIT) Kharagpur
- Indian Institute of Technology (IIT) Bombay
- Indian Institute of Technology (IIT) Delhi
- Indian Institute of Technology (IIT) Madras
- National Institute of Industrial Engineering (NITIE), Mumbai
- National Institute of Technology (NIT) Trichy
- Indian Institute of Technology (IIT) Gandhinagar

10. **Materials Science and Engineering:**

- Indian Institute of Technology (IIT) Kharagpur
- Indian Institute of Technology (IIT) Bombay
- Indian Institute of Technology (IIT) Madras
- Indian Institute of Technology (IIT) Delhi
- Indian Institute of Technology (IIT) Roorkee
- National Institute of Technology (NIT) Rourkela
- Indian Institute of Technology (IIT) Hyderabad

11. **Textile Disciplines**

- Indian Institute of Technology (IIT) Delhi
- Indian Institute of Technology (IIT) Kharagpur
- Indian Institute of Technology (IIT) Madras
- National Institute of Fashion Technology (NIFT)
- Institute of Chemical Technology (ICT) Mumbai

- National Institute of Design (NID)

- Jawahar Lal Nehru Technical University (JNTU) Hyderabad

- National Institute of Technology, Jalandhar

Most preferred higher technical education institutions other than India

Here is a branch-wise list of potential institutions outside India for pursuing higher technical education:

1. **Mechanical Engineering:**

   - Massachusetts Institute of Technology (MIT), USA

   - Stanford University, USA

   - University of California, Berkeley, USA

   - Imperial College London, UK

   - ETH Zurich, Switzerland

   - University of Cambridge, UK

   - University of Tokyo, Japan

2. **Electrical Engineering:**
   - Stanford University, USA
   - University of California, Berkeley, USA
   - Massachusetts Institute of Technology (MIT), USA
   - ETH Zurich, Switzerland
   - University of Illinois Urbana-Champaign, USA
   - University of Cambridge, UK
   - University of Tokyo, Japan

3. **Civil Engineering:**
   - University of California, Berkeley, USA
   - Massachusetts Institute of Technology (MIT), USA
   - Stanford University, USA
   - University of Cambridge, UK
   - Imperial College London, UK
   - ETH Zurich, Switzerland
   - University of Melbourne, Australia

4. **Chemical Engineering:**
   - Massachusetts Institute of Technology (MIT), USA
   - Stanford University, USA
   - University of California, Berkeley, USA
   - University of Cambridge, UK
   - ETH Zurich, Switzerland
   - California Institute of Technology (Caltech), USA
   - University of Tokyo, Japan

5. **Computer Engineering:**
   - Massachusetts Institute of Technology (MIT), USA
   - Stanford University, USA
   - University of California, Berkeley, USA
   - Carnegie Mellon University, USA
   - ETH Zurich, Switzerland
   - University of Cambridge, UK
   - University of Toronto, Canada

6. **Aerospace Engineering:**
   - Massachusetts Institute of Technology (MIT), USA
   - California Institute of Technology (Caltech), USA
   - Stanford University, USA
   - University of Michigan, USA
   - Imperial College London, UK
   - ETH Zurich, Switzerland
   - University of Tokyo, Japan

7. **Biomedical Engineering:**
   - Massachusetts Institute of Technology (MIT), USA
   - Stanford University, USA
   - Johns Hopkins University, USA
   - University of California, San Diego, USA
   - ETH Zurich, Switzerland
   - University of Cambridge, UK
   - University of Toronto, Canada

8. **Environmental Engineering:**
   - Stanford University, USA
   - University of California, Berkeley, USA
   - Massachusetts Institute of Technology (MIT), USA
   - ETH Zurich, Switzerland
   - University of Cambridge, UK
   - Imperial College London, UK
   - University of Melbourne, Australia

9. **Industrial Engineering:**
   - Georgia Institute of Technology, USA
   - University of Michigan, USA
   - Stanford University, USA
   - Massachusetts Institute of Technology (MIT), USA
   - University of California, Berkeley, USA
   - University of Cambridge, UK
   - ETH Zurich, Switzerland

10. **Materials Science and Engineering:**
    - Massachusetts Institute of Technology (MIT), USA
    - Stanford University, USA
    - University of California, Berkeley, USA
    - University of Cambridge, UK
    - ETH Zurich, Switzerland
    - California Institute of Technology (Caltech), USA
    - University of Tokyo, Japan

11. Textile Disciplines

- Massachusetts Institute of Technology (MIT), USA
- University of California, Davis, USA
- North Carolina State University, USA
- University of Leeds, UK
- University of Manchester, UK
- Royal Melbourne Institute of Technology (RMIT), Australia
- University of Borås, Sweden
- Politecnico di Milano, Italy
- Aalto University, Finland

Most preferred higher technical education private institutions of India

Here's the list of some of the most preferred private technical institutions in India for higher studies:

- Birla Institute of Technology and Science (BITS), Pilani
- Vellore Institute of Technology (VIT), Vellore

- Manipal Academy of Higher Education (MAHE), Manipal
- Shiv Nadar University, Greater Noida
- Amrita Vishwa Vidyapeetham, Coimbatore
- SRM Institute of Science and Technology (SRMIST), Chennai
- Thapar University, Patiala
- O. P. Jindal Global University, Sonipat
- Dhirubhai Ambani Institute of Information and Communication Technology (DA-IICT), Gandhinagar
- Chandigarh University, Chandigarh

Disclaimer

The list of institutions provided above is intended to offer a general overview of prominent higher education institutions in India for various engineering branches. While the institutions mentioned are renowned for their academic and research capabilities, this list is not exhaustive from subjects and countries point of view and does not imply endorsement or ranking. The choice of institution should be based on individual research and consideration of various factors, including program specifics, faculty expertise, campus facilities, location, and personal career goals. Prospective students are advised to conduct thorough research, consult official institutional resources, and seek guidance from academic advisors or industry professionals to make informed decisions about their higher education options.

Country-Specific Tests and Requirements in Textile Discipline:

Apart from GATE and GRE there are some country specific entrance examinations in Textiles and related specializations such as design, fashion management etc. Here's is the list of such entrance examination where the aspirants may venture into.

- **India:**
  - **NIFT Entrance Exam:** For admission to various textile programs at the National Institute of Fashion Technology (NIFT).
  - **NID Entrance Exam:** For design programs at the National Institute of Design (NID), including textile design.

- **United Kingdom:**
  - **UKCAT/BMAT:** Some universities may use these tests for design and management courses related to textiles.

- **Germany:**
  - **TestAS (Test for Academic Studies):** May be required for international students applying to textile engineering programs.

- **Italy:**
  - **Institutions like Politecnico di Milano** may have specific design or technical entrance requirements for textile programs.

- **France:**
  - **Concours des Grandes Écoles:** Some prestigious French institutions may have their own competitive exams for admission to specialized programs in textile design and engineering.
  - **Entrance Tests for Design Schools:** Schools like École de la Chambre Syndicale de la Couture Parisienne or Institut Français de la Mode (IFM) may have specific entrance exams assessing design aptitude, creativity, and technical skills.
  - **Language Proficiency Tests:** For non-French speakers, demonstrating French language proficiency through exams like DELF/DALF might be required for some programs.

When applying to textile disciplines, ensure to check the specific requirements of each institution and program, as they can vary significantly.

Entrance Examinations for Higher Education in Management

For pursuing management programs, particularly MBA programs, various entrance examinations are used globally. Here's a list of prominent entrance exams for management programs:

1. **GMAT (Graduate Management Admission Test)**
   - **Purpose:** Widely used for admission to MBA and other management programs worldwide.
   - **Details:** Tests analytical writing, integrated reasoning, quantitative, and verbal skills.

2. **GRE (Graduate Record Examination)**
   - **Purpose:** Accepted by many business schools as an alternative to the GMAT for MBA and management programs.
   - **Details:** Assesses verbal reasoning, quantitative reasoning, and analytical writing skills.

3. **CAT (Common Admission Test)**
   - **Purpose:** Primarily used for admission to MBA programs in India.
   - **Details:** Tests quantitative ability, verbal ability, and logical reasoning.

4. **XAT (Xavier Aptitude Test)**
   - **Purpose:** Used for admission to management programs in India, particularly at Xavier Institute of Management.
   - **Details:** Tests quantitative ability, verbal ability, and analytical and logical reasoning.

5. **CMAT (Common Management Admission Test)**

   - **Purpose:** Conducted by the National Testing Agency (NTA) in India for admission to MBA programs.

   - **Details:** Tests quantitative techniques, logical reasoning, language comprehension, and general awareness.

6. **MAT (Management Aptitude Test)**

   - **Purpose:** Used for admission to various MBA programs in India.

   - **Details:** Tests language comprehension, mathematical skills, data analysis, and intelligence and critical reasoning.

7. **GRE General Test**

   - **Purpose:** Accepted by many business schools globally as an alternative to GMAT for MBA programs.

   - **Details:** Assesses general aptitude in verbal reasoning, quantitative reasoning, and analytical writing.

8. **TAMAT (Tokyo MBA Admission Test)**

   - **Purpose:** Used for admission to MBA programs in Japan, particularly for international students.

   - **Details:** Tests general knowledge, analytical skills, and reasoning.

9. **EMAT (Executive Management Aptitude Test)**

   - **Purpose:** Used for executive MBA programs to assess professional experience and management potential.

   - **Details:** Focuses on managerial experience, leadership potential and analytical abilities.

10. **GATE (Graduate Aptitude Test in Engineering)**

- **Purpose:** While primarily for engineering and science, some management programs accept GATE scores.

- **Details:** Tests knowledge in specific technical subjects.

11. **ISAT (Indian School of Business Admission Test)**

- **Purpose:** Used by the Indian School of Business (ISB) for admission to its management programs.

- **Details:** Includes sections on quantitative ability, verbal ability, and analytical reasoning.

12. **Executive Assessment**

- **Purpose:** Used by some business schools for executive MBA programs.

- **Details:** Assesses the applicant's managerial experience, decision-making, and problem-solving skills.

13. **Language Proficiency Tests (for non-native speakers)**

- **Purpose:** For non-native English speakers, tests like TOEFL or IELTS may be required to demonstrate English language proficiency.

- **Details:** TOEFL tests reading, listening, speaking, and writing skills, while IELTS assesses similar skills with a focus on academic English.

Nut Shell: Each program and institution may have its own specific entrance requirements, so it's essential to check the individual requirements of the business schools to which you are applying.

CHAPTER 7

Entrepreneurship and Startups

Entrepreneurship and startups represent the dynamic intersection of innovation, risk-taking, and creativity. At its core, entrepreneurship is about identifying opportunities and transforming ideas into viable businesses, often in the face of uncertainty and limited resources. Startups, which are typically characterized by their pursuit of scalable and repeatable business models, exemplify this spirit by challenging traditional market norms and introducing groundbreaking solutions. These ventures drive economic growth, foster technological advancements, and contribute to a vibrant ecosystem of innovation. As entrepreneurs navigate the complex landscape of launching and scaling new enterprises, they not only contribute to their own success but also play a crucial role in shaping the future of industries and societies.

7.1 Introduction to Entrepreneurship

Entrepreneurship is the driving force behind the creation and evolution of businesses, characterized by the ability to identify opportunities and transform them into successful ventures. At its essence, entrepreneurship involves more than just starting a new company; it encompasses the spirit of innovation, risk-taking, and strategic thinking. Entrepreneurs are individuals who leverage their vision and creativity to solve problems, meet market needs, or capitalize on emerging trends, often in ways that disrupt conventional practices and challenge the status quo.

The journey of entrepreneurship begins with an idea—whether it's a novel product, a unique service, or an innovative business model. This idea must then be developed through meticulous planning, market research, and the creation of a viable business plan. Entrepreneurs must navigate various stages of business development, from securing initial funding and building a team to scaling operations and managing growth.

Entrepreneurship is not limited to creating new businesses but also includes the act of revitalizing existing enterprises and fostering innovation within established organizations. It requires a blend of perseverance, adaptability, and strategic foresight, as entrepreneurs must constantly pivot and adapt to changing market conditions and emerging opportunities.

The impact of entrepreneurship extends beyond individual success. Entrepreneurs drive economic growth by generating employment, introducing new technologies, and enhancing productivity. They contribute to a dynamic and competitive market environment that benefits consumers and stimulates further innovation. In essence, entrepreneurship is a powerful engine of progress, shaping industries, economies, and societies through the transformative potential of new ideas and entrepreneurial action.

7.2 Identifying Opportunities and Market Needs

Identifying opportunities and market needs is a cornerstone of entrepreneurship and a critical step in launching a successful business. This process involves recognizing gaps or inefficiencies in the market and discerning areas where new solutions or improvements can create value. The ability to spot these opportunities requires a combination of keen observation, market research, and a deep understanding of consumer behavior.

1. **Observation and Trend Analysis**: Effective entrepreneurs often start by observing the world around them, noting changes in technology, consumer preferences, and industry trends. This observation might involve tracking emerging technologies, shifts in societal attitudes, or evolving regulatory landscapes. By staying informed about these trends, entrepreneurs can anticipate future needs and identify potential areas for innovation.

2. **Market Research**: Thorough market research is essential for understanding the specific needs and pain points of target audiences. This research can be conducted through surveys, interviews, focus groups, and analysis of existing data. By gathering insights directly from potential customers, entrepreneurs can pinpoint what consumers are looking for, what they find lacking in current offerings, and how they prioritize their needs.

3. **Competitive Analysis**: Evaluating the competitive landscape helps entrepreneurs understand how existing players address market needs and where there might be room for differentiation. By analyzing competitors' strengths and weaknesses, entrepreneurs can identify gaps in the market or areas where they can offer a superior solution. This involves examining competitors' products, pricing strategies, customer feedback, and market positioning.

4. **Problem Identification**: At the heart of identifying opportunities is the ability to recognize problems that need solving. Entrepreneurs should look for issues that affect consumers or businesses, such as inefficiencies, unmet needs, or

emerging challenges. Understanding the problem deeply allows entrepreneurs to design solutions that truly address these issues and provide tangible benefits.

5. **Validation**: Once potential opportunities are identified, validating these opportunities is crucial to ensure they are viable. This involves testing assumptions through prototypes, pilot programs, or market trials. Feedback from these initial tests can help refine the concept, assess market demand, and determine the feasibility of scaling the solution.

6. **Leveraging Networks**: Engaging with industry experts, mentors, and other entrepreneurs can provide valuable insights and perspectives on market needs and opportunities. Networking can expose entrepreneurs to new ideas, trends, and feedback that might not be apparent through independent research.

Nut Shell: Identifying opportunities and market needs is a multifaceted process that combines observation, research, analysis, and validation. By understanding and addressing real consumer problems and market gaps, entrepreneurs can create solutions that resonate with their target audience and drive successful business outcomes. This proactive approach not only enhances the likelihood of entrepreneurial success but also contributes to broader innovation and economic development.

7.2.1 Precautions

1. **Conduct Thorough Market Research**

   - **Avoid Assumptions:** Don't rely solely on assumptions or anecdotal evidence. Base your insights on comprehensive data and research.

   - **Understand the Market:** Study industry trends, consumer behavior, and competitive landscape. Use surveys, interviews, and market reports to gather information.

2. **Evaluate Market Size and Potential**

   - **Check Market Viability:** Assess whether the market is large enough to support your business and if it's growing.

   - **Consider Saturation:** Ensure the market isn't oversaturated with similar offerings that could limit your potential success.

3. **Identify and Validate Customer Needs**

   - **Engage with Target Audience:** Directly interact with potential customers to understand their pain points and needs.

   - **Test Assumptions:** Use prototypes or pilot programs to validate whether your solution effectively addresses the identified needs.

4. **Analyze the Competitive Landscape**

   - **Study Competitors:** Identify existing competitors, their strengths, weaknesses, and market positions.

   - **Differentiate Your Offerings:** Ensure your business provides unique value or differentiation compared to existing solutions.

5. **Assess Feasibility and Resources**

   - **Evaluate Costs:** Analyze the cost structure and financial requirements of your business idea.

   - **Resource Availability:** Ensure you have access to the necessary resources, including capital, talent, and technology.

6. **Understand Regulatory and Legal Requirements**

   - **Compliance:** Be aware of industry regulations, legal requirements, and potential barriers to entry.

   - **Licensing and Permits:** Ensure you have the necessary licenses and permits to operate legally in your target market.

7. **Consider Technological Trends**

   - **Adopt Innovations:** Stay updated with technological advancements that could impact your industry or create new opportunities.

- **Plan for Disruption:** Be prepared for potential technological disruptions that could affect your business model.

8. **Manage Risks**

    - **Identify Risks:** Evaluate potential risks and challenges that could impact your business.

    - **Mitigation Strategies:** Develop strategies to mitigate these risks, including contingency plans and insurance.

9. **Seek Feedback and Mentorship**

    - **Get Expert Advice:** Consult with mentors, industry experts, or advisors to gain valuable insights and feedback.

    - **Iterate and Improve:** Use feedback to refine your idea and business strategy.

10. **Monitor and Adapt**

    - **Track Progress:** Continuously monitor market conditions, customer feedback, and performance metrics.

    - **Be Flexible:** Be willing to adapt your approach based on new information and changing circumstances.

Nut Shell: Carefully considering these precautions, you can better identify viable opportunities and address market needs effectively, setting a strong foundation for your entrepreneurial endeavors.

7.3 Developing a Business Idea

Developing a business idea is a dynamic and iterative process that begins with recognizing a potential opportunity and evolves through careful research and strategic planning. It involves identifying unmet needs or problems within a market, brainstorming innovative solutions, and validating these ideas through market analysis and customer feedback.

The goal is to transform a conceptual vision into a viable business model, considering factors such as market demand, competition, and resource availability. By following a structured approach, aspiring entrepreneurs can refine their ideas, mitigate risks, and lay the groundwork for a successful and sustainable business venture.

Developing a business idea involves a series of thoughtful and strategic steps that help transform a concept into a viable business model. Here's a detailed look at the process:

1. **Idea Generation**

   - **Brainstorming:** Start with creative brainstorming sessions to generate a range of ideas. Consider personal interests, industry trends, or gaps in the market.

   - **Observation:** Look for problems or inefficiencies in daily life or within specific industries that could be addressed with innovative solutions.

   - **Research:** Explore existing solutions and identify their limitations to uncover areas for improvement or differentiation.

2. **Market Research**

   - **Industry Analysis:** Study the industry landscape, including market size, growth trends, and key players. Understand the current state and future outlook of the sector.

   - **Customer Research:** Conduct surveys, interviews, or focus groups to gather insights into customer needs, preferences, and pain points.

   - **Competitive Analysis:** Identify direct and indirect competitors. Analyze their strengths, weaknesses, market positioning, and customer feedback to find opportunities for differentiation.

3. **Idea Validation**

- **Develop a Value Proposition:** Clearly define the unique value your idea offers to customers. How does it solve their problems or meet their needs better than existing solutions?

- **Create a Prototype or MVP:** Develop a minimal viable product (MVP) or prototype to test the feasibility of your idea. This allows you to gather real-world feedback and make improvements.

- **Test with Target Audience:** Share your MVP or prototype with a segment of your target market to validate your assumptions and gather feedback on usability, effectiveness, and overall appeal.

4. **Business Model Development**

- **Define Your Business Model:** Determine how your business will generate revenue. This could involve direct sales, subscription models, licensing, or other revenue streams.

- **Create a Business Plan:** Outline your business goals, target market, value proposition, revenue model, marketing strategy, and financial projections. This plan serves as a roadmap for your business and helps attract investors or partners.

5. **Feasibility Analysis**

- **Financial Assessment:** Evaluate the financial requirements of your business, including startup costs, operating expenses, and projected revenue. Determine how you will fund your venture, whether through personal savings, loans, or investors.

- **Resource Planning:** Assess the resources you need, such as technology, talent, and physical space. Ensure you have access to these resources or a plan to acquire them.

6. **Legal and Regulatory Considerations**

   - **Business Structure:** Decide on the legal structure of your business (e.g., sole proprietorship, partnership, and corporation) and understand its implications for liability and taxes.

   - **Licenses and Permits:** Identify and obtain any necessary licenses, permits, or registrations required to operate legally in your industry and location.

   - **Intellectual Property:** Consider protecting your intellectual property through patents, trademarks, or copyrights if applicable.

7. **Market Entry Strategy**

   - **Marketing Plan:** Develop a strategy for reaching your target audience. This includes branding, advertising, digital marketing, and public relations.

   - **Sales Strategy:** Define your sales approach, including distribution channels, pricing strategy, and customer acquisition tactics.

   - **Launch Plan:** Plan the launch of your business, including key milestones, marketing campaigns, and operational setup.

8. **Implementation and Scaling**

   - **Operational Setup:** Establish your business operations, including supply chain management, staffing, and production processes.

- **Monitor Performance:** Track key performance indicators (KPIs) and metrics to assess the effectiveness of your strategies and make data-driven decisions.

- **Iterate and Improve:** Continuously gather feedback, analyze performance, and make adjustments to improve your product, services, and business operations.

9. **Growth and Expansion**

- **Explore Opportunities:** Identify opportunities for growth, such as new markets, product lines, or strategic partnerships.

- **Scale Operations:** Develop strategies for scaling your operations to handle increased demand while maintaining quality and efficiency leading to a matured business model.

7.3.1 Internal and External Factors that influence the Business Idea

When developing and refining a business idea, it's essential to consider both internal and external factors that can significantly influence its viability and success. Here's an overview of these factors:

A. Internal Factors

1. Skills and Expertise

- **Personal Expertise:** The skills, knowledge, and experience of the founders and team members play a critical role in shaping the business idea. A deep understanding of the industry or market can enhance the idea's feasibility and execution.

- **Team Dynamics:** The ability to collaborate effectively, manage conflicts, and leverage diverse skills within the team influences the development and implementation of the business idea.

2. **Resources and Capabilities**

   - **Financial Resources:** Available capital for startup costs, operations, and growth initiatives impacts the ability to develop and scale the business idea.

   - **Technology and Equipment:** Access to necessary technology, tools, and infrastructure affects the execution and efficiency of the business operations.

   - **Human Resources:** The talent, expertise, and organizational structure within the team contribute to the development and management of the business idea.

3. **Company Culture and Vision**

   - **Mission and Values:** The core mission, values, and vision of the company influence how the business idea is shaped and pursued.

   - **Innovation Culture:** A culture that fosters creativity, experimentation, and risk-taking can enhance the development of innovative ideas.

4. **Operational Capabilities**

   - **Processes and Systems:** The effectiveness of internal processes and systems for product development, marketing, sales, and customer service impacts the execution of the business idea.

   - **Supply Chain Management:** The ability to manage suppliers, logistics, and inventory influences the feasibility and scalability of the business idea.

B. External Factors

1. **Market Conditions**

   - **Demand and Supply:** Market demand for the product or service and the availability of similar offerings affect the potential success of the business idea.

- **Economic Conditions:** Economic factors such as inflation, interest rates, and economic growth impact consumer spending and investment opportunities.

2. **Competitive Landscape**

- **Competitors:** The number, strength, and strategies of existing competitors influence how your business idea differentiates itself and captures market share.

- **Market Saturation:** High levels of competition or market saturation can affect the viability and attractiveness of the business idea.

3. **Regulatory and Legal Environment**

- **Regulations:** Industry-specific regulations, standards, and compliance requirements affect how the business idea is developed and implemented.

- **Intellectual Property:** The availability of patents, trademarks, or copyrights, and the protection of intellectual property impact the competitive edge and innovation potential of the business idea.

4. **Technological Trends**

- **Innovation and Technology:** Advances in technology can create new opportunities or disrupt existing markets, influencing the relevance and potential of the business idea.

- **Adoption Rates:** The rate at which new technologies or innovations are adopted by consumers and businesses impacts the timing and approach for implementing the business idea.

5. **Social and Cultural Factors**

- **Consumer Preferences:** Changes in consumer preferences, attitudes, and behavior of the social fabric influence the acceptance and demand for the business idea.

- **Cultural Trends:** Social trends, lifestyle changes, and cultural shifts can affect the relevance and appeal of the business idea to different demographic groups.

6. **Economic and Political Factors**

   - **Economic Stability:** Economic stability or volatility impacts consumer confidence, purchasing power, and investment climate.

   - **Political Environment:** Political stability, policies, and government support or restrictions can influence the business environment and regulatory landscape.

7. **Environmental Factors**

   - **Sustainability:** Increasing emphasis on environmental sustainability can affect consumer expectations and regulatory requirements.

   - **Environmental Impact:** Consideration of the environmental impact of your business operations and product offerings can influence public perception and compliance.

Nut Shell: Understanding and analyzing these internal and external factors help in refining the business idea, anticipating potential challenges, and making informed decisions for a successful venture.

7.4 Funding and Financial Management

Funding and financial management are pivotal components of building and sustaining a successful business. Securing adequate funding is essential for turning a business idea into reality, supporting operations, and facilitating growth. Effective financial management, on the other hand, ensures that resources are allocated efficiently, financial risks are mitigated, and long-term profitability is achieved.

From navigating various funding sources such as venture capital, loans, and grants, to implementing robust financial strategies and controls, understanding these aspects is crucial for maintaining financial health and achieving business objectives. Proper management of finances not only supports day-to-day operations but also positions a business for scalability and resilience in a competitive market.

7.4.1 Funding

Funding is a critical aspect of starting and growing a new business. It involves acquiring the necessary capital to launch operations, sustain activities, and expand. The pattern and sources of funding can vary depending on the business stage, industry, and specific needs. Here's a detailed look at the various funding sources and patterns for new businesses:

1. Self-Funding (Bootstrapping)

Description:

- **Personal Savings:** Entrepreneurs use their own savings to finance their startup. This approach allows for greater control and ownership but can be risky if the business does not succeed.

- **Family and Friends:** Support from family and friends can provide initial capital, often in the form of loans or equity investments.

Advantages:

- Full control over the business without external interference.

- No obligation to repay or share ownership if the funding is a gift.

Disadvantages:

- Limited to the personal financial resources of the entrepreneur.

- Risk of straining personal relationships if the business faces difficulties.

2. Seed Funding

Description:

- **Angel Investors:** Wealthy individuals who provide capital in exchange for equity or convertible debt. They often offer mentorship and guidance.

- **Seed Funds:** Specialized investment funds that focus on early-stage startups, providing capital in exchange for equity.

Advantages:

- Access to capital that can help develop a prototype or MVP.

- Potential mentorship and network connections from investors.

Disadvantages:

- Dilution of ownership and control due to equity given away.

- Pressure to achieve milestones and returns for investors.

3. Venture Capital (VC)

Description:

- **Venture Capitalists:** Professional investors who provide funding to startups with high growth potential in exchange for equity. VC funding typically occurs in multiple rounds (Series A, B, C, etc.).

Advantages:

- Significant capital that can support rapid growth and scaling.

- Strategic support and industry expertise from venture capital firms.

Disadvantages:

- High level of scrutiny and due diligence required.

- Loss of significant ownership and control due to equity stakes.

4. Bank Loans and Credit

Description:

- **Traditional Bank Loans:** Financial institutions offer loans that must be repaid with interest over a specified period. Secured loans require collateral.
- **Lines of Credit:** Flexible borrowing options where businesses can draw funds up to a certain limit as needed.

Advantages:

- Retain full ownership of the business.
- Predictable repayment schedules and interest rates.

Disadvantages:

- Requires a solid credit history and business plan.
- Debt obligations that must be repaid regardless of business performance.

5. Government Grants and Subsidies

Description:

- **Grants:** Funds provided by government agencies or organizations that do not need to be repaid. Often awarded for specific purposes such as research, development, or community impact.
- **Subsidies:** Financial assistance provided to support certain activities or sectors, such as innovation or green technology.

Advantages:

- Non-repayable funds that can reduce financial burden.
- Potential for credibility and increased visibility.

Disadvantages:

- Competitive application processes with specific requirements.

- Limited to particular uses and may involve strict compliance and reporting.

6. Crowd Funding

Description:

- **Equity Crowd funding:** Individuals invest in exchange for equity shares in the company through online platforms.
- **Reward-Based Crowd funding:** Contributors receive non-financial rewards, such as products or services, in exchange for their support.

Advantages:

- Access to capital without traditional financing methods.
- Opportunity to validate the business idea and build a customer base.

Disadvantages:

- Requires significant effort in marketing and promotion.
- Potential for intellectual property concerns and public exposure.

7. Strategic Partnerships and Joint Ventures

Description:

- **Partnerships:** Collaborations with other businesses or organizations to share resources, reduce costs, or enter new markets.
- **Joint Ventures:** Temporary alliances where two or more parties create a new entity to pursue specific business objectives.

Advantages:

- Shared resources, expertise, and risks.
- Access to new markets or technologies.

Disadvantages:

- Potential for conflicts of interest and operational challenges.
- Shared control and decision-making.

8. Incubators and Accelerators

Description:

- **Incubators:** Programs that support early-stage startups with resources, mentoring, and networking opportunities, often in exchange for equity.
- **Accelerators:** Intensive programs designed to rapidly scale startups over a defined period, providing funding, mentorship, and access to investors.

Advantages:

- Structured support and mentorship to accelerate growth.
- Networking opportunities with investors and industry experts.

Disadvantages:

- Equity dilution and program fees.
- Time-limited support and intense pressure to achieve milestones.

7.4.2 Funding Pattern and Strategy

1. **Pre-Seed Stage:**
   - **Funding Sources:** Personal savings, family and friends, early angel investors.
   - **Focus:** Product development, market research, and initial validation.

2. **Seed Stage:**
   - **Funding Sources:** Angel investors, seed funds, crowdfunding.
   - **Focus:** Building a prototype, initial market entry, and early customer acquisition.

3. **Early Stage:**

   - **Funding Sources:** Venture capital, strategic partnerships.

   - **Focus:** Scaling operations, expanding market reach, and achieving profitability.

4. **Growth Stage:**

   - **Funding Sources:** Venture capital, private equity, bank loans.

   - **Focus:** Scaling on a larger scale, entering new markets, and preparing for an exit strategy (e.g., IPO or acquisition).

Nut Shell: Understanding these funding sources and patterns helps entrepreneurs choose the best financing options for their specific needs and stage of growth. Effective funding strategies align with the business's goals, operational needs, and long-term vision.

7.4.3 Schemes of Government of India

The Government of India offers a range of schemes and programs to support and fund entrepreneurs at various stages of their business journey. These schemes aim to foster innovation, support startups, and promote entrepreneurship across different sectors. Here's an overview of some notable flagship schemes of Government of India for funding entrepreneurs in India:

1. **Startup India Initiative**

   Description:

   - **Objective:** To promote and support startups through various benefits, including funding, tax exemptions, and regulatory relief.

   - **Key Features:**

     - **Funding Support:** Access to a fund of funds for startups (FFS) managed by SIDBI.

- **Tax Benefits:** Tax exemptions for three years and compliance with self-certification.

- **Ease of Doing Business:** Faster patent registration and regulatory clearances.

Eligibility:

- New startups recognized by the Department for Promotion of Industry and Internal Trade (DPIIT).

Website: Startup India

2. **Pradhan Mantri Mudra Yojana (PMMY)**

Description:

- **Objective:** To provide financial support to small businesses and startups through micro-financing.

- **Key Features:**

    - **Loan Categories:** A (up to ₹50,000), B (₹50,000 to ₹5 Lakh), and C (₹5 Lakh to ₹10 Lakh).

    - **Interest Rates:** Competitive and subsidized rates.

    - **Collateral-Free:** Loans are provided without the need for collateral.

Eligibility:

- Small businesses, including sole proprietorships, partnerships, and enterprises.

Website: Mudra Yojana

3. **Stand Up India Scheme**

Description:

- **Objective:** To promote entrepreneurship among women and SC/ST communities by providing financial support.

- **Key Features:**
  - **Loan Amount:** Provides loans ranging from ₹10 Lakh to ₹1 Crore for setting up green-field enterprises.
  - **Coverage:** Loans cover the cost of plant, machinery, and equipment.

Eligibility:

- SC/ST and women entrepreneurs starting a new business.

Website: Stand Up India

4. **ATAL Innovation Mission (AIM)**

Description:

- **Objective:** To promote innovation and support startups through various programs and funding opportunities.
- **Key Features:**
  - **AIM's Programs:** Includes ATAL Incubation Centers (AICs), ATAL Community Innovation Centers (ACICs), and ATAL New India Challenges.
  - **Funding and Support:** Provides grants and support to incubators, accelerators, and innovators.

Eligibility:

- Startups, innovators, and incubators as per specific program criteria.

Website: ATAL Innovation Mission

5. **National Small Industries Corporation (NSIC) Schemes**

Description:

- **Objective:** To support small businesses with financing, technology, and marketing assistance.

- **Key Features:**
  - **Credit Support:** Provides credit facilities to small enterprises.
  - **Technology Transfer:** Offers technology support and consultancy.
  - **Marketing Assistance:** Helps with marketing and procurement support.

Eligibility:

- Small and medium-sized enterprises (SMEs) across various sectors.

Website: NSIC

6. Technology Development Board (TDB) Schemes

Description:

- **Objective:** To support the commercialization of innovative technologies.

- **Key Features:**
  - **Financial Assistance:** Provides loans, grants, and equity support for technology development.
  - **Focus Areas:** Includes technology upgrade, R&D, and commercialization.

Eligibility:

- Startups and enterprises involved in technology development and innovation.

Website: Technology Development Board

7. NABARD Schemes

Description:

- **Objective:** To provide financial assistance for rural development and agriculture-related enterprises.

- **Key Features:**
  - **Financial Products:** Includes refinancing, microfinance, and rural entrepreneurship programs.
  - **Support:** Provides loans and grants for rural and agribusiness ventures.

Eligibility:

- Rural entrepreneurs, agricultural startups, and rural development projects.

Website: NABARD

8. Digital India Program

Description:

- **Objective:** To encourage and support digital entrepreneurship and technology-driven startups.
- **Key Features:**
  - **Funding Opportunities:** Various funding and incentive schemes under the Digital India program.
  - **Support:** Infrastructure and technology support for digital startups.

Eligibility:

- Technology-driven startups and digital enterprises.

Website: Digital India

9. Prime Minister's Employment Generation Program (PMEGP)

Description:

- **Objective:** To generate employment opportunities through the establishment of new micro-enterprises.

- **Key Features:**
  - **Loan Amount:** Provides financial assistance for setting up new enterprises.
  - **Subsidy:** Offers a subsidy on the loan amount for specific sectors and regions.

Eligibility:

- Individuals, particularly in rural and semi-urban areas, with no prior enterprise experience.

Website: PMEGP

10. Skill Development Schemes

Description:

- **Objective:** To support skill development and entrepreneurship through various training and funding programs.
- **Key Features:**
  - **Training Programs:** Includes training and capacity-building programs for entrepreneurs.
  - **Funding Support:** Provides financial assistance for skill development initiatives.

Eligibility:

- Individuals and organizations involved in skill development and training.

Website: Skill Development

Nut Shell: These schemes provide diverse funding options and support mechanisms for entrepreneurs at different stages of their business journey. Entrepreneurs should review the eligibility criteria, application procedures, and specific benefits of each scheme to find the most suitable option for their needs.

7.5 Building and Leading a Startup Team

Building and leading a startup team is a fundamental aspect of transforming a business idea into a successful enterprise. Assembling a cohesive and skilled team is crucial for driving innovation, executing strategies, and achieving growth objectives. Effective leadership in a startup involves not only recruiting individuals with the right expertise and cultural fit but also fostering a collaborative environment where creativity and productivity thrive. A strong startup team is characterized by clear communication, mutual trust, and a shared vision, enabling the organization to navigate challenges, seize opportunities, and adapt to an ever-evolving market. By prioritizing team dynamics and leadership, entrepreneurs can lay the foundation for a resilient and high-performing startup.

7.5.1 Building Startup Team

Building a successful startup team involves several critical steps that ensure you attract, retain, and effectively lead the right people to achieve your business goals. Here's a detailed guide to the process:

1. **Define the Vision and Culture**

   Clarify Your Vision:

   - **Mission and Goals:** Articulate the startup's mission, long-term goals, and core values. This vision will guide the recruitment and management of your team.

   - **Culture:** Establish the company culture you want to foster, including values, work ethics, and behavioral norms.

   Communicate Clearly:

   - **Vision Statement:** Create a compelling vision statement that reflects the startup's goals and inspires potential team members.

   - **Cultural Fit:** Ensure that every team member aligns with and contributes positively to the startup's culture.

2. **Identify Key Roles and Responsibilities**

   Determine Needs:

   - **Role Definition:** Identify the key roles and responsibilities necessary to achieve your startup's objectives. This may include technical roles, marketing, sales, and operational positions.

   - **Skill Set:** Define the required skills, experience, and attributes for each role.

   Prioritize Roles:

   - **Critical Positions:** Focus on filling critical roles first, such as co-founders or key technical positions that are essential to the startup's success.

3. **Recruit the Right Talent**

   Develop a Recruitment Strategy:

   - **Job Descriptions:** Create detailed and attractive job descriptions that highlight the role's responsibilities, required skills, and growth opportunities.

- **Sourcing Channels:** Use various channels for recruitment, including job boards, social media, industry networks, and recruitment agencies.

Screen and Interview:

- **Screening Process:** Review resumes and applications to shortlist candidates based on skills, experience, and cultural fit.

- **Interviews:** Conduct thorough interviews to assess candidates' technical abilities, problem-solving skills, and compatibility with the startup's values.

Evaluate Fit:

- **Skills Assessment:** Use practical tests or assignments to evaluate candidates' abilities.

- **Cultural Fit:** Assess candidates' alignment with the company culture through behavioral questions and team interactions.

4. **Onboard and Integrate**

Effective On-boarding:

- **Orientation:** Provide a comprehensive on-boarding process that includes training on company policies, culture, and role-specific responsibilities.

- **Mentorship:** Assign mentors or buddy systems to help new hires integrate smoothly into the team and understand the startup's dynamics.

Set Expectations:

- **Clear Goals:** Define short-term and long-term goals for new team members. Ensure they understand their role in achieving the startup's objectives.

- **Feedback Mechanism:** Establish regular feedback sessions to address any issues and support ongoing development.

5. **Foster a Collaborative Environment**

Build Team Dynamics:

- **Team Building Activities:** Organize team-building exercises to enhance collaboration, communication, and trust among team members.

- **Open Communication:** Promote a culture of open communication where team members feel comfortable sharing ideas, feedback, and concerns.

Encourage Innovation:

- **Creative Freedom:** Allow team members to contribute ideas and solutions, fostering a sense of ownership and creativity.

- **Recognize Contributions:** Acknowledge and reward individual and team achievements to maintain motivation and engagement.

6. **Provide Leadership and Support**

Lead by Example:

- **Demonstrate Values:** Exhibit the values and behaviors you expect from your team. Your leadership style should reflect the startup's culture and vision.

- **Decision-Making:** Make informed decisions while considering the input and expertise of your team.

Offer Support:

- **Professional Development:** Provide opportunities for skill development and career growth through training, workshops, and mentoring.

- **Resources:** Ensure your team has the tools, resources, and support needed to perform effectively.

7. **Monitor and Adapt**

Evaluate Performance:

- **Performance Reviews:** Conduct regular performance reviews to assess individual and team progress toward goals. Provide constructive feedback and set new objectives.

- **Adjust Roles:** Be flexible and willing to adjust roles and responsibilities as the startup evolves and grows.

Address Challenges:

- **Conflict Resolution:** Handle conflicts and issues promptly and fairly to maintain a positive work environment.

- **Continuous Improvement:** Regularly assess team dynamics and processes to identify areas for improvement and implement changes as needed.

8. **Retain Top Talent**

Create a Positive Work Environment:

- **Work-Life Balance:** Promote a healthy work-life balance to enhance job satisfaction and reduce burnout.

- **Career Growth:** Offer opportunities for advancement and professional development to retain and motivate top talent.

Incentives and Recognition:

- **Compensation:** Provide competitive salaries and benefits that align with industry standards.

- **Recognition:** Recognize and reward outstanding performance to keep team members engaged and committed.

By following these steps, you can build a strong, cohesive startup team capable of driving your business forward and adapting to the challenges and opportunities that come with entrepreneurship.

7.5.2 Leading a Startup Team

Leading a startup team effectively is arduous task for driving the business toward its goals and ensuring that the team operates cohesively and efficiently. As a leader, your role extends beyond just managing tasks and projects; it involves inspiring, guiding, and supporting your team. A true leader eliminates the hurdles encountered in managing a startup. Here's a detailed look at the steps involved in leading a startup team:

1. **Establish a Clear Vision, Mission, Value Statements and Goals**

   Communicate the Vision:

   - **Articulate Vision:** Clearly define and communicate the startup's vision, mission, value statements and long-term goals. Ensure that every team member understands and aligns with this vision.

   - **Set Expectations:** Outline what success looks like and how individual and team efforts contribute to achieving these goals.

   Define Objectives:

   - **Short-Term and Long-Term Goals:** Set clear, achievable objectives for both the short term (e.g., quarterly targets) and long term (e.g., annual milestones).

   - **Key Performance Indicators (KPIs):** Establish KPIs to measure progress and success.

2. **Build a Strong Team Culture**

   Foster Collaboration:

   - **Encourage Teamwork:** Promote a collaborative environment where team members work together and support each other.

- **Open Communication:** Facilitate open lines of communication, encouraging feedback and dialogue.

Promote Values:

- **Model Behavior:** Demonstrate the values and behaviors you expect from your team. Lead by example in terms of work ethic, integrity, and professionalism.

- **Recognize and Reward:** Celebrate team achievements and recognize individual contributions to reinforce positive behaviors and morale.

3. **Empower and Support Team Members**

   Delegate Effectively:

   - **Assign Responsibilities:** Delegate tasks and responsibilities according to team members' strengths and skills. Trust your team to take ownership of their roles.

   - **Provide Autonomy:** Allow team members the freedom to make decisions and solve problems within their areas of responsibility.

   Offer Support:

   - **Provide Resources:** Ensure that team members have the tools, resources, and information needed to perform their tasks effectively.

   - **Mentorship:** Offer guidance and mentorship to help team members develop their skills and advance their careers.

4. **Foster Innovation and Creativity**

   Encourage Experimentation:

   - **Support Risk-Taking:** Create an environment where team members feel comfortable experimenting with new ideas and approaches without fear of failure.

- **Solicit Ideas:** Actively seek input and suggestions from team members to drive innovation and problem-solving.

Create a Learning Culture:

- **Promote Continuous Learning:** Encourage ongoing learning and development through training, workshops, and self-study.

- **Share Knowledge:** Facilitate knowledge sharing and best practices within the team.

5. **Manage Performance and Provide Feedback**

Set Performance Metrics:

- **Track Progress:** Regularly monitor progress against goals and KPIs. Use performance data to inform decisions and identify areas for improvement.

- **Assess Performance:** Conduct performance reviews to evaluate individual and team performance.

Deliver Constructive Feedback:

- **Provide Regular Feedback:** Offer timely and specific feedback on performance. Focus on both strengths and areas for improvement.

- **Encourage Development:** Use feedback sessions as opportunities for coaching and professional growth.

6. **Address Challenges and Conflicts**

Resolve Issues Promptly:

- **Identify Problems:** Recognize and address challenges or conflicts as they arise. Avoid letting issues fester or negatively impact team dynamics.

- **Facilitate Resolution:** Use conflict resolution strategies to address and resolve disputes fairly and constructively.

Adapt and Evolve:

- **Be Flexible:** Adapt your leadership style and strategies in response to changing circumstances or feedback from the team.

- **Continuous Improvement:** Regularly assess and refine processes and practices to enhance team performance and effectiveness.

7. **Ensure Alignment and Communication**

Maintain Alignment:

- **Regular Check-Ins:** Hold regular meetings to discuss progress, align on objectives, and address any issues. Ensure that everyone is on the same page.

- **Transparency:** Keep the team informed about key decisions, changes, and developments within the startup.

Facilitate Effective Communication:

- **Communication Channels:** Utilize appropriate communication tools and channels to keep the team connected and engaged.

- **Active Listening:** Practice active listening to understand team members' perspectives and concerns.

8. **Lead by Example**

Demonstrate Leadership:

- **Exhibit Commitment:** Show dedication to the startup's mission and goals. Your enthusiasm and commitment can inspire and motivate the team.

- **Maintain Integrity:** Uphold high ethical standards and demonstrate reliability and accountability.

Manage Stress and Resilience:

- **Stay Composed:** Handle pressure and setbacks with resilience and composure. Your ability to manage stress can influence the team's morale and confidence.

9. **Develop and Grow the Team**

   Identify Development Needs:

- **Skill Assessment:** Regularly assess the skills and development needs of team members. Identify areas where additional training or support may be required.

- **Career Growth:** Provide opportunities for career advancement and professional growth within the startup.

Promote Team Well-Being:

- **Work-Life Balance:** Encourage a healthy work-life balance to prevent burnout and ensure long-term productivity and satisfaction.

- **Support Well-Being:** Offer support for personal well-being and mental health, fostering a positive work environment.

By following these steps, you can lead your startup team effectively, fostering a collaborative and productive environment that drives the business toward its goals while supporting and developing your team members.

7.6 Challenges and Risks in Startups

Startups are inherently fraught with challenges and risks, reflecting the high-stakes nature of pioneering new ventures. Entrepreneurs often face a complex array of obstacles, from securing adequate funding and managing cash flow to navigating market uncertainties and scaling operations. The fast-paced environment of a startup demands agility and resilience, as founders must contend with intense competition, evolving consumer preferences, and unforeseen disruptions.

Additionally, risks related to regulatory compliance, technology adoption, and talent retention can further complicate the journey. Understanding and proactively addressing these challenges is crucial for steering a startup towards success and achieving long-term sustainability.

7.6.1 Challenges in Startup

Startups face a myriad of challenges that can significantly impact their chances of success. These challenges often arise from the inherent uncertainties and risks associated with launching and scaling a new business. Here's a detailed look at some of the most common and critical challenges that startups encounter:

1. **Securing Funding**

   Challenge:

   - **Access to Capital:** Obtaining sufficient funding to cover startup costs and sustain operations is a major hurdle. Startups often struggle to secure investments from venture capitalists, angel investors, or financial institutions.

   - **Cash Flow Management:** Managing cash flow effectively is crucial, as startups may face periods of high expenditure before generating revenue.

   Impact:

   - Insufficient funding can limit a startup's ability to develop products, hire talent, and scale operations.

2. **Market Uncertainty**

   Challenge:

   - **Market Validation:** Startups often face uncertainty regarding the market demand for their products or services. Validating the market and identifying a target audience can be challenging.

- **Competitive Landscape:** Competing against established players and other startups can be daunting, especially if market dynamics are rapidly changing.

Impact:

- Incorrect market assumptions or poor market fit can lead to product failures and financial losses.

3. **Building a Strong Team**

Challenge:

- **Talent Acquisition:** Attracting and retaining skilled and motivated team members can be difficult, particularly when competing with larger, established companies that offer higher salaries and benefits.

- **Team Dynamics:** Ensuring effective collaboration and maintaining team morale in a high-pressure startup environment requires strong leadership and management skills.

Impact:

- A weak or misaligned team can hinder progress, reduce productivity, and impact overall business performance.

4. **Product Development**

Challenge:

- **Innovation and Execution:** Developing a product or service that meets market needs and stands out from competitors requires significant time, effort, and resources.

- **Iterative Changes:** Startups often need to pivot or iterate on their product based on market feedback, which can be resource-intensive and time-consuming.

Impact:

- Poor product development or delays in launching can lead to missed market opportunities and reduced competitiveness.

5. **Scaling Operations**

Challenge:

- **Operational Efficiency:** Scaling operations effectively while maintaining quality and customer satisfaction is a complex task. Startups must manage supply chains, production processes, and customer support efficiently.

- **Infrastructure:** Investing in the necessary infrastructure and technology to support growth can strain financial and operational resources.

Impact:

- Ineffective scaling can lead to operational bottlenecks, customer dissatisfaction, and financial strain.

6. **Navigating Legal and Regulatory Requirements**

Challenge:

- **Compliance:** Startups must navigate a complex regulatory environment, including industry-specific regulations, tax obligations, and employment laws.

- **Intellectual Property:** Protecting intellectual property and managing legal risks associated with patents, trademarks, and copyrights are essential but often challenging.

Impact:

- Legal and regulatory issues can result in costly fines, legal disputes, and operational disruptions.

7. **Managing Risk**

   Challenge:

   - **Risk Assessment:** Identifying and managing risks, including financial, operational, and strategic risks, is crucial for startup survival.

   - **Contingency Planning:** Developing effective contingency plans for potential setbacks and uncertainties is often overlooked but vital.

   Impact:

   - Unmanaged risks can lead to business failures, financial losses, and reputational damage.

8. **Customer Acquisition and Retention**

   Challenge:

   - **Marketing and Sales:** Developing and executing effective marketing and sales strategies to attract and retain customers can be challenging, especially with limited budgets.

   - **Customer Engagement:** Building and maintaining strong relationships with customers to ensure long-term loyalty requires continuous effort and adaptation.

   Impact:

   - Poor customer acquisition and retention strategies can result in low revenue and high churn rates.

9. **Adapting to Technology Changes**

   Challenge:

   - **Technological Advancements:** Keeping up with rapid technological advancements and integrating new technologies into the business can be challenging.

- **Cyber security:** Ensuring robust cyber security measures to protect sensitive data and maintain trust is increasingly important.

Impact:

- Technology-related issues can lead to operational inefficiencies, data breaches, and competitive disadvantages.

10. Managing Work-Life Balance

Challenge:

- **Work Pressure:** The intense pressure and long hours commonly associated with startups can lead to burnout and affect personal well-being.

- **Stress Management:** Balancing the demands of running a startup with personal life requires effective stress management strategies.

Impact:

- Burnout and poor work-life balance can impact productivity, decision-making, and overall team morale.

11. Establishing a Market Presence

Challenge:

- **Brand Building:** Building a strong brand identity and establishing a market presence amidst competition can be challenging.

- **Market Penetration:** Gaining market share and achieving visibility in a crowded market requires strategic marketing and sales efforts.

Impact:

- Failure to establish a strong market presence can limit growth potential and customer acquisition.

Nut Shell: Addressing these challenges requires a combination of strategic planning, adaptability, and resilience. By proactively managing these obstacles and seeking solutions, startups can improve their chances of achieving long-term success and stability.

7.6.2 Strategic Planning and Implementation Addressing Challenges

Strategic planning is essential for effectively addressing the challenges faced by startups. A well-thought-out strategic plan helps in anticipating potential issues, setting clear goals, and creating actionable steps to overcome obstacles. Here's a broad guide to strategic planning for addressing startup challenges:

1. **Securing Funding**

   Strategic Actions:

   - **Develop a Detailed Business Plan:** Create a comprehensive business plan that outlines your startup's vision, market opportunity, financial projections, and growth strategy. This plan will help attract investors and secure funding.

   - **Diversify Funding Sources:** Explore various funding options such as venture capital, angel investors, crowd-funding, grants, and loans. Diversifying your funding sources can reduce reliance on a single source and increase financial stability.

   - **Build Relationships:** Network with potential investors, attend industry events, and participate in pitch competitions to build relationships and gain visibility.

   Implementation:

   - **Regular Financial Reviews:** Conduct regular financial reviews to track cash flow, manage expenses, and ensure that funding is utilized effectively.

- **Investor Updates:** Provide regular updates to investors on progress, milestones, and financial performance to build trust and maintain support.

2. **Market Uncertainty**

Strategic Actions:

- **Conduct Market Research:** Perform thorough market research to understand customer needs, market trends, and competitive dynamics. Use this information to validate your business idea and refine your value proposition.

- **Develop a Minimum Viable Product (MVP):** Launch an MVP to test market assumptions and gather feedback from early adopters. Use this feedback to iterate and improve your product.

- **Monitor Competitors:** Continuously monitor competitors to stay informed about their strategies and adapt your approach accordingly.

Implementation:

- **Agile Methodology:** Adopt an agile approach to product development and marketing, allowing for quick adjustments based on market feedback and changes.

- **Scenario Planning:** Develop multiple scenarios and contingency plans to address potential market changes and uncertainties.

3. **Building a Strong Team**

Strategic Actions:

- **Define Team Roles:** Clearly define roles and responsibilities for each team member based on their skills and expertise. Ensure that roles align with the startup's goals and needs.

- **Recruitment Strategy:** Develop a recruitment strategy that highlights the startup's mission, culture, and growth opportunities to attract top talent. Use employee referrals, industry networks, and targeted job postings.

- **Foster Team Culture:** Create a positive work environment that promotes collaboration, open communication, and mutual respect. Encourage team-building activities and provide opportunities for professional development.

Implementation:

- **On-boarding Process:** Implement a structured onboarding process to integrate new hires effectively and align them with the startup's culture and objectives.

- **Performance Management:** Set clear performance goals and conduct regular reviews to provide feedback and support team members' growth.

4. **Product Development**

Strategic Actions:

- **Develop a Product Roadmap:** Create a product roadmap that outlines key milestones, development phases, and timelines. This will help in managing development processes and ensuring timely delivery.

- **Customer Feedback Loop:** Establish mechanisms to gather and analyze customer feedback throughout the development process. Use this feedback to make informed decisions and refine the product.

- **Invest in R&D:** Allocate resources for research and development to innovate and stay ahead of market trends.

Implementation:

- **Iterative Development:** Use iterative development practices such as Agile or Scrum to make continuous improvements based on feedback and testing.

- **Quality Assurance:** Implement robust quality assurance processes to ensure that the product meets standards and delivers value to customers.

5. **Scaling Operations**

Strategic Actions:

- **Develop Scalable Processes:** Design and implement scalable processes and systems that can handle increased demand without compromising quality. Focus on automating repetitive tasks and optimizing workflows.

- **Invest in Technology:** Invest in technology and infrastructure that supports growth, such as customer relationship management (CRM) systems, enterprise resource planning (ERP) systems, and scalable cloud solutions.

- **Build Strategic Partnerships:** Form strategic partnerships with suppliers, distributors, and service providers to enhance capabilities and expand reach.

Implementation:

- **Monitor Metrics:** Track key operational metrics such as production capacity, customer satisfaction, and supply chain efficiency to identify areas for improvement.

- **Scale Gradually:** Scale operations in phases to manage growth effectively and avoid overextension.

6. **Navigating Legal and Regulatory Requirements**

Strategic Actions:

- **Consult Legal Experts:** Work with legal experts to understand and comply with industry-specific regulations, intellectual property laws, and employment laws.

- **Establish Compliance Procedures:** Develop and implement compliance procedures to ensure that all legal and regulatory requirements are met.

- **Protect Intellectual Property:** Register trademarks, patents, and copyrights to protect your intellectual property and prevent infringement.

Implementation:

- **Regular Audits:** Conduct regular legal and regulatory audits to identify and address any compliance issues.

- **Update Policies:** Keep legal and compliance policies up-to-date with changing regulations and industry standards.

7. **Managing Risk**

Strategic Actions:

- **Risk Assessment:** Perform a comprehensive risk assessment to identify potential risks across various areas such as financial, operational, and strategic.

- **Develop a Risk Management Plan:** Create a risk management plan that outlines strategies for mitigating identified risks and managing potential disruptions.

- **Implement Contingency Plans:** Develop contingency plans for critical risks to ensure that you can respond effectively in case of unforeseen events.

Implementation:

- **Regular Reviews:** Regularly review and update the risk management plan to address new risks and changes in the business environment.

- **Training:** Provide risk management training to team members to ensure they are aware of potential risks and know how to respond.

8. **Customer Acquisition and Retention**

Strategic Actions:

- **Develop Marketing Strategies:** Create targeted marketing strategies to reach your ideal customers. Utilize digital marketing, content marketing, and social media to build brand awareness and drive customer acquisition.

- **Enhance Customer Experience:** Focus on delivering exceptional customer service and creating positive experiences to retain customers and encourage repeat business.

- **Implement Loyalty Programs:** Develop customer loyalty programs and incentives to reward repeat customers and foster long-term relationships.

Implementation:

- **Monitor Metrics:** Track customer acquisition costs, retention rates, and customer satisfaction to evaluate the effectiveness of marketing and retention strategies.

- **Adapt Strategies:** Continuously adapt marketing and retention strategies based on customer feedback and performance data.

9. Adapting to Technology Changes

Strategic Actions:

- **Stay Informed:** Keep up with technological advancements and industry trends to identify opportunities for innovation and improvement.

- **Invest in Technology Upgrades:** Invest in technology upgrades and new tools that enhance operational efficiency and competitiveness.

- **Ensure Cyber-security:** Implement robust cyber-security measures to protect data and maintain trust with customers and partners.

Implementation:

- **Regular Assessments:** Regularly assess and update technology infrastructure to ensure it meets current and future needs.

- **Training:** Provide training to team members on new technologies and best practices for cyber-security.

10. Managing Work-Life Balance

Strategic Actions:

- **Promote Work-Life Balance:** Encourage a healthy work-life balance by offering flexible work arrangements, promoting time off, and fostering a supportive work environment.

- **Support Well-Being:** Provide resources and support for mental health and well-being, such as counseling services and wellness programs.

- **Set Boundaries:** Establish clear boundaries between work and personal life to prevent burnout and maintain productivity.

Implementation:

- **Monitor Well-Being:** Regularly check in with team members to assess their well-being and address any concerns related to work-life balance.

- **Encourage Time Off:** Encourage employees to take regular breaks and time off to recharge and maintain a healthy work-life balance.

Nut Shell: *adopting these strategic actions and implementing them effectively, startups can address challenges proactively, mitigate risks, and enhance their chances of long-term success and sustainability.*

7.6.3 Risks in Startups: Definitions, Key Factors and Mitigation Strategies

Startups inherently involve various risks that can impact their viability and success. Understanding and managing these risks is crucial for navigating the uncertain landscape of entrepreneurship. Here's an in-depth look at the key risks faced by startups:

1. **Financial Risk**

   Definition:

   - Financial risk involves the uncertainty surrounding a startup's financial health and its ability to manage cash flow, secure funding, and maintain profitability.

   Key Factors:

   - **Funding Shortages:** Difficulty in securing sufficient funding or investment can hinder operations and growth.

   - **Cash Flow Problems:** Poor cash flow management can lead to operational challenges and inability to meet financial obligations.

- **High Burn Rate:** Excessive spending relative to revenue can deplete resources quickly.

Mitigation Strategies:

- **Develop a Solid Financial Plan:** Create detailed financial projections and budgets. Monitor cash flow regularly and adjust spending as needed.

- **Diversify Funding Sources:** Seek multiple funding avenues, such as venture capital, angel investors, loans, and grants.

- **Maintain Financial Reserves:** Keep a financial buffer to manage unexpected expenses or downturns.

2. **Market Risk**

Definition:

- Market risk involves uncertainties related to market demand, competition, and customer preferences that can affect a startup's success.

Key Factors:

- **Market Demand:** Misjudging market demand or failing to validate the product-market fit can lead to low sales and revenue.

- **Competitive Pressure:** Intense competition from established players or other startups can impact market share and profitability.

- **Market Trends:** Rapid changes in market trends and consumer preferences can render a product or service obsolete.

Mitigation Strategies:

- **Conduct Thorough Market Research:** Understand customer needs, market trends, and competitive landscape through research and analysis.

- **Validate Product-Market Fit:** Use MVPs and pilot programs to test and refine your product based on customer feedback.

- **Stay Agile:** Be prepared to pivot or adapt your business model in response to market changes.

3. **Operational Risk**

Definition:

- Operational risk pertains to the potential disruptions in daily business operations, including supply chain issues, production problems, and technology failures.

Key Factors:

- **Supply Chain Disruptions:** Issues with suppliers or logistics can affect production and delivery schedules.

- **Operational Inefficiencies:** Inefficient processes or inadequate infrastructure can impact productivity and service quality.

- **Technology Failures:** Reliance on technology introduces risks related to system failures, data breaches, and cybersecurity threats.

Mitigation Strategies:

- **Develop Robust Processes:** Implement efficient and scalable processes for operations, production, and delivery.

- **Build Strong Supplier Relationships:** Establish reliable supply chain partners and have contingency plans in place.

- **Invest in Technology:** Ensure that technology infrastructure is secure and up-to-date. Implement regular system backups and cybersecurity measures.

4. Legal and Regulatory Risk

Definition:

- Legal and regulatory risk involves compliance with laws, regulations, and industry standards, which can affect operations, intellectual property, and business practices.

Key Factors:

- **Regulatory Compliance:** Non-compliance with industry regulations, tax laws, and employment laws can result in fines, legal disputes, and operational setbacks.

- **Intellectual Property Issues:** Failure to protect intellectual property or potential infringement claims can impact competitive advantage and business operations.

- **Contractual Disputes:** Disputes with partners, suppliers, or customers over contracts can lead to legal challenges and financial losses.

Mitigation Strategies:

- **Consult Legal Experts:** Work with legal professionals to ensure compliance with applicable laws and regulations.

- **Protect Intellectual Property:** Register trademarks, patents, and copyrights to safeguard your intellectual property.

- **Draft Clear Contracts:** Create clear and comprehensive contracts with partners, suppliers, and customers to minimize the risk of disputes.

5. Strategic Risk

Definition:

- Strategic risk involves uncertainties related to the startup's strategic decisions and business model, which can impact long-term success and growth.

Key Factors:

- **Incorrect Strategy:** Pursuing an ineffective business strategy or entering a saturated market can hinder growth and profitability.

- **Poor Decision-Making:** Strategic decisions made without adequate data or analysis can lead to unfavorable outcomes.

- **Execution Challenges:** Difficulties in executing strategic plans or achieving set objectives can affect overall business performance.

Mitigation Strategies:

- **Develop a Strategic Plan:** Create a well-defined strategic plan with clear goals, objectives, and action plans.

- **Use Data-Driven Decisions:** Base strategic decisions on thorough analysis, market research, and data insights.

- **Monitor and Adjust:** Regularly review and adjust your strategy based on performance metrics and changing market conditions.

6. **Reputational Risk**

Definition:

- Reputational risk involves the potential damage to a startup's reputation due to negative events, customer dissatisfaction, or public perception.

Key Factors:

- **Negative Publicity:** Negative media coverage, customer complaints, or product recalls can harm the startup's reputation.

- **Customer Service Issues:** Poor customer service or failure to address customer concerns can lead to negative reviews and decreased trust.

- **Ethical Concerns:** Ethical lapses or questionable business practices can damage the startup's public image.

Mitigation Strategies:

- **Focus on Customer Satisfaction:** Provide excellent customer service and address complaints or issues promptly.

- **Manage Public Relations:** Develop a strong public relations strategy to handle negative events and maintain a positive image.

- **Adhere to Ethical Standards:** Uphold high ethical standards and transparency in all business practices.

7. **Talent Risk**

Definition:

- Talent risk pertains to the challenges related to acquiring, retaining, and managing skilled employees, which are crucial for a startup's success.

Key Factors:

- **Talent Acquisition:** Difficulty in attracting qualified candidates or competing with larger companies for talent can impact team building.

- **Employee Retention:** High turnover rates or dissatisfaction among employees can disrupt operations and affect team morale.

- **Skill Gaps:** Lack of necessary skills or expertise within the team can hinder progress and innovation.

Mitigation Strategies:

- **Develop a Strong Employer Brand:** Highlight your startup's mission, culture, and growth opportunities to attract top talent.

- **Implement Retention Strategies:** Offer competitive compensation, benefits, and professional development opportunities to retain employees.

- **Provide Training and Development:** Invest in employee training and development to address skill gaps and enhance team capabilities.

8. **Competitive Risk**

Definition:

- Competitive risk involves the challenges posed by existing and emerging competitors that can impact market share, pricing, and overall competitiveness.

Key Factors:

- **Competitive Pressure:** Intense competition can lead to price wars, reduced margins, and loss of market share.

- **New Entrants:** New competitors entering the market can disrupt existing dynamics and pose additional challenges.

- **Competitive Advantage:** Failing to maintain or establish a competitive advantage can weaken market position.

Mitigation Strategies:

- **Analyze Competitors:** Regularly analyze competitors' strategies, strengths, and weaknesses to inform your own approach.

- **Innovate Continuously:** Focus on innovation and differentiation to maintain a competitive edge.

- **Build Strong Relationships:** Develop strong relationships with customers, partners, and industry influencers to enhance market position.

Nut Shell: ***By recognizing these risks and implementing effective strategies to manage and mitigate those risks, startups can improve their chances of navigating the complexities of entrepreneurship and achieving long-term success.***

7.6.4 Risk Management Strategies

Effective risk management is crucial for startups to navigate uncertainties and mitigate potential threats to their business. Implementing robust risk management strategies helps in identifying, assessing, and addressing risks proactively. Here's a detailed guide to risk management strategies for startups:

1. **Risk Identification**

   Objective:

   - To identify potential risks that could impact the startup's operations, financial health, or strategic goals.

   Strategies:

   - **Conduct Risk Assessments:** Regularly perform risk assessments to identify internal and external risks. This can include brainstorming sessions, expert consultations, and SWOC (Strengths, Weaknesses, Opportunities, and Challenges) analysis.

   - **Engage Stakeholders:** Involve key stakeholders such as employees, partners, and advisors in identifying risks, as they may provide valuable insights from different perspectives.

   - **Review Historical Data:** Analyze past incidents and industry trends to identify recurring risks and potential vulnerabilities.

2. **Risk Assessment**

   Objective:

   - To evaluate the likelihood and impact of identified risks and prioritize them based on their potential effect on the startup.

   Strategies:

   - **Risk Matrix:** Use a risk matrix to assess risks based on their probability of occurrence and potential impact. This helps in categorizing risks into high, medium, or low priority.

   - **Quantitative Analysis:** Apply quantitative methods such as statistical analysis or modeling to measure the potential financial impact of risks.

   - **Qualitative Analysis:** Use qualitative methods such as expert judgment or scenario analysis to assess risks that are difficult to quantify.

3. **Risk Mitigation**

   Objective:

   - To develop and implement strategies to reduce the likelihood or impact of identified risks.

   Strategies:

   - **Risk Avoidance:** Modify business processes or strategies to avoid certain risks altogether. For example, choosing not to enter a highly competitive market.

   - **Risk Reduction:** Implement measures to reduce the probability or impact of risks. This can include adopting best practices, enhancing security measures, or improving operational efficiencies.

- **Risk Sharing:** Share the risk with other parties through partnerships, insurance, or outsourcing. For instance, outsourcing certain functions to specialized firms can mitigate operational risks.

- **Risk Acceptance:** In some cases, accepting the risk might be the most viable option. This involves acknowledging the risk and preparing to manage it if it occurs.

4. **Risk Monitoring and Review**

Objective:

- To continuously monitor and review risks to ensure that risk management strategies remain effective and relevant.

Strategies:

- **Regular Monitoring:** Implement regular monitoring processes to track identified risks and detect any new risks. Use key risk indicators (KRIs) to signal potential issues.

- **Risk Reviews:** Conduct periodic risk reviews to evaluate the effectiveness of risk management strategies and make necessary adjustments. This can be done through scheduled risk assessment meetings or audits.

- **Update Risk Register:** Maintain and update a risk register or risk management database to keep track of risks, mitigation measures, and changes in risk status.

5. **Contingency Planning**

Objective:

- To prepare for and respond to unforeseen events or emergencies that could disrupt business operations.

Strategies:

- **Develop Contingency Plans:** Create detailed contingency plans for high-priority risks. These plans should outline specific actions to take in response to different risk scenarios.

- **Conduct Drills:** Regularly conduct drills or simulations to test contingency plans and ensure that the team is prepared to handle emergencies.

- **Establish Communication Protocols:** Develop communication protocols for informing stakeholders and managing public relations in the event of a crisis.

6. **Risk Communication**

Objective:

- To ensure that risk-related information is effectively communicated to all relevant stakeholders.

Strategies:

- **Develop a Communication Plan:** Create a risk communication plan that outlines how risk information will be shared with employees, investors, customers, and other stakeholders.

- **Foster Transparency:** Promote transparency in communicating risks and risk management efforts to build trust and confidence among stakeholders.

- **Provide Training:** Train employees on risk awareness and response procedures to ensure that they understand their roles in managing risks.

7. **Risk Culture and Leadership**

   Objective:

   - To build a risk-aware culture within the startup and ensure that leadership supports effective risk management practices.

   Strategies:

   - **Promote a Risk-Aware Culture:** Encourage a culture where risk awareness is embedded in everyday operations and decision-making. This includes promoting open discussion about risks and learning from past experiences.

   - **Leadership Involvement:** Ensure that senior leadership is actively involved in risk management efforts and sets an example for the rest of the organization.

   - **Establish Risk Ownership:** Assign specific individuals or teams responsibility for managing particular risks and ensure accountability.

8. **Risk Transfer**

   Objective:

   - To transfer the financial impact of certain risks to third parties, thereby reducing the startup's exposure.

   Strategies:

   - **Insurance:** Obtain insurance coverage for various types of risks, such as property damage, liability, and business interruption. Ensure that insurance policies are adequate and tailored to the startup's needs.

   - **Contracts and Agreements:** Use contractual agreements to transfer risk to other parties. For example, include indemnification clauses or liability limits in contracts with suppliers and partners.

9. **Legal and Compliance**

Objective:

- To ensure compliance with legal and regulatory requirements and manage legal risks effectively.

Strategies:

- **Stay Informed:** Keep up-to-date with relevant laws and regulations that affect the startup's industry and operations.

- **Consult Legal Experts:** Work with legal professionals to ensure compliance and address potential legal issues.

- **Implement Compliance Programs:** Develop and implement compliance programs and policies to ensure adherence to legal and regulatory requirements.

10. **Financial Risk Management**

Objective:

- To manage financial risks related to funding, cash flow, and investment.

Strategies:

- **Financial Controls:** Implement robust financial controls and procedures to manage expenses, monitor cash flow, and ensure accurate financial reporting.

- **Budgeting and Forecasting:** Develop detailed budgets and financial forecasts to anticipate future financial needs and plan for potential financial risks.

- **Diversification:** Diversify revenue streams and funding sources to reduce reliance on a single source of income or investment.

Nut Shell: *Adopting these risk management strategies, startups can proactively address potential risks, minimize their impact, and enhance their ability to navigate the uncertainties of entrepreneurship successfully.*

7.7 Resources and Support for Entrepreneurs

Entrepreneurs embarking on the journey of building a startup often encounter numerous challenges that require more than just innovation and determination. Access to resources and support plays a pivotal role in transforming a vision into a thriving business. From financial backing and mentorship to networking opportunities and educational resources, these elements provide the critical infrastructure needed for entrepreneurs to succeed.

By leveraging various forms of support—whether through government schemes, industry associations, educational institutions, or community networks—entrepreneurs can gain valuable insights, reduce risks, and accelerate their growth.

Here's an elaborate look at the various types of resources and support available to entrepreneurs:

1. **Financial Resources**

   Types of Financial Support:

   - **Venture Capital:** Investment from venture capital firms in exchange for equity. This is often suited for high-growth startups with significant scaling potential.

   - **Angel Investors:** High-net-worth individuals who invest their personal funds into startups, typically in exchange for equity or convertible debt.

   - **Grants and Subsidies:** Non-repayable funds provided by governments, foundations, or organizations to support specific business activities or innovations.

   - **Bank Loans:** Traditional loans from financial institutions that must be repaid with interest. Banks often require a solid business plan and collateral.

- **Crowd-funding:** Raising small amounts of money from a large number of people, typically via online platforms like Kickstarter or Indiegogo.

Strategies for Accessing Financial Resources:

- **Develop a Comprehensive Business Plan:** A well-prepared business plan helps attract investors by clearly outlining the business model, market potential, and financial projections.

- **Network with Investors:** Attend industry events, pitch competitions, and networking meet-ups to connect with potential investors and funding sources.

- **Apply for Grants and Competitions:** Research and apply for relevant grants, subsidies, and startup competitions that align with your business goals.

2. **Mentorship and Advisory Support**

Types of Mentorship and Advisory Support:

- **Mentors:** Experienced professionals who provide guidance, advice, and support based on their own entrepreneurial experiences.

- **Advisory Boards:** A group of industry experts who offer strategic advice and insights to help guide the startup's growth and decision-making.

- **Incubators and Accelerators:** Programs that provide mentorship, resources, and support to early-stage startups in exchange for equity or fees. They often include structured mentoring and training.

Strategies for Accessing Mentorship:

- **Seek Out Mentors:** Look for mentors through industry associations, startup communities, and personal networks. Don't hesitate to reach out to potential mentors for guidance.

- **Join Incubators and Accelerators:** Apply to programs that offer structured support and access to a network of mentors, advisors, and industry experts.

- **Participate in Networking Events:** Engage in startup meet-ups, industry conferences, and workshops to connect with potential advisors and mentors.

3. **Educational Resources and Training**

Types of Educational Resources:

- **Business Courses and Workshops:** Educational programs offered by universities, business schools, or online platforms that cover various aspects of entrepreneurship, from business strategy to financial management.

- **Online Learning Platforms:** Platforms such as NPTEL – SWAYAM, COURSERA, UDEMY, and LinkedIn Learning offer courses on a wide range of topics relevant to entrepreneurs.

- **Industry Certifications:** Professional certifications and training programs that provide specialized knowledge and skills applicable to specific industries or business functions.

Strategies for Accessing Educational Resources:

- **Enroll in Relevant Courses:** Choose courses or workshops that align with your business needs and personal development goals.

- **Leverage Online Resources:** Utilize online learning platforms to access a variety of educational materials and training programs.

- **Seek Industry-Specific Training:** Look for certifications and training programs that offer specialized knowledge relevant to your industry.

4. **Networking and Community Support**

   Types of Networking and Community Support:

   - **Startup Communities:** Local or online communities where entrepreneurs can connect, share experiences, and support each other.

   - **Industry Associations:** Organizations that offer resources, networking opportunities, and industry-specific insights.

   - **Professional Organizations:** Groups that provide access to a network of professionals, including potential partners, clients, and collaborators.

   Strategies for Building Networks:

   - **Join Startup Groups:** Participate in local or online startup groups and forums to connect with other entrepreneurs and industry professionals.

   - **Attend Industry Events:** Take part in conferences, trade shows, and networking events to build relationships and stay informed about industry trends.

   - **Engage in Online Communities:** Utilize social media platforms and online forums to engage with communities relevant to your business.

5. **Legal and Compliance Resources**

   Types of Legal and Compliance Support:

   - **Legal Advisors:** Attorneys or legal firms that provide advice on business formation, intellectual property, contracts, and compliance.

   - **Compliance Tools:** Software and services that help startups comply with regulations, manage documentation, and maintain legal standards.

- **Government Resources:** Government agencies and programs that offer guidance on regulatory compliance, business registration, and industry-specific requirements.

Strategies for Accessing Legal Support:

- **Consult Legal Professionals:** Work with legal advisors to ensure that all legal and regulatory requirements are met.

- **Utilize Compliance Tools:** Implement tools and software designed to assist with compliance and regulatory management.

- **Research Government Programs:** Explore government resources and programs that provide legal and compliance assistance for startups.

6. **Technology and Infrastructure**

Types of Technology and Infrastructure Support:

- **Technology Platforms:** Software and tools that support business operations, including customer relationship management (CRM), project management, and accounting software.

- **Office Space and Equipment:** Co-working spaces, virtual offices, and equipment leasing options that provide the physical infrastructure needed for operations.

- **Technical Support:** Services and support for technology-related issues, including IT support and cyber-security solutions.

Strategies for Leveraging Technology:

- **Adopt Relevant Tools:** Choose technology platforms that align with your business needs and enhance operational efficiency.

- **Explore Co-Working Spaces:** Consider co-working spaces or virtual offices to reduce overhead costs and access shared resources.

- **Invest in Technical Support:** Ensure that you have access to reliable technical support for managing and maintaining your technology infrastructure.

7. **Market and Business Development**

Types of Market and Business Development Support:

- **Market Research Services:** Firms and tools that provide insights into market trends, customer behavior, and competitive analysis.

- **Business Development Programs:** Initiatives and programs designed to help startups with market entry, growth strategies, and sales development.

- **Customer Acquisition Platforms:** Tools and services that assist in acquiring and retaining customers, including digital marketing and lead generation services.

Strategies for Enhancing Business Development:

- **Conduct Market Research:** Use market research services to gain insights into your target market and refine your business strategies.

- **Participate in Business Development Programs:** Engage in programs that offer support for scaling and expanding your business.

- **Utilize Customer Acquisition Tools:** Leverage digital marketing platforms and tools to drive customer acquisition and retention.

CHAPTER 8

Resume and Cover Letter Writing

Crafting a compelling resume and cover letter is essential for making a strong impression in today's competitive job market. Your resume serves as a succinct summary of your professional experience, skills, and accomplishments, designed to catch the eye of potential employers and open doors to interviews. It is a strategic document that highlights your strengths and relevant qualifications, often tailored for specific job applications to align with the employer's needs.

Meanwhile, a well-written cover letter provides a personalized narrative that goes beyond the bullet points of your resume. It allows you to articulate your enthusiasm for the role, demonstrate a deeper understanding of the company's culture and goals, and illustrate how your unique background makes you an ideal fit.

Together, these documents create a powerful first impression, showcasing not only your suitability for the position but also your genuine interest in the company. By thoughtfully crafting both your resume and cover letter, you can effectively communicate your value and increase your chances of advancing in the hiring process.

8.1 Characteristics of a Strong Resume

1. **Relevance**

   - **Tailored Content**: The resume should be customized for each job application, highlighting skills, experiences, and achievements relevant to the specific position and industry.

   - **Targeted Keywords**: Incorporate industry-specific terms and keywords from the job description to pass Applicant Tracking Systems (ATS) and resonate with recruiters.

2. **Clarity and Conciseness**

   - **Clear Structure**: Use a logical format with distinct sections such as Summary, Experience, Skills, Education, and Certifications. Ensure each section is clearly labeled.

3. **Professional Appearance**

   - **Clean Layout**: Utilize a clean, professional design with consistent fonts, margins, and spacing. Avoid excessive graphics or complicated layouts.

   - **Readable Fonts**: Professional and easily readable fonts (e.g., Arial, Calibri) in a standard size (e.g., 10-12 pt) to enhance readability.

4. **Quantifiable Achievements**

   - **Specific Metrics**: Include quantifiable results to demonstrate the impact of your work (e.g., "Increased sales by 25%" or "Reduced processing time by 30%").

5. **Accuracy and Honesty**

   - **Error-Free Content**: Ensure the resume is free from spelling, grammar, and punctuation errors. Proofread thoroughly or use tools to check for mistakes.

6. **Strong Summary or Objective**

   - **Compelling Introduction**: Start with a strong summary or objective statement that succinctly outlines your career goals and key qualifications, setting the stage for the rest of the resume.

7. **Relevant Skills and Experience**

   - **Skills Section**: Include a dedicated section for relevant skills that match the job requirements, such as technical skills, soft skills, and industry-specific competencies.

8. **Educational and Professional Development**

   - **Education**: Clearly list your educational background, including degrees, institutions, and graduation dates. Mention any honors or relevant coursework if applicable.

9. **Customization for ATS**

   - **Keyword Optimization**: Use keywords and phrases from the job description to ensure your resume is optimized for ATS and increases the chances of passing initial screenings.

10. **Contact Information**

    - **Up-to-Date Details**: Provide current and accurate contact information, including a professional email address and phone number. Ensure these details are easily visible at the top of the resume.

Nut Shell: Focusing on these quality parameters, you can create a resume that effectively showcases your qualifications, aligns with job requirements, and stands out to both automated systems and human recruiters.

8.2 Crafting a Strong Resume

8.2.1 Resume for Graduating Student (Campus Interview)

Crafting an effective resume for a campus interview as a graduating student involves highlighting your academic achievements, relevant experiences, and skills in a way that appeals to potential employers. Here are some tailored tips to help you create a standout resume:

1. **Highlight Academic Achievements**

   - **Emphasize Relevant Coursework**: Include courses that are directly related to the job or industry you're applying for. Mention specific projects or assignments that demonstrate your skills.

   - **Showcase Academic Honors**: List any awards, scholarships, or honors you've received. These can help highlight your dedication and excellence in your field.

2. **Focus on Internships and Projects**

   - **Detail Internships**: Include any internships or part-time roles relevant to your field. Highlight your responsibilities, achievements, and the skills you developed.

   - **Include Key Projects**: Describe significant academic or personal projects that demonstrate your practical skills, problem-solving abilities, and knowledge in your area of study.

3. **Highlight Skills and Competencies**

   - **Technical Skills**: List any technical skills or software proficiencies that are relevant to the job. For example, programming languages, data analysis tools, or design software.

- **Soft Skills**: Include soft skills like communication, teamwork, and leadership. Provide examples of how you've demonstrated these skills through group projects, presentations, or extracurricular activities.

4. **Include Extracurricular Activities**

- **Leadership Roles**: Mention any leadership positions in student organizations, clubs, or societies. This demonstrates initiative and the ability to manage responsibilities.

- **Relevant Involvements**: Highlight involvement in activities or volunteer work that relates to the job or industry. This can provide insight into your interests and dedication.

5. **Craft a Strong Summary Statement**

- **Career Objective or Summary**: Start with a brief summary or objective statement that outlines your career goals and what you bring to the table. Tailor this to reflect your aspirations and the position you're targeting.

6. **Use Action Verbs and Metrics**

- **Dynamic Language**: Use action verbs like "developed," "led," "analyzed," or "designed" to convey your experiences effectively.

- **Quantify Achievements**: Whenever possible, quantify your accomplishments (e.g., "Coordinated a team of 5 for a marketing campaign that increased social media engagement by 30%").

7. **Keep It Concise and Focused**

- **One Page**: As a graduating student, aim to keep your resume to one page. Be concise and focus on the most relevant experiences and skills.

- **Clear Layout**: Use a clean and professional layout with clear headings, bullet points, and consistent formatting to make your resume easy to read.

8. **Proofread and Review**

   - **Error-Free**: Carefully proofread your resume to eliminate any spelling, grammar, or formatting errors. Consider having a mentor, career advisor, or peer review it as well.

9. **Include Contact Information**

   - **Professional Contact Details**: Ensure your contact information is up-to-date and includes a professional email address and phone number. Make this information easily accessible at the top of your resume.

10. **Tailor for the Role**

    - **Research the Employer**: Understand the company and the role you're applying for. Tailor your resume to emphasize experiences and skills that align with the employer's needs and values.

Nut Shell: focusing on these tips, you can create a resume that effectively highlights your qualifications and makes a strong impression during campus interviews.

8.1.2 Resume for Switching a Job

Creating a strong resume is crucial for catching the attention of hiring managers and landing interviews. Here are some essential tips to help you craft an effective resume for changing the job or job profile:

1. **Tailor Your Resume to the Job**: Customize your resume for each position you apply for. Use keywords from the job description to ensure that your resume aligns with the specific skills and experiences the employer is looking for.

2. **Use a Clear, Professional Format**: Choose a clean, professional layout that is easy to read. Use consistent fonts, bullet points, and headings. Ensure that your formatting enhances readability and does not distract from the content.

3. **Start with a Strong Summary or Objective**: Begin with a brief summary or objective that highlights your key qualifications and career goals. This should be tailored to the specific role and provide a snapshot of your professional identity.

4. **Focus on Achievements, Not Just Duties**: Highlight your accomplishments in previous roles rather than just listing job duties. Use quantifiable metrics (e.g., "increased sales by 20%") to demonstrate the impact of your work.

5. **Use Action Verbs**: Begin each bullet point with a strong action verb to convey your responsibilities and achievements more dynamically. Words like "developed," "managed," or "implemented" can make your contributions stand out.

6. **Keep It Concise**: Aim to keep your resume to one or two pages. Be concise and prioritize the most relevant information. Avoid including unnecessary details that do not contribute to your qualifications for the position.

7. **Include Relevant Skills and Keywords**: Identify and include key skills and industry-specific terms that are relevant to the job. This can help your resume pass through ATS and catch the attention of recruiters.

8. **Proofread for Errors**: Ensure your resume is free from spelling, grammar, and formatting errors. Typos can create a negative impression and suggest a lack of attention to detail.

9. **Highlight Education and Certifications**: List your educational background and any relevant certifications or professional

development courses. Include dates and institutions to provide context.

10. **Incorporate a Professional Design**: If you have the skills, consider using a professional design tool to create a visually appealing resume. Ensure that any design elements enhance readability and are not overly complex.

8.1.1 Dos and Don'ts in Creating Strong Resume

Creating a quality resume involves balancing professionalism, clarity, and relevance. Here's a guide to the essential dos and don'ts to help you craft a resume that stands out for the right reasons:

Dos

1. **Do Tailor Your Resume**: Customize your resume for each job application. Highlight experiences and skills that are most relevant to the specific position and company.

2. **Do Use Clear and Concise Language**: Write in a straightforward manner using bullet points and short phrases. Avoid long paragraphs to make it easier for hiring managers to scan your resume quickly.

3. **Do Quantify Your Achievements**: Use numbers and specific metrics to demonstrate your impact. For example, "Increased customer satisfaction by 15%" provides a clearer picture of your accomplishments.

4. **Do Include Relevant Keywords**: Incorporate industry-specific terms and keywords from the job description. This helps your resume pass through ATS and catch the attention of recruiters.

5. **Do Focus on Professional Design**: Use a clean, professional format with consistent fonts, headings, and spacing. Ensure your resume is visually appealing and easy to read.

6. **Do Proofread Your Resume**: Check for spelling, grammar, and punctuation errors. A polished, error-free resume reflects attention to detail and professionalism.

7. **Do Highlight Transferable Skills**: If you're changing industries or roles, emphasize skills that are applicable across different fields, such as project management, communication, or leadership etc.

8. **Do Include a Summary or Objective**: Start with a brief summary or objective statement that outlines your career goals and key qualifications. This sets the tone and provides context for the rest of your resume.

Don'ts

1. **Don't Use Generic Resumes**: Avoid sending out the same resume for every job application. A generic resume may not effectively address the specific requirements of each role.

2. **Don't Include Irrelevant Information**: Exclude details that don't pertain to the job you're applying for, such as unrelated work experiences or outdated skills.

3. **Don't Use Unprofessional Formatting**: Steer clear of overly complex designs, flashy fonts, or unusual layouts. These can distract from your content and may not be ATS - friendly.

4. **Don't Lie or Exaggerate**: Be truthful about your qualifications and experiences. Misrepresentations can be easily uncovered and could damage your credibility and chances of landing the job.

5. **Don't Use Jargon or Buzzwords**: Avoid excessive jargon or buzzwords that might be unclear or overused. Focus on clear, straightforward language that accurately reflects your skills and experiences.

6. **Don't Neglect Contact Information**: Ensure your contact details are current and prominently displayed. Include a professional email address and phone number.

7. **Don't Overlook Gaps in Employment**: Address significant gaps in your work history, if possible. Be prepared to explain them in a way that shows how you remained productive or how the experience has contributed to your growth.

8. **Don't Forget to Update Your Resume**: Regularly revise your resume to include your latest accomplishments, roles, and skills. An outdated resume may not reflect your most recent achievements and qualifications.

8.2 Writing an Effective Cover Letter

An effective cover letter is an integral component of your job application, complementing your resume and providing a personalized introduction to potential employers. Here are the key characteristics of an effective cover letter:

1. **Tailored to the Job and Company**
   - **Customized Content**: Address the specific job you're applying for and the company you're targeting. Mention the job title and how you found out about the position.
   - **Company-Specific Insights**: Demonstrate that you've researched the company. Reference its values, culture, or recent achievements to show your genuine interest and fit.

2. **Strong Opening**
   - **Engaging Introduction**: Start with a compelling opening that grabs the reader's attention. Mention your enthusiasm for the role and briefly outline why you're a strong candidate.

- **Personal Connection**: If possible, reference a mutual connection or mention a recent company development that excited you.

3. **Clear and Concise**

   - **Focused Content**: Keep your cover letter to one page. Be concise and avoid repetition. Clearly articulate your main points and qualifications.

   - **Organized Structure**: Use a clear structure with distinct paragraphs: introduction, body (highlighting key qualifications), and conclusion.

4. **Emphasizes Relevant Skills and Achievements**

   - **Skill Alignment**: Highlight how your skills and experiences align with the job requirements. Use specific examples to demonstrate your abilities and accomplishments.

   - **Quantifiable Results**: Whenever possible, include quantifiable achievements (e.g., "Led a team that increased sales by 20%") to underscore your impact.

5. **Professional Tone and Language**

   - **Appropriate Language**: Use professional and courteous language. Avoid jargon or complex vocabulary. Ensure that your tone reflects the company culture—formal for traditional industries and slightly more casual for creative fields, if appropriate.

   - **Positive and Confident**: Express enthusiasm and confidence without coming across as arrogant. Show that you're eager to contribute to the company's success.

6. **Demonstrates Knowledge of the Role and Company**

   - **Role-Specific Insights**: Show that you understand the responsibilities and requirements of the position. Explain how your background makes you a perfect fit for the role.

- **Company Knowledge**: Convey that you've researched the company. Mention aspects of its mission, values, or recent projects that resonate with you.

7. **Highlights Your Unique Value**

   - **Differentiation**: Explain what makes you unique compared to other candidates. Focus on what you can offer that others might not, and how your unique skills or experiences align with the company's needs.

   - **Personal Impact**: Describe how you can contribute to the company's goals or solve specific challenges they may be facing.

8. **Effective Closing**

   - **Call to Action**: End with a strong closing that invites the reader to take action. Express your desire for an interview and indicate your willingness to provide additional information.

   - **Gratitude**: Thank the reader for considering your application. Acknowledge their time and express your eagerness to discuss how you can contribute to the team.

9. **Error-Free**

   - **Proofread Thoroughly**: Ensure that your cover letter is free from spelling, grammar, and punctuation errors. Carefully review your letter or have someone else proofread it.

10. **Professional Formatting**

    - **Consistent Format**: Use a professional format with a clear header, appropriate salutation, and consistent font. Align your cover letter with the same formatting style as your resume for a cohesive look.

8.3 Tailoring Applications for Distinct Roles

Tailoring your application for different roles is important for standing out in a competitive job market. A tailored application demonstrates that you've put thought into how your skills and experiences align with the specific requirements of each position. Here's a step-by-step guide on how to customize your resume and cover letter for various roles:

1. **Analyze the Job Description**

   - **Identify Key Requirements**: Carefully review the job description to identify the essential skills, qualifications, and responsibilities. Note any specific keywords or phrases used.

   - **Understand the Company Culture**: Research the company's mission, values, and work environment to understand what they're looking for in a candidate.

2. **Customize Your Resume**

   - **Highlight Relevant Experience**: Adjust the "Experience" section of your resume to emphasize roles and accomplishments that are most relevant to the job. Rearrange bullet points or add new ones to better match the job description.

   - **Incorporate Keywords**: Include keywords and phrases from the job description in your resume. This helps your resume get noticed by Applicant Tracking Systems (ATS) and resonates with hiring managers.

   - **Adapt the Summary Statement**: Modify your resume's summary or objective statement to reflect the specific role you're applying for. Mention the job title and how your skills and goals align with the position.

3. **Tailor Your Cover Letter**

   - **Personalize the Introduction**: Address the cover letter to the hiring manager by name, if possible. Mention the specific job title and how you learned about the position.

   - **Align Your Qualifications**: Use the cover letter to explain how your background and skills match the specific requirements of the job. Provide examples that demonstrate your suitability for the role.

   - **Showcase Company Fit**: Highlight your knowledge of the company and explain why you're interested in working there. Mention any company-specific details that connect with your personal values or career goals.

4. **Emphasize Relevant Skills and Achievements**

   - **Select Key Skills**: Focus on skills that are directly relevant to the job. If the job emphasizes project management, for example, highlight your experience in leading projects.

   - **Quantify Achievements**: Use numbers and metrics to quantify your accomplishments. Tailor these achievements to reflect the impact they would have in the new role.

5. **Adjust Your Professional Tone and Language**

   - **Match the Job's Tone**: If the job posting uses formal language, mirror that tone in your application. For a more creative role, you might adopt a slightly more casual and engaging style.

   - **Reflect the Company Culture**: Ensure that the tone of your application matches the company's culture. If the company values innovation, emphasize your creative solutions and forward-thinking approach.

6. **Address Any Potential Concerns**

    - **Explain Career Changes**: If you're changing industries or roles, use your cover letter to explain how your previous experiences are relevant and how they prepare you for the new role.

    - **Highlight Transferable Skills**: Emphasize skills that are transferable across different roles or industries. This helps bridge any gaps between your previous experience and the new job requirements.

7. **Proofread and Finalize**

    - **Check for Consistency**: Ensure that both your resume and cover letter are consistently tailored for the role and company. Double-check that all references to the job title and company are accurate.

    - **Eliminate Errors**: Proofread your documents for spelling, grammar, and formatting errors. A well-polished application reflects professionalism and attention to detail.

8. **Follow Up**

    - **Send a Follow-Up Email**: After submitting your application, consider sending a brief follow-up email to express your continued interest in the position. Mention that you've tailored your application to reflect the job requirements and reiterate your enthusiasm for the role.

8.4 Showcasing Projects and Achievements

Showcasing projects and achievements effectively on your resume and cover letter is crucial for demonstrating your practical experience, skills, and contributions. Here's how to highlight these elements to make a strong impression:

1. **Choose Relevant Projects and Achievements**
   - **Align with Job Requirements**: Select projects and achievements that are directly relevant to the job you're applying for. This demonstrates that you have the specific experience and skills the employer is looking for.
   - **Highlight Impact**: Focus on accomplishments that had a significant impact or resulted in measurable outcomes. This shows that you not only participated in projects but also contributed to their success.

2. **Detail Your Role and Contributions**
   - **Be Specific About Your Role**: Clearly define your role in each project or achievement. Use action verbs to describe what you did (e.g., "led," "developed," "implemented").
   - **Describe Your Contributions**: Provide details about your responsibilities and contributions. This helps the reader understand your level of involvement and expertise.

3. **Use Quantifiable Metrics**
   - **Include Numbers and Data**: Where possible, quantify your achievements with numbers, percentages, or other measurable outcomes. For example, "Increased website traffic by 40%" or "Managed a team of 10 to deliver a project 2 weeks ahead of schedule."
   - **Showcase Results**: Highlight the results of your work to demonstrate the value you brought to the project or organization.

4. **Present Projects and Achievements Clearly**
   - **Create a Dedicated Section**: On your resume, consider creating separate sections for "Projects" and "Achievements"

if they are significant and varied. This makes it easier for employers to see your key contributions.

- **Use Bullet Points**: List projects and achievements using bullet points for clarity and ease of reading. Start each bullet with a strong action verb and focus on outcomes.

5. **Provide Context and Background**

- **Explain the Project**: Briefly describe the context of the project. Mention the objective, scope, and any relevant background information to help the reader understand the significance of your contribution.

- **Clarify the Challenge**: If applicable, outline any challenges or constraints you faced during the project. This can provide insight into your problem-solving skills and resilience.

6. **Showcase Collaborative Efforts**

- **Acknowledge Teamwork**: If you worked as part of a team, mention this and explain your specific role. Highlight any leadership or coordination responsibilities you had.

- **Focus on Individual Impact**: While acknowledging teamwork, emphasize your individual contributions and how they drove the success of the project.

7. **Highlight Awards and Recognitions**

- **Mention Honors**: If your projects or achievements received awards or formal recognition, include this information. It adds credibility and shows that your work was valued by others.

- **Include Certificates or Badges**: If you received certifications or badges related to the achievements, list them to provide tangible proof of your accomplishments.

8. **Integrate Projects and Achievements in Your Cover Letter**

   - **Connect to the Role**: In your cover letter, reference specific projects and achievements that demonstrate how your experience aligns with the job requirements.

   - **Narrate Success Stories**: Use the cover letter to tell a compelling story about your most significant projects or achievements. Explain how these experiences have prepared you for the role you're applying for.

9. **Update Regularly**

   - **Keep Information Current**: Regularly update your resume and cover letter with new projects and achievements. This ensures that your application reflects your most recent and relevant experiences.

10. **Proofread and Revise**

    - **Ensure Accuracy**: Double-check all details related to your projects and achievements for accuracy. Ensure that numbers and descriptions are correct and clearly presented.

    - **Revise for Clarity**: Review your resume and cover letter to ensure that your projects and achievements are presented in a clear and compelling manner.

CHAPTER 9

Interview Preparation

In the competitive landscape of job hunting, where every detail counts, meticulous preparation for an interview can be the decisive factor between success and missed opportunity. This chapter delves into the crucial preparatory steps that lay the groundwork for a compelling interview performance. From understanding the company's culture and aligning your skills with the job requirements to mastering the art of self-presentation and practicing strategic responses to common questions, preparation is not just about readiness—it's about transforming potential into performance.

Effective preparation begins with comprehensive research, allowing you to tailor your responses and demonstrate genuine enthusiasm for the role. It involves anticipating potential questions and crafting thoughtful answers that highlight your strengths while addressing potential weaknesses.

Additionally, preparation extends beyond the content of your responses to include the subtleties of body language, attire, and punctuality. By honing these elements, you set the stage to showcase not only your qualifications but also your proactive commitment to excelling in the role. Ultimately, thorough preparation empowers you to navigate the interview with confidence, turning each interaction into an opportunity to affirm your suitability for the position and make a lasting impression on your prospective employer.

9.1 Types of Interviews

Job interviews for engineering graduates can vary widely depending on the industry, company, and role. Here are some common types of interviews that engineering graduates might encounter:

1. **Technical Interviews**

   - **Purpose:** To assess your technical skills and problem-solving abilities relevant to the engineering role.

   - **Format:** These interviews often include technical questions, problem-solving exercises, and coding challenges (for software engineering roles). You might be asked to solve engineering problems on a whiteboard or a computer.

   - **Preparation:** Review fundamental concepts in your field, practice coding problems, and solve engineering problems related to your discipline.

2. **Behavioral Interviews**

   - **Purpose:** To evaluate your soft skills, such as teamwork, leadership, and communication, and how you handle various work situations.

   - **Format:** Questions are often framed around past experiences, such as "Tell me about a time when you faced a challenge," using the STAR method (Situation, Task, Action, Result) to structure your responses.

- **Preparation:** Reflect on your past experiences, and prepare to discuss specific examples that highlight your skills and achievements.

3. **Case Interviews**

   - **Purpose:** To test your problem-solving skills and ability to apply engineering principles to real-world scenarios.

   - **Format:** You might be presented with a case study or scenario and asked to analyze the problem, propose solutions, and discuss your thought process.

   - **Preparation:** Practice case studies related to your field, focusing on problem analysis, solution development, and clear communication of your thought process.

4. **Panel Interviews**

   - **Purpose:** To gather diverse perspectives from multiple interviewers and assess how well you interact with different stakeholders.

   - **Format:** You will be interviewed by a panel of interviewers, which might include engineers, managers, and HR representatives. Questions can range from technical to behavioral.

   - **Preparation:** Practice responding to multiple people, and be ready to handle questions from different perspectives.

5. **Group Interviews**

   - **Purpose:** To assess your teamwork, communication, and leadership skills in a group setting.

   - **Format:** You may be placed in a group with other candidates and given a task or problem to solve collaboratively. Interviewers observe how you interact and contribute.

- **Preparation:** Develop your teamwork skills, practice working in groups, and be prepared to demonstrate your ability to collaborate effectively.

6. **Technical Presentation Interviews**

    - **Purpose:** To evaluate your ability to present technical information clearly and effectively.

    - **Format:** You might be asked to prepare and deliver a presentation on a technical topic relevant to the role. This could be followed by questions from the interviewers.

    - **Preparation:** Choose a relevant topic, practice your presentation skills, and prepare to answer questions about your presentation.

7. **Phone or Video Interviews**

    - **Purpose:** To conduct an initial screening or preliminary assessment, often when candidates are not local.

    - **Format:** These interviews are conducted over the phone or via video conferencing tools. They can include both technical and behavioral questions.

    - **Preparation:** Ensure you have a quiet environment, test your technology, and prepare answers to common questions. Practice speaking clearly and confidently.

8. **On-Site Interviews**

    - **Purpose:** To assess your fit within the company and the specific team, and to see your problem-solving skills in a real work environment.

    - **Format:** Typically includes a mix of technical interviews, site tours, and meetings with team members. You might be asked to complete technical tasks or case studies.

- **Preparation:** Familiarize yourself with the company's work environment, and be ready to participate in technical exercises and meet with various team members.

9. **Internship or Co-op Interviews**

- **Purpose:** To assess your suitability for a temporary or part-time role that provides practical experience.

- **Format:** These interviews often focus on your academic background, interest in the field, and any relevant coursework or projects.

- **Preparation:** Highlight your academic projects, relevant coursework, and enthusiasm for gaining practical experience.

Nut Shell: Preparing for these various types of interviews, engineering graduates can effectively demonstrate their technical expertise, problem-solving skills, and fit for the role, increasing their chances of securing their desired position.

9.2 Preparing for Interview

Preparing for an interview during campus placements involves a series of strategic steps designed to maximize your chances of success. Here's a structured approach to ensure you're thoroughly prepared:

1. **Understand the Company and Role**

- **Research the Company:** Gather information about the company's history, mission, values, culture, and recent news. Understand their products or services and their position in the industry.

- **Study the Job Description:** Analyze the job role you're applying for, including key responsibilities, required skills, and qualifications. Align these with your own experiences and skills.

2. **Prepare Your Resume and Documents**

   - **Update Your Resume:** Ensure your resume is current, clearly formatted, and tailored to the role. Highlight relevant skills, experiences, and achievements.

   - **Gather Required Documents:** Prepare any additional documents requested by the company, such as transcripts, certificates, or portfolio samples.

3. **Practice Common Interview Questions**

   - **Behavioral Questions:** Prepare for questions about past experiences using the STAR method (Situation, Task, Action, Result) to structure your responses.

   - **Technical Questions:** For technical roles, review relevant concepts and practice problem-solving exercises related to your field.

   - **Situational Questions:** Think through hypothetical scenarios related to the role and prepare how you might address them.

4. **Develop Your Personal Pitch**

   - **Elevator Pitch:** Craft a brief, compelling summary of who you are, your background, and what you're looking for in a role. This should be concise and engaging.

5. **Prepare Questions for the Interviewer**

   - **Insightful Questions:** Prepare thoughtful questions about the company, team dynamics, or the role to demonstrate your interest and engagement.

6. **Practice Mock Interviews**

   - **Simulate the Interview:** Conduct mock interviews with friends, family, or mentors to practice your responses, body language, and overall demeanor.

- **Seek Feedback:** Use feedback from these practice sessions to refine your answers and presentation.

7. **Plan Your Attire**

- **Dress Professionally:** Choose an outfit that is appropriate for the company culture and role. Ensure it is clean, well-fitted, and free of distractions.

8. **Logistics and Timing**

- **Know the Details:** Confirm the date, time, and format (in-person or virtual) of the interview. Plan your route if it's in-person, or test your technology if it's virtual.

- **Arrive Early:** Aim to arrive at least 10-15 minutes early for an in-person interview. For virtual interviews, log in a few minutes early to address any technical issues.

9. **Prepare Mentally and Physically**

- **Get Rest:** Ensure you have a good night's sleep before the interview.

- **Stay Calm:** Practice relaxation techniques to manage anxiety and maintain composure.

10. **Follow-Up**

- **Send a Thank-You Note:** After the interview, send a polite thank-you email expressing appreciation for the opportunity and reiterating your interest in the role.

Nut Shell: Diligently following these steps, you will be well-prepared to handle the interview process with confidence and professionalism, making a strong impression on potential employers during your campus placement.

9.3 Common Interview Questions and How to answer them

During a personal interview in a placement drive, candidates are typically asked a range of questions designed to assess their suitability for the role and their fit within the company's culture. Here are some commonly asked questions, along with insights into what interviewers are looking for:

9.3.1 Behavioral Questions

Behavioral questions are a common feature of placement interviews, designed to assess how candidates have handled various situations in the past and to predict how they might behave in similar circumstances in the future. These questions focus on your experiences, actions, and outcomes rather than hypothetical scenarios. Here's a comprehensive guide on the types of behavioral questions you might encounter and how to prepare for them:

A. Types of Behavioral Questions

1. **Problem-Solving:**

   - **Example Question:** "Can you describe a time when you faced a significant challenge at work or school? How did you handle it, and what was the outcome?"

   - **Purpose:** To assess your problem-solving skills and how you deal with obstacles.

2. **Teamwork:**

   - **Example Question:** "Tell me about a time when you worked as part of a team. What was your role, and how did you contribute to the team's success?"

   - **Purpose:** To evaluate your ability to work collaboratively and your role within a team.

3. **Leadership:**

   - **Example Question:** "Describe a situation where you had to take the lead on a project or task. How did you motivate others and ensure the project was completed successfully?"

   - **Purpose:** To gauge your leadership qualities and ability to manage and inspire others.

4. **Conflict Resolution:**

   - **Example Question:** "Give me an example of a conflict you encountered with a colleague or team member. How did you resolve it?"

   - **Purpose:** To understand how you handle interpersonal conflicts and find solutions.

5. **Time Management:**

   - **Example Question:** "Describe a time when you had multiple deadlines to meet. How did you prioritize your tasks and manage your time effectively?"

   - **Purpose:** To assess your organizational and time management skills.

6. **Decision-Making:**

   - **Example Question:** "Can you provide an example of a difficult decision you had to make? What was the process you followed to make the decision?"

   - **Purpose:** To evaluate your decision-making process and the reasoning behind your choices.

7. **Adaptability:**

   - **Example Question:** "Tell me about a time when you had to adapt to a significant change or unexpected situation. How did you handle it?"

- **Purpose:** To assess your flexibility and ability to adjust to new or challenging circumstances.

8. **Achievement:**

   - **Example Question:** "Describe a project or accomplishment that you are particularly proud of. What steps did you take to achieve it?"

   - **Purpose:** To understand what you consider as achievements and how you reached your goals.

9. **Customer Service:**

   - **Example Question:** "Provide an example of a time when you dealt with a difficult customer or client. How did you handle the situation and ensure their satisfaction?"

   - **Purpose:** To evaluate your customer service skills and ability to handle difficult interactions.

B. Preparing for Behavioral Questions

1. **Use the STAR Method:**

   - **Situation:** Describe the context or background of the situation you faced.

   - **Task:** Explain your role and what you needed to accomplish.

   - **Action:** Detail the specific steps you took to address the situation.

   - **Result:** Share the outcome of your actions and what you learned from the experience.

2. **Reflect on Past Experiences:**

   - Think about various situations from your academic, work, or extracurricular activities where you demonstrated skills related to the behavioral questions. Prepare specific examples for each type of question.

3. **Be Honest and Specific:**

   - Provide genuine examples from your experience, and be specific about your role and contributions. Avoid vague or generic responses.

4. **Practice Your Responses:**

   - Rehearse your answers to common behavioral questions to gain confidence and ensure your responses are clear and concise.

5. **Showcase Key Skills:**

   - Focus on demonstrating core competencies such as leadership, teamwork, problem-solving, and adaptability through your examples.

C. Sample Behavioral Answers

1. **Problem-Solving:**

   - **Situation:** During a group project, our team faced a critical issue with a tight deadline.

   - **Task:** I was responsible for coordinating the team and finding a solution to meet the deadline.

   - **Action:** I organized an emergency meeting; delegated tasks based on team members' strengths, and created a revised timeline.

   - **Result:** We successfully completed the project on time, and our final presentation received positive feedback from the client.

2. **Teamwork:**

   - **Situation:** I worked on a team project for a class where we needed to develop a marketing plan.

- **Task:** My role was to lead the research phase and collaborate with team members to integrate our findings into the plan.

- **Action:** I coordinated meetings, gathered data, and communicated effectively with the team to ensure everyone's contributions were included.

- **Result:** The project was well-received, and we achieved a high grade for our cohesive and thorough marketing strategy.

9.3.2 Situational Questions

Situational questions in placement interviews are designed to assess how candidates might handle hypothetical scenarios they could encounter in the workplace. These questions evaluate your problem-solving skills, decision-making abilities, and how you approach various challenges. Here's a guide to common situational questions and strategies for responding effectively:

A. Common Situational Questions

1. **Handling Tight Deadlines:**

   - **Example Question:** "Imagine you are working on a project with a tight deadline, and you realize that you won't be able to complete it on time. How would you handle this situation?"

   - **Purpose:** To assess your time management skills and ability to prioritize tasks under pressure.

2. **Dealing with Conflicts:**

   - **Example Question:** "Suppose you are working on a team project and have a disagreement with a team member about the approach to take. How would you resolve this conflict?"

   - **Purpose:** To evaluate your conflict resolution skills and ability to work collaboratively with others.

3. **Managing Multiple Priorities:**

   - **Example Question:** "If you were assigned multiple tasks with competing deadlines, how would you prioritize and manage your workload?"

   - **Purpose:** To test your organizational skills and ability to manage competing priorities effectively.

4. **Responding to Unexpected Changes:**

   - **Example Question:** "Imagine you are halfway through a project when your manager informs you of a major change in the project scope. How would you adapt to this change?"

   - **Purpose:** To evaluate your adaptability and flexibility in response to unexpected changes.

5. **Handling a Difficult Customer or Client:**

   - **Example Question:** "You are working in customer service, and a customer is upset about a product or service. How would you handle their complaint?"

   - **Purpose:** To assess your customer service skills and ability to manage challenging interactions professionally.

6. **Leading a Team:**

   - **Example Question:** "If you were leading a team and a critical team member was not contributing their fair share, how would you address the situation?"

   - **Purpose:** To evaluate your leadership and management skills, including how you handle team dynamics and accountability.

7. **Making Ethical Decisions:**

   - **Example Question:** "You discover that a colleague is engaging in unethical behavior that could harm the company. What steps would you take in this situation?"

- **Purpose:** To test your integrity and decision-making when faced with ethical dilemmas.

8. **Implementing New Ideas:**

   - **Example Question:** "Suppose you have an idea for improving a process at work, but you know it may face resistance from your colleagues. How would you go about implementing your idea?"

   - **Purpose:** To assess your creativity, initiative, and ability to persuade and collaborate with others.

9. **Handling Mistakes:**

   - **Example Question:** "If you made a mistake that negatively impacted a project or team, how would you address the situation and prevent it from happening again?"

   - **Purpose:** To evaluate your accountability, problem-solving skills, and willingness to learn from errors.

10. **Working Under Pressure:**

    - **Example Question:** "You are under a lot of pressure to deliver results quickly. How do you maintain your productivity and ensure high-quality work?"

    - **Purpose:** To assess how you handle stress and maintain performance standards under pressure.

B. Preparing for Situational Questions

1. **Understand the STAR Method:**

   - **Situation:** Set the context by describing the scenario.

   - **Task:** Explain your role and the challenges you faced.

   - **Action:** Detail the specific steps you took to address the situation.

- **Result:** Describe the outcome of your actions and any lessons learned.

2. **Practice Common Scenarios:**

- Think of various hypothetical situations related to your field or the role you're applying for. Practice how you would respond to these scenarios using the STAR method.

3. **Focus on Key Skills:**

- Emphasize skills relevant to the role, such as problem-solving, leadership, teamwork, adaptability, and communication, in your responses.

4. **Be Specific and Realistic:**

- Provide detailed and realistic answers based on your experiences or logical approaches to hypothetical situations. Avoid vague responses.

5. **Showcase Your Problem-Solving Abilities:**

- Demonstrate your ability to think critically and logically about how you would handle various challenges, providing clear examples of your approach.

6. **Remain Positive and Professional:**

- Approach each scenario with a positive and professional attitude, showing your ability to stay calm and focused even in challenging situations.

C. Sample Answers

1. **Handling Tight Deadlines:**

- **Situation:** "During a major project at my previous internship, we faced a tight deadline due to unexpected delays."

- **Task:** "My task was to ensure that all components of the project were completed on time."

- **Action:** "I reassessed the project timeline, prioritized critical tasks, and delegated responsibilities among team members. I also communicated with the client to manage their expectations."

- **Result:** "We completed the project on time, and the client was pleased with our proactive communication and the final deliverables."

2. **Dealing with Conflicts:**

- **Situation:** "In a group project, I disagreed with a team member about the direction of our presentation."

- **Task:** "My role was to find a resolution and ensure we could move forward as a team."

- **Action:** "I initiated a discussion to understand their perspective, proposed a compromise that incorporated elements from both viewpoints, and facilitated a vote to reach a consensus."

- **Result:** "The team agreed on the revised approach, which led to a successful presentation and improved team dynamics."

Nut Shell: ***Preparing thoroughly for situational questions and using structured responses, you can demonstrate your problem-solving skills and readiness for the role you're applying for.***

9.3.3 Traditional / General Questions

Traditional or general questions in placement interviews are designed to gauge a candidate's overall suitability for a role, their career aspirations, and their fit within the organization's culture. These questions typically focus on your background, experiences, and personal attributes rather than specific situational or behavioral scenarios. Here's a guide to common traditional or general questions and tips for answering them effectively:

A. Common Traditional/General Questions

1. **Tell Me About Yourself:**

   - **Example Question:** "Can you give me a brief overview of your background and experience?"

   - **Purpose:** To get an initial understanding of your qualifications, career path, and key experiences.

   - **Tip:** Provide a concise summary of your academic background, relevant experiences, and key skills. Tailor your answer to highlight aspects most relevant to the role you're applying for.

2. **Why Do You Want to Work Here?**

   - **Example Question:** "What interests you about this company and this particular role?"

   - **Purpose:** To assess your motivation and whether you have done your research on the company.

   - **Tip:** Demonstrate your knowledge of the company's values, culture, and recent developments. Connect these to your own career goals and interests.

3. **What are Your Strengths and Weaknesses?**

   - **Example Question:** "Can you discuss your greatest strengths and areas for improvement?"

   - **Purpose:** To evaluate self-awareness and how your strengths align with the job requirements, as well as how you address your weaknesses.

   - **Tip:** Choose strengths that are relevant to the job and provide specific examples. For weaknesses, mention an area you're working on improving and the steps you're taking to address it.

4. **Where do You See Yourself in Five Years?**

   - **Example Question:** "What are your long-term career goals and how does this position fit into them?"

   - **Purpose:** To gauge your career aspirations and whether they align with the company's growth opportunities.

   - **Tip:** Outline realistic career goals and how the role you're applying for will help you achieve them. Show enthusiasm for both the position and the company's trajectory.

5. **Why should we hire you?**

   - **Example Question:** "What makes you a good fit for this role and our company?"

   - **Purpose:** To understand why you believe you are the best candidate for the job.

   - **Tip:** Highlight your unique qualifications, experiences, and skills that make you stand out. Relate these directly to the job requirements and company needs.

6. **Tell Me About a Time You Demonstrated Leadership:**

   - **Example Question:** "Can you provide an example of a time when you took on a leadership role?"

   - **Purpose:** To assess your leadership qualities and ability to take initiative.

   - **Tip:** Use specific examples where you led a project or team, detailing your actions and the outcomes achieved.

7. **How Do You Handle Stress and Pressure?**

   - **Example Question:** "Describe how you manage stress and maintain productivity in high-pressure situations."

- **Purpose:** To evaluate your ability to cope with stress and perform effectively under pressure.

- **Tip:** Share specific strategies you use to manage stress, such as prioritization, time management, or relaxation techniques. Provide examples of how these strategies have worked for you.

8. **What Are Your Salary Expectations?**

   - **Example Question:** "What are your salary expectations for this role?"

   - **Purpose:** To understand your compensation requirements and if they align with the company's budget.

   - **Tip:** Research industry standards and company norms beforehand. Provide a salary range based on your research and express flexibility if needed.

9. **Can You Describe a Time When You Faced a Challenge?**

   - **Example Question:** "Tell me about a challenging situation you encountered and how you dealt with it."

   - **Purpose:** To evaluate your problem-solving skills and resilience.

   - **Tip:** Use the STAR method to outline the situation, your task, the actions you took, and the result. Focus on a challenge relevant to the role you're applying for.

10. **How Do You Stay Motivated?**

    - **Example Question:** "What motivates you to perform at your best?"

    - **Purpose:** To understand what drives you and how you maintain enthusiasm for your work.

- **Tip:** Discuss what aspects of your work or career drive you, such as goals, achievements, or the impact of your work. Relate this motivation to the role and company.

B. Preparing for Traditional/General Questions

1. **Self-Assessment:**

   - Reflect on your experiences, strengths, weaknesses, career goals, and achievements. Prepare concise and relevant responses for common questions.

2. **Research the Company:**

   - Understand the company's mission, values, culture, and recent developments. Use this information to tailor your responses and demonstrate your genuine interest.

3. **Practice Your Responses:**

   - Rehearse answers to common questions to gain confidence and ensure your responses are clear and articulate.

4. **Be Honest and Authentic:**

   - Provide honest and genuine responses that reflect your true self and your real experiences.

5. **Highlight Relevant Skills and Experiences:**

   - Focus on aspects of your background that are most relevant to the position you're applying for.

*Nut Shell: **Preparing effectively for these traditional or general questions, you can present yourself as a well-rounded and suitable candidate for the role, demonstrating both your qualifications and your fit with the company's values and goals.***

9.3.4 Technical Questions

Technical questions in placement interviews are designed to assess your knowledge, skills, and problem-solving abilities related to your specific field or role. These questions can vary widely depending on the industry, job function, and level of expertise required. Here's a guide to common technical questions and tips on how to prepare for them effectively:

A. Common Technical Questions

1. **Conceptual Understanding:**

   - **Example Question:** "Can you explain the differences between TCP and UDP?"

   - **Purpose:** To evaluate your understanding of fundamental concepts in your field.

   - **Tip:** Provide clear, concise explanations with examples to demonstrate your grasp of the subject.

2. **Problem-Solving:**

   - **Example Question:** "How would you optimize the performance of a SQL query?"

   - **Purpose:** To assess your ability to apply technical knowledge to solve practical problems.

   - **Tip:** Discuss specific techniques or tools you would use, such as indexing, query optimization strategies, or database design improvements.

3. **Technical Skills:**

   - **Example Question:** "What is your experience with version control systems like Git? Can you explain how branching and merging work?"

   - **Purpose:** To gauge your hands-on experience with essential tools and technologies.

   - **Tip:** Describe your experience with the tool, including specific tasks you've performed, and explain technical processes in a straightforward manner.

4. **Coding and Algorithms:**

   - **Example Question:** "Can you write a function to reverse a linked list?"

   - **Purpose:** To test your coding skills and understanding of algorithms and data structures.

   - **Tip:** Practice coding problems on platforms like LeetCode or HackerRank. Be prepared to write code on a whiteboard or in an online coding environment during the interview.

5. **System Design:**

   - **Example Question:** "How would you design a scalable system for handling real-time notifications?"

   - **Purpose:** To evaluate your ability to design systems and understand architectural principles.

   - **Tip:** Discuss system components, scalability considerations, and trade-offs. Use diagrams if possible to illustrate your design.

6. **Technical Troubleshooting:**

   - **Example Question:** "If a web application is experiencing slow response times, what steps would you take to diagnose and fix the issue?"

   - **Purpose:** To assess your problem-solving approach and technical troubleshooting skills.

   - **Tip:** Outline a systematic approach, including checking server logs, analyzing performance metrics, and identifying potential bottlenecks.

7. **Knowledge of Tools and Technologies:**

   - **Example Question:** "What are the main features of [specific technology or tool and how have you used them in your projects?"

- **Purpose:** To assess your familiarity with specific tools or technologies relevant to the role.
- **Tip:** Provide examples of how you've applied the technology in real projects, highlighting specific features and benefits.

8. **Data Analysis:**

   - **Example Question:** "How would you handle missing values in a dataset? What techniques might you use for data imputation?"
   - **Purpose:** To evaluate your skills in data analysis and statistical methods.
   - **Tip:** Discuss various techniques such as mean imputation, median imputation, or using predictive models for data imputation.

9. **Security Practices:**

   - **Example Question:** "What are some common security vulnerabilities in web applications, and how can they be mitigated?"
   - **Purpose:** To assess your understanding of security best practices and potential vulnerabilities.
   - **Tip:** Discuss specific vulnerabilities like SQL injection or XSS and provide solutions or practices to mitigate these risks.

10. **Industry-Specific Questions:**

    - **Example Question:** For a mechanical engineering role: "Can you explain the working principle of a heat exchanger?"
    - **Purpose:** To test your knowledge of industry-specific concepts and principles.
    - **Tip:** Provide detailed explanations based on your knowledge and experience in the field.

B. Preparing for Technical Questions

1. Review Core Concepts:

- Revisit fundamental concepts and principles related to your field. Use textbooks, online resources, and practice problems to refresh your knowledge.

2. Practice Coding and Problem-Solving:

- Work on coding problems and algorithms regularly to improve your problem-solving skills. Use platforms like LeetCode, HackerRank, or CodeSignal to practice.

3. Understand the Job Requirements:

- Review the job description to understand the technical skills and knowledge required for the role. Focus your preparation on these areas.

4. Study System Design and Architecture:

- Read up on system design principles and architecture patterns. Practice designing systems and understanding scalability, reliability, and performance considerations.

5. Familiarize Yourself with Tools and Technologies:

- Gain hands-on experience with tools and technologies mentioned in the job description. Work on projects or contribute to open-source initiatives to build your skills.

6. Prepare for Technical Troubleshooting:

- Develop a structured approach to troubleshooting technical issues. Practice diagnosing problems and proposing solutions based on your experience.

7. Use Online Resources:

- Utilize online tutorials, courses, and forums to deepen your understanding of specific technologies or concepts.

8. **Mock Interviews:**

   - Conduct mock interviews with peers or mentors to simulate the interview experience and receive feedback on your performance.

C. Sample Answers

1. **Coding and Algorithms:**

   - **Question:** "Write a function to find the maximum element in an array."

   - **Answer:**

```python
python
Copy code
def find_max(arr):
    if not arr:
        return None
    max_val = arr[0]
    for num in arr:
        if num > max_val:
            max_val = num
    return max_val
```

2. **System Design:**

   - **Question:** "Design a URL shortening service."

   - **Answer:** "I would design the system with a front-end service to handle user requests, a back-end service to process URL shortening and redirection, and a database to store mappings between short and long URLs. I would use a hash function to generate short URLs and implement a caching layer to improve performance. The system should be scalable to handle high traffic and include monitoring for reliability."

D. Sample Technical Questions in Textile Discipline

1. **Fiber and Fabric Properties:**

   - **Example Question:** "Can you explain the difference between natural and synthetic fibers? What are the advantages and disadvantages of each?"

   - **Purpose:** To assess your understanding of fiber types and their properties.

   - **Tip:** Discuss characteristics such as moisture absorption, strength, durability, and environmental impact. Provide examples of each fiber type and their typical applications.

2. **Textile Manufacturing Processes:**

   - **Example Question:** "Describe the process of yarn spinning. What are the different types of spinning methods, and how do they affect the yarn properties?"

   - **Purpose:** To evaluate your knowledge of textile production processes.

   - **Tip:** Explain the steps involved in spinning, such as carding, drafting, and twisting. Compare methods like ring spinning and open-end spinning, and discuss how they influence yarn characteristics like strength and texture.

3. **Fabric Structure and Weaving:**

   - **Example Question:** "What is the difference between a plain weave and a twill weave? How do these weaves affect the fabric's appearance and properties?"

   - **Purpose:** To assess your understanding of fabric construction and weave types.

   - **Tip:** Describe the basic patterns and properties of plain weave and twill weave, including their impact on fabric strength, texture, and durability. Use diagrams if possible to illustrate the differences.

4. **Dyeing and Finishing Techniques:**

   - **Example Question:** "What are the common methods of dyeing textiles, and how do you choose a method based on the type of fabric and desired outcome?"

   - **Purpose:** To evaluate your knowledge of textile dyeing and finishing processes.

   - **Tip:** Discuss methods like batch dyeing, continuous dyeing, and piece dyeing. Explain factors such as fiber type, dye type, and application method that influence the choice of dyeing technique.

5. **Textile Testing and Quality Control:**

   - **Example Question:** "What are some standard tests conducted to assess the quality of textiles, and why are they important?"

   - **Purpose:** To assess your familiarity with textile testing and quality control measures.

   - **Tip:** Mention tests such as tensile strength, abrasion resistance, colorfastness, and shrinkage. Explain how these tests ensure the fabric meets industry standards and performance requirements.

6. **Sustainability in Textiles:**

   - **Example Question:** "How can textile manufacturers reduce their environmental impact, and what are some examples of sustainable practices in the industry?"

   - **Purpose:** To evaluate your understanding of sustainability issues and practices in textile manufacturing.

- **Tip:** Discuss practices such as using eco-friendly dyes, recycling waste materials, adopting water-efficient processes, and incorporating sustainable fibers. Provide examples of companies or initiatives focused on sustainability.

7. **Textile Machinery and Technology:**

- **Example Question:** "Can you describe the working principle of a weaving loom and its various components?"

- **Purpose:** To assess your technical knowledge of textile machinery.

- **Tip:** Explain the main components of a weaving loom, such as the warp beam, weft yarn, reed, and heddles. Describe how these components work together to produce woven fabrics.

8. **Advanced Textile Applications:**

- **Example Question:** "What are smart textiles, and what are some of their potential applications in the future?"

- **Purpose:** To gauge your knowledge of emerging trends and technologies in textiles.

- **Tip:** Define smart textiles and discuss their ability to respond to environmental stimuli. Provide examples such as conductive fabrics, shape-memory alloys, or textiles with embedded sensors.

9. **Textile Production Challenges:**

- **Example Question:** "What are some common challenges faced in large-scale textile production, and how can they be addressed?"

- **Purpose:** To assess your problem-solving skills and understanding of production issues.

- **Tip:** Identify challenges such as quality control, production efficiency, and supply chain management. Discuss strategies to address these challenges, such as process optimization, quality assurance protocols, and effective supply chain management.

10. **Fabric Performance Testing:**

    - **Example Question:** "How do you test for fabric durability, and what factors influence the longevity of a textile product?"

    - **Purpose:** To evaluate your understanding of fabric performance and durability testing.

    - **Tip:** Describe tests like abrasion resistance and pilling resistance. Discuss factors such as fiber content; weave structure, and finishing treatments that impact fabric durability.

E. Preparing for Technical Questions in Textiles

1. **Review Core Concepts:**

    - Study fundamental principles related to fibers, yarns, fabrics, dyeing, finishing, and textile machinery.

2. **Understand Industry Trends:**

    - Stay updated on recent advancements in textile technology, sustainability practices, and emerging trends in the industry.

3. **Practice Problem-Solving:**

    - Work on case studies or hypothetical scenarios related to textile production challenges to hone your problem-solving skills.

4. **Familiarize Yourself with Machinery:**

    - Gain hands-on experience or theoretical knowledge about textile machinery and production processes.

5. **Use Visual Aids:**

   - Prepare diagrams or sketches to help illustrate complex concepts, such as fabric weaves or machinery components.

*Nut Shell: **Preparing thoroughly for these technical questions and practicing your responses, you can demonstrate your technical proficiency and problem-solving abilities effectively during placement interviews.***

9.3.5 Case Questions

Case questions in placement interviews are designed to evaluate your problem-solving skills, analytical thinking, and ability to approach complex business scenarios. These questions often involve real-world problems or hypothetical situations where you need to analyze data, propose solutions, and justify your recommendations. Here's a guide to common types of case questions and tips for addressing them effectively:

A. Common Case Questions

1. **Market Entry:**

   - **Example Question:** "A company wants to enter a new international market. What factors should they consider, and how would you evaluate the potential success of this move?"

   - **Purpose:** To assess your ability to analyze market conditions, competition, and strategic planning.

   - **Tip:** Consider factors such as market size, growth potential, competition, regulatory environment, and cultural differences. Use frameworks like PESTEL (Political, Economic, Social, Technological, Environmental, and Legal) analysis to structure your response.

2. **Business Expansion:**

   - **Example Question:** "A retail company is looking to expand its product line. How would you determine which new products to introduce, and what steps would you take to ensure successful integration?"

- **Purpose:** To evaluate your strategic thinking and ability to assess product opportunities.

- **Tip:** Analyze market trends, customer needs, and competitive landscape. Use tools like SWOC (Strengths, Weaknesses, Opportunities, and Challenges) analysis and conduct feasibility studies to support your recommendations.

3. **Operational Efficiency:**

   - **Example Question:** "A manufacturing plant is experiencing high production costs. What steps would you take to identify and reduce these costs?"

   - **Purpose:** To test your problem-solving skills and knowledge of operational processes.

   - **Tip:** Examine cost drivers, process inefficiencies, and potential areas for improvement. Use techniques like value stream mapping and root cause analysis to pinpoint issues and propose cost-saving measures.

4. **Financial Analysis:**

   - **Example Question:** "A company is considering investing in a new project. How would you evaluate the financial viability of this investment?"

   - **Purpose:** To assess your financial analysis skills and understanding of investment evaluation.

   - **Tip:** Use financial metrics such as Net Present Value (NPV), Internal Rate of Return (IRR), and Payback Period. Analyze cash flows, investment costs, and potential returns to determine the project's feasibility.

5. **Customer Segmentation:**

   - **Example Question:** "A company wants to improve its marketing strategy by targeting specific customer segments. How would you approach the segmentation process and develop targeted marketing strategies?"

   - **Purpose:** To evaluate your ability to segment markets and create effective marketing strategies.

   - **Tip:** Identify segmentation criteria such as demographics, psychographics, and behavior. Propose targeted marketing campaigns and strategies based on the needs and preferences of each segment.

6. **Crisis Management:**

   - **Example Question:** "A company has faced a major public relations crisis. How would you handle the situation and restore the company's reputation?"

   - **Purpose:** To test your crisis management and communication skills.

   - **Tip:** Develop a crisis management plan that includes immediate response actions, communication strategies, and long-term reputation management. Emphasize transparency, accountability, and customer engagement.

7. **Product Launch:**

   - **Example Question:** "A tech company is launching a new gadget. What factors should be considered in the launch strategy, and how would you ensure a successful market entry?"

   - **Purpose:** To assess your ability to plan and execute a successful product launch.

- **Tip:** Consider product positioning, target market, marketing channels, and distribution strategies. Develop a launch plan that includes pre-launch activities, promotional campaigns, and post-launch evaluations.

8. **Competitive Analysis:**

   - **Example Question:** "How would you analyze the competitive landscape for a new business entering the market, and what strategies would you recommend to gain a competitive advantage?"

   - **Purpose:** To evaluate your understanding of competitive analysis and strategic positioning.

   - **Tip:** Use tools like Porter's Five Forces to analyze competition, market entry barriers, and industry dynamics. Recommend strategies based on competitive strengths and weaknesses, market opportunities, and differentiation.

9. **Sales Strategy:**

   - **Example Question:** "A company's sales are declining. What steps would you take to identify the cause of the decline and develop a plan to increase sales?"

   - **Purpose:** To assess your ability to diagnose and address sales performance issues.

   - **Tip:** Analyze sales data, customer feedback, and market trends. Propose actions such as revising sales strategies, improving customer relationships, or enhancing product offerings.

10. **Supply Chain Optimization:**

    - **Example Question:** "A company is experiencing delays in its supply chain. How would you identify the root causes of these delays and propose solutions to improve efficiency?"

- **Purpose:** To evaluate your knowledge of supply chain management and problem-solving skills.

- **Tip:** Investigate supply chain processes, supplier performance, and logistics. Use tools like supply chain mapping and performance metrics to identify bottlenecks and recommend improvements.

B. Preparing for Case Questions

1. **Understand the Problem:**

   - Carefully read and analyze the case question. Identify the key issues and objectives before formulating your response.

2. **Use Structured Frameworks:**

   - Employ analytical frameworks such as SWOT, PESTEL, or Porter's Five Forces to organize your thoughts and provide a structured analysis.

3. **Break Down the Problem:**

   - Divide the case into manageable components and address each one systematically. This helps in developing a comprehensive solution.

4. **Analyze Data and Facts:**

   - Use any provided data or facts to support your analysis. If data is not provided, state any assumptions you are making and how they impact your recommendations.

5. **Develop Solutions:**

   - Propose practical and actionable solutions based on your analysis. Consider the feasibility, impact, and potential risks of your recommendations.

6. **Communicate Clearly:**

   - Present your findings and recommendations clearly and logically. Use visual aids like charts or graphs if applicable.

7. **Practice Case Studies:**

   - Work on practice case studies or mock interviews to refine your problem-solving and presentation skills.

Nut Shell: Preparing thoroughly for case questions and practicing structured problem-solving techniques, you can demonstrate your analytical abilities and strategic thinking during placement interviews.

9.3.6 Stress Questions

Stress questions in placement interviews are designed to test your ability to handle pressure, maintain composure, and think clearly under challenging or high-stress conditions. These questions often involve hypothetical or real-life stressful situations where your responses can reveal your coping mechanisms, problem-solving skills, and emotional resilience. Here's a guide to common stress questions and how to handle them effectively:

A. Common Stress Questions

1. **Handling Tight Deadlines:**

   - **Example Question:** "Describe a time when you had to meet a tight deadline. How did you handle the pressure, and what was the outcome?"

   - **Purpose:** To assess your ability to manage time and perform under pressure.

   - **Tip:** Share specific examples where you successfully met a deadline. Highlight your time management strategies, prioritization skills, and how you ensured quality despite the pressure.

2. **Conflict Resolution:**

    - **Example Question:** "Tell me about a time when you had a disagreement with a team member. How did you resolve the conflict, and what was the result?"

    - **Purpose:** To evaluate your conflict resolution and interpersonal skills under stress.

    - **Tip:** Describe the conflict situation objectively, focusing on your approach to resolving it. Emphasize communication, empathy, and finding a mutually acceptable solution.

3. **Handling Multiple Tasks:**

    - **Example Question:** "How do you manage multiple tasks or projects with competing deadlines? Can you provide an example?"

    - **Purpose:** To understand your ability to juggle various responsibilities and stay organized.

    - **Tip:** Discuss your strategies for task management, such as prioritization, delegation, and effective planning. Provide an example demonstrating how you handled multiple tasks successfully.

4. **Responding to Criticism:**

    - **Example Question:** "How do you handle constructive criticism or feedback? Can you give an example of a time when you received feedback and how you responded?"

    - **Purpose:** To assess your receptiveness to feedback and your ability to use it constructively.

    - **Tip:** Share an instance where you received feedback, focusing on how you addressed it positively and used it to improve your performance or skills.

5. **Adapting to Change:**

   - **Example Question:** "Describe a situation where you had to adapt to a significant change at work or in a project. How did you handle it?"

   - **Purpose:** To evaluate your flexibility and adaptability in the face of change.

   - **Tip:** Provide an example of how you adjusted to changes, highlighting your problem-solving approach and how you maintained effectiveness despite the changes.

6. **Decision-Making under Pressure:**

   - **Example Question:** "Tell me about a time when you had to make a difficult decision quickly. What was the situation, and what was the outcome?"

   - **Purpose:** To assess your decision-making skills and ability to handle pressure.

   - **Tip:** Describe the decision-making process, including how you evaluated options and made the decision. Highlight the positive outcome or lessons learned from the experience.

7. **Managing Workload:**

   - **Example Question:** "If you were assigned a project that was beyond your expertise and you had limited time to complete it, how would you approach the situation?"

   - **Purpose:** To understand your approach to tackling challenges and managing unfamiliar tasks.

   - **Tip:** Explain how you would leverage resources, seek assistance, and break down the project into manageable parts. Emphasize your willingness to learn and adapt.

8. **Dealing with Failure:**

   - **Example Question:** "Can you describe a time when you failed to achieve a goal? How did you handle the situation and what did you learn from it?"

   - **Purpose:** To evaluate your ability to handle setbacks and learn from failures.

   - **Tip:** Share an example of a failure, focusing on your reaction, how you addressed the situation, and the lessons you learned. Highlight your resilience and growth mindset.

9. **Managing Stressful Situations:**

   - **Example Question:** "How do you deal with stress or high-pressure situations in your daily work?"

   - **Purpose:** To understand your personal stress management techniques and coping strategies.

   - **Tip:** Discuss your methods for managing stress, such as exercise, time management, or relaxation techniques. Provide examples of how these methods have helped you stay focused and effective.

10. **Handling Unexpected Issues:**

   - **Example Question:** "How would you handle an unexpected issue or problem that arises during a critical phase of a project?"

   - **Purpose:** To assess your problem-solving skills and ability to remain calm under unexpected circumstances.

   - **Tip:** Describe a situation where you successfully managed an unexpected issue. Highlight your problem-solving approach, communication with stakeholders, and how you resolved the problem.

B. Preparing for Stress Questions

1. Reflect on Past Experiences:

- Review past situations where you faced stress or pressure and analyze how you handled them. Prepare specific examples to illustrate your skills and strategies.

2. Practice Your Responses:

- Rehearse answers to common stress questions to gain confidence and ensure clarity in your responses.

3. Focus on Positive Outcomes:

- Emphasize the positive results or lessons learned from stressful situations. Demonstrate how you have grown or improved as a result.

4. Stay Calm and Composed:

- During the interview, take a moment to gather your thoughts before responding. Maintain a calm and composed demeanor to show your ability to handle stress effectively.

5. Use the STAR Method:

- Structure your responses using the STAR method (Situation, Task, Action, and Result) to provide a clear and concise explanation of how you managed stressful situations.

6. Demonstrate Emotional Resilience:

- Show that you can maintain your effectiveness and professionalism even under pressure. Highlight your coping mechanisms and problem-solving abilities.

Nut Shell: Preparing thoroughly for stress questions and practicing your responses, you can effectively demonstrate your ability to handle pressure and navigate challenging situations during placement interviews.

9.3.7 Competency-based Questions

Competency-based questions in placement interviews are designed to assess specific skills and behaviors that are crucial for success in the role you're applying for. These questions typically focus on how you've demonstrated key competencies in your past experiences. They often follow a structured format and aim to uncover how your skills and experiences align with the job requirements. Here's a guide to common competency-based questions and how to effectively respond to them:

A. Common Competency-Based Questions

1. **Teamwork:**

    - **Example Question:** "Can you provide an example of a time when you worked successfully as part of a team?"

    - **Purpose:** To evaluate your ability to collaborate and work effectively with others.

    - **Tip:** Use the STAR method (Situation, Task, Action, Result) to describe a specific team project. Highlight your role, how you contributed, and the outcome of the team's efforts.

2. **Leadership:**

    - **Example Question:** "Describe a situation where you had to lead a team or project. What was your approach and what were the results?"

    - **Purpose:** To assess your leadership and management skills.

    - **Tip:** Provide an example where you took initiative, led a team, or managed a project. Emphasize how you motivated and guided your team and the impact of your leadership.

3. **Problem-Solving:**

    - **Example Question:** "Tell me about a time when you faced a significant problem at work. How did you resolve it?"

- **Purpose:** To gauge your problem-solving abilities and analytical skills.

- **Tip:** Explain the problem you encountered, the steps you took to solve it, and the results of your actions. Focus on your problem-solving process and the successful outcome.

4. **Communication:**

   - **Example Question:** "Give an example of a time when you had to communicate complex information to someone who did not understand it. How did you handle it?"

   - **Purpose:** To assess your communication skills and ability to convey information clearly.

   - **Tip:** Describe a situation where you effectively communicated complex ideas or information. Explain how you adapted your communication style to the audience and the results of your approach.

5. **Time Management:**

   - **Example Question:** "Can you provide an example of how you managed multiple priorities or deadlines? What strategies did you use?"

   - **Purpose:** To evaluate your time management and organizational skills.

   - **Tip:** Share an example of a time when you successfully managed multiple tasks or deadlines. Highlight the techniques you used to prioritize and stay organized.

6. **Adaptability:**

   - **Example Question:** "Describe a time when you had to adapt to a significant change at work. How did you handle it?"

   - **Purpose:** To assess your ability to adapt to change and remain flexible.

- **Tip:** Provide an example where you successfully adapted to a change, such as a new process or unexpected challenge. Discuss how you managed the transition and the positive results.

7. **Initiative:**

   - **Example Question:** "Tell me about a time when you took the initiative to improve a process or solve a problem. What was the impact?"

   - **Purpose:** To gauge your proactive approach and ability to take initiative.

   - **Tip:** Describe a situation where you identified an opportunity for improvement or a problem and took proactive steps to address it. Emphasize the positive impact of your actions.

8. **Customer Service:**

   - **Example Question:** "Give an example of a time when you provided excellent customer service. How did you ensure customer satisfaction?"

   - **Purpose:** To assess your customer service skills and commitment to client satisfaction.

   - **Tip:** Share a specific example where you went above and beyond to meet customer needs. Highlight the steps you took to ensure a positive experience and the outcome.

9. **Decision-Making:**

   - **Example Question:** "Describe a situation where you had to make a difficult decision. What factors did you consider, and what was the result?"

   - **Purpose:** To evaluate your decision-making skills and ability to handle complex situations.

- **Tip:** Explain the context of the decision, the factors you considered, and how you arrived at your conclusion. Discuss the outcome and what you learned from the experience.

10. **Conflict Resolution:**

    - **Example Question:** "Tell me about a time when you had a conflict with a colleague or team member. How did you resolve it?"

    - **Purpose:** To assess your ability to handle conflicts and maintain positive working relationships.

    - **Tip:** Provide an example of a conflict situation, how you approached resolving it, and the outcome. Emphasize your communication and problem-solving skills in resolving the conflict.

B. Preparing for Competency-Based Questions

1. **Identify Key Competencies:**

   - Review the job description to identify key competencies required for the role. These might include teamwork, leadership, problem-solving, communication, and more.

2. **Reflect on Your Experiences:**

   - Think about past experiences where you demonstrated these competencies. Prepare specific examples that highlight your skills and achievements.

3. **Use the STAR Method:**

   - Structure your responses using the STAR method:

     - **Situation:** Describe the context or background.

     - **Task:** Explain the task or challenge you faced.

     - **Action:** Detail the actions you took.

- **Result:** Highlight the outcomes and results of your actions.

4. **Practice Your Responses:**

   - Rehearse your responses to common competency-based questions to gain confidence and ensure clarity in your answers.

5. **Be Specific and Relevant:**

   - Provide specific examples relevant to the competency being asked about. Focus on concrete actions you took and the impact they had.

6. **Demonstrate Growth and Learning:**

   - Highlight how you've learned from your experiences and how these lessons have helped you develop professionally.

Nut Shell: ***Preparing thoroughly and using the STAR method to structure your responses, you can effectively showcase your competencies and demonstrate how you are well-suited for the role during placement interviews.***

9.3.8 Questions about strengths and weaknesses

Questions about strengths and weaknesses are common in placement interviews as they help employers gauge self-awareness, honesty, and how well you fit into their organizational culture. Here's how to approach these questions effectively:

A. Strengths Questions

Common Questions:

- "What are your greatest strengths?"

- "Can you provide examples of how your strengths have helped you succeed in your previous roles or projects?"

- "How do you leverage your strengths to contribute to a team or project?"

Tips for Answering:

- **Identify Relevant Strengths:** Choose strengths that are directly relevant to the role you're applying for. Common strengths include problem-solving skills, leadership, communication, teamwork, adaptability, and technical expertise.

- **Provide Examples:** Use specific examples to illustrate how your strengths have led to successful outcomes. For instance, if you claim to have strong problem-solving skills, describe a situation where you successfully addressed a complex issue.

- **Quantify Achievements:** Whenever possible, quantify your achievements to provide concrete evidence of your strengths. For example, "My organizational skills helped me manage a project that resulted in a 20% increase in efficiency."

Sample Answer:

- **Question:** "What is your greatest strength?"

- **Answer:** "One of my greatest strengths is my ability to solve complex problems. For example, during my internship at XYZ Company, I was tasked with improving the efficiency of a process that was causing delays. I analyzed the workflow, identified bottlenecks, and proposed a new system that reduced processing time by 30%. This experience not only enhanced my problem-solving skills but also demonstrated my ability to implement effective solutions."

B. Weaknesses Questions

Common Questions:

- "What are your greatest weaknesses?"

- "Can you describe a time when your weakness affected your work, and how did you handle it?"
- "How are you working to improve your weaknesses?"

Tips for Answering:

- **Be Honest but Tactful:** Choose a real weakness, but one that won't undermine your candidacy for the role. Avoid mentioning critical skills that are essential for the job.
- **Show Improvement:** Emphasize what steps you've taken to address your weakness. This demonstrates your willingness to grow and improve.
- **Focus on Development:** Highlight how your efforts to overcome your weakness have led to personal or professional development.

Sample Answer:

- **Question:** "What is your greatest weakness?"
- **Answer:** "One area I've been working on is my tendency to take on too many tasks at once. I've found that this can lead to feeling overwhelmed and occasionally missing deadlines. To address this, I've started using project management tools and techniques to better organize my tasks and prioritize effectively. This approach has helped me improve my time management and ensure that I meet deadlines more consistently."

C. General Guidelines

Self-Awareness:

- Demonstrate that you are aware of your strengths and weaknesses. Self-awareness is a key trait that employers look for.

Relevance to the Role:

- Tailor your answers to align with the requirements of the role. Ensure your strengths are relevant and your weaknesses do not detract from your suitability for the job.

Positive Spin:

- Even when discussing weaknesses, frame them in a positive light by focusing on your commitment to personal growth and development.

Practice and Preparation:

- Prepare and practice your responses to these questions to ensure you can answer confidently and concisely during the interview.

*Nut Shell: **Thoughtfully addressing questions about your strengths and weaknesses, you can effectively demonstrate your suitability for the role and your commitment to personal and professional growth.***

9.3.9 Culture-fit Questions

Culture fit questions in placement interviews are designed to assess whether your values, behaviors, and work style align with the company's culture and values. These questions help employers determine if you will thrive in their work environment and contribute positively to the team dynamic. Here's a guide to common culture fit questions and how to approach them:

A. Common Culture Fit Questions

1. **Work Environment Preferences:**

   - **Example Question:** "Describe your ideal work environment. What type of company culture do you thrive in?"
   - **Purpose:** To understand if your preferred work environment aligns with the company's culture.

- **Tip:** Research the company's culture and values before the interview. Tailor your response to highlight aspects of the company's environment that resonate with you. For example, if the company values innovation, discuss how you thrive in creative and dynamic settings.

2. **Team Collaboration:**

   - **Example Question:** "Can you provide an example of a time when you worked effectively in a team? What role did you play, and how did you contribute?"

   - **Purpose:** To assess your ability to collaborate and fit into team dynamics.

   - **Tip:** Share a specific example that highlights your teamwork skills and how you adapted to different roles within the team. Emphasize qualities such as communication, collaboration, and respect for others' ideas.

3. **Conflict Resolution:**

   - **Example Question:** "Tell me about a time when you had a conflict with a colleague. How did you handle the situation, and what was the outcome?"

   - **Purpose:** To evaluate how you handle interpersonal conflicts and work within a team.

   - **Tip:** Describe a situation where you managed a conflict constructively. Focus on your communication skills, ability to listen, and approach to finding a resolution that maintained positive working relationships.

4. **Alignment with Company Values:**

   - **Example Question:** "What aspects of our company's mission and values resonate with you the most, and why?"

- **Purpose:** To determine if your personal values align with the company's mission and values.

- **Tip:** Demonstrate your understanding of the company's mission and values. Explain how these align with your own beliefs and experiences. For example, if the company values sustainability, discuss any relevant experiences or passions you have for environmental issues.

5. **Adaptability to Change:**

   - **Example Question:** "Describe a situation where you had to adapt to significant changes at work. How did you handle it?"

   - **Purpose:** To assess your flexibility and ability to thrive in a changing environment.

   - **Tip:** Provide an example of how you successfully adapted to change. Highlight your openness to new ideas, willingness to learn, and how you maintained productivity despite changes.

6. **Motivation and Work Ethic:**

   - **Example Question:** "What motivates you to perform well at work? How do you stay engaged and productive?"

   - **Purpose:** To understand what drives you and how it fits with the company's expectations.

   - **Tip:** Discuss specific factors that motivate you, such as achieving goals, recognition, or working on challenging projects. Relate these motivations to the company's culture and how they align with your role.

7. **Handling Work-Life Balance:**

   - **Example Question:** "How do you manage work-life balance, and what strategies do you use to maintain it?"

- **Purpose:** To assess if your approach to work-life balance fits with the company's expectations and culture.

- **Tip:** Explain how you prioritize tasks and manage your time effectively to maintain a healthy work-life balance. Show that you understand the importance of both productivity and personal well-being.

8. **Feedback and Development:**

   - **Example Question:** "How do you handle feedback and criticism? Can you provide an example of how feedback has helped you improve?"

   - **Purpose:** To evaluate your receptiveness to feedback and commitment to professional growth.

   - **Tip:** Share an example where you received constructive feedback and used it to improve your performance. Highlight your openness to learning and development.

9. **Work Style Preferences:**

   - **Example Question:** "How would you describe your work style? How do you ensure you are meeting your team's expectations?"

   - **Purpose:** To determine if your work style complements the team's dynamics and the company's work culture.

   - **Tip:** Describe your work style in terms of organization, communication, and collaboration. Relate it to how you ensure you meet or exceed expectations and contribute effectively to the team.

10. **Cultural Contributions:**

    - **Example Question:** "How do you contribute to creating a positive work culture? Can you give an example?"

- **Purpose:** To assess how you contribute to and enhance the company culture.

- **Tip:** Provide examples of how you have positively impacted previous work environments. Highlight qualities such as team spirit, inclusivity, and fostering a supportive atmosphere.

B. Preparing for Culture Fit Questions

1. **Research the Company:**

   - Learn about the company's culture, mission, values, and work environment through their website, social media, and any available company reviews.

2. **Reflect on Your Fit:**

   - Consider your own values, work style, and past experiences to determine how they align with the company's culture.

3. **Prepare Specific Examples:**

   - Develop examples from your past experiences that demonstrate how you align with the company's culture and values.

4. **Practice Your Responses:**

   - Rehearse your answers to culture fit questions to ensure you can articulate how your background and values align with the company's expectations.

5. **Be Genuine:**

   - Be honest and authentic in your responses. Employers value genuine answers that reflect true alignment with their culture.

Nut Shell:** **Preparing thoughtful responses to culture fit questions and demonstrating how your values and work style align with the company, you can effectively show that you are a strong cultural match for the organization.

9.3.10 Future-oriented Questions

Future-oriented questions in placement interviews are designed to understand your long-term goals, career aspirations, and how you envision your growth within the company. These questions help employers gauge your motivation, ambition, and whether your future plans align with the company's trajectory and opportunities. Here's how to effectively respond to future-oriented questions:

A. Common Future-Oriented Questions

1. **Career Goals:**

   - **Example Question:** "Where do you see yourself in five years? How does this position fit into your career plan?"

   - **Purpose:** To assess your long-term career goals and how this role aligns with those goals.

   - **Tip:** Articulate clear and realistic career goals that align with the company's growth and opportunities. Explain how the position you're applying for will help you develop the skills and experiences needed to achieve those goals.

2. **Professional Development:**

   - **Example Question:** "What skills or experiences are you looking to gain from this role? How do you plan to develop these skills?"

   - **Purpose:** To understand your commitment to professional development and how you plan to leverage the role for growth.

   - **Tip:** Identify specific skills or experiences you wish to gain that are relevant to the role. Discuss how you plan to acquire these through on-the-job experiences, training, or other professional development activities.

3. **Vision for Contribution:**

   - **Example Question:** "How do you plan to contribute to the company's goals and success over the next few years?"

   - **Purpose:** To gauge your understanding of the company's goals and how you envision making an impact.

   - **Tip:** Demonstrate knowledge of the company's objectives and outline how your skills, experiences, and ambitions will help you contribute to these goals. Be specific about the value you plan to bring.

4. **Career Advancement:**

   - **Example Question:** "What steps will you take to advance in your career, and how does this role help you achieve those steps?"

   - **Purpose:** To assess your proactive approach to career advancement and how the role fits into your growth strategy.

   - **Tip:** Outline your career advancement strategy, including short-term and long-term goals. Explain how the role will provide the necessary experience, skills, or opportunities to support your advancement.

5. **Adapting to Change:**

   - **Example Question:** "How do you plan to adapt to changes and challenges in your industry over the next few years?"

   - **Purpose:** To evaluate your ability to anticipate and adapt to industry changes and challenges.

   - **Tip:** Discuss how you stay informed about industry trends and your strategies for adapting to changes. Highlight your flexibility, willingness to learn, and approach to staying relevant in your field.

6. **Long-Term Projects:**

   - **Example Question:** "If given the opportunity, what long-term projects or initiatives would you like to pursue within the company?"

   - **Purpose:** To understand your interest in taking on significant projects and your vision for contributing to the company's success.

   - **Tip:** Propose a project or initiative that aligns with the company's goals or current challenges. Explain how you would approach it and how it aligns with your career interests.

7. **Leadership Aspirations:**

   - **Example Question:** "Do you have any aspirations for leadership roles in the future? How do you plan to prepare for them?"

   - **Purpose:** To assess your leadership potential and your plans for developing leadership skills.

   - **Tip:** If you aspire to leadership, describe your vision for a leadership role and how you plan to develop the necessary skills, such as through mentorship, training, or taking on leadership responsibilities in current roles.

8. **Company's Future:**

   - **Example Question:** "Where do you see the company going in the next few years, and how do you see yourself contributing to that vision?"

   - **Purpose:** To gauge your understanding of the company's future direction and how you see yourself playing a role in it.

   - **Tip:** Research the company's strategic goals and future plans. Discuss how your skills and experiences align with these plans and how you envision contributing to the company's success.

9. **Personal Development:**

   - **Example Question:** "What are your personal development goals for the next few years, and how does this position align with them?"

   - **Purpose:** To understand your personal growth objectives and how the role supports them.

   - **Tip:** Identify personal development goals that are relevant to the position. Explain how the role provides opportunities for achieving these goals and how this aligns with your overall career trajectory.

10. **Impact and Legacy:**

    - **Example Question:** "What kind of impact would you like to make in this role, and what kind of legacy do you hope to leave?"

    - **Purpose:** To assess your ambition and the kind of contributions you hope to make.

    - **Tip:** Discuss the specific impact you aim to have in the role and how you plan to achieve it. Reflect on the legacy you hope to create and how it aligns with the company's values and objectives.

B. Preparing for Future-Oriented Questions

1. **Research the Company:**

   - Understand the company's goals, values, and future plans. This will help you align your answers with the company's vision.

2. **Reflect on Your Goals:**

   - Clarify your own career aspirations and how they align with the role and company.

3. **Develop a Vision:**

   - Think about how you want to contribute to the company's success and how the role fits into your long-term career plans.

4. **Practice Articulation:**

   - Practice explaining how the role supports your career goals and what you hope to achieve in the future.

5. **Show Flexibility:**

   - Be open to discussing how you can adapt and grow within the company, even if your future goals evolve over time.

Nut Shell: Preparing thoughtful and forward-looking responses to these questions, you can demonstrate your ambition, alignment with the company's vision, and readiness to contribute meaningfully to the organization's future success.

9.4 Preparing for Technical Assessment Top of Form

As the gateway to showcasing your engineering expertise and problem-solving prowess, technical assessments play a pivotal role in the hiring process for engineering roles. This chapter delves into the essential strategies for excelling in technical evaluations, which often include coding challenges, problem-solving exercises, and practical applications of engineering principles. Preparing for a technical assessment requires a thorough understanding of relevant concepts, rigorous practice, and a strategic approach to problem-solving.

By mastering the foundational skills, familiarizing yourself with common assessment formats, and honing your ability to think critically under pressure, you can approach these evaluations with confidence and precision. This chapter provides a comprehensive guide to navigating technical assessments effectively, transforming them from daunting hurdles into opportunities to demonstrate your technical acumen and analytical capabilities.

Preparing for a technical assessment involves a structured approach to ensure you can effectively demonstrate your skills and knowledge. Here's a detailed guide on the steps you should take:

1. **Understand the Assessment Format**

   - **Review Instructions:** Read any provided materials or instructions carefully to understand the format, tools, and types of questions or problems you'll encounter.

   - **Identify the Focus:** Determine whether the assessment will focus on coding, engineering principles, problem-solving, or practical applications.

2. **Review Core Concepts**

   - **Study Key Topics:** Refresh your knowledge of fundamental concepts relevant to the assessment, such as algorithms, data structures, electrical circuits, or software design patterns.

   - **Consult Resources:** Use textbooks, online tutorials, and educational platforms to review concepts and clarify any doubts.

3. **Practice with Sample Problems**

   - **Solve Practice Questions:** Work through sample problems or past assessment papers to familiarize you with the type of questions and the level of difficulty.

   - **Use Online Platforms:** Engage with soft platforms for practice engineering-specific problems.

4. **Work on Time Management**

   - **Simulate Test Conditions:** Practice solving problems under timed conditions to improve your ability to manage time effectively during the assessment.

   - **Prioritize Tasks:** Learn to identify and tackle easier problems first, allowing more time for complex challenges.

5. **Develop a Problem-Solving Strategy**

   - **Understand the Problem:** Carefully read and analyze each problem before jumping to solutions. Break down the problem into manageable parts.

   - **Plan Your Approach:** Outline your strategy for solving the problem.

   - **Implement and Test:** Write your solution, ensuring you test it with various input cases to verify its correctness and efficiency.

6. **Practice Coding or Technical Skills (For Computer engineering pupil)**

   - **Code Regularly:** Regular coding practice helps reinforce syntax and problem-solving skills. Work on a variety of problems to build versatility.

   - **Use Debugging Tools:** Familiarize yourself with debugging tools and techniques to quickly identify and fix issues in your code.

7. **Prepare Your Environment**

   - **Set Up Tools:** Ensure your development environment or any required tools are properly set up and functioning before the assessment.

- **Check Technical Requirements:** Verify that you have the necessary software, hardware, and internet connectivity, especially for remote assessments.

8. **Review and Refine Your Solutions**

   - **Self-Review:** After solving problems, review your solutions for efficiency and accuracy. Look for opportunities to optimize or improve your code.

   - **Seek Feedback:** If possible, get feedback on your solutions from peers or mentors to gain insights into areas for improvement.

9. **Stay Calm and Focused**

   - **Manage Stress:** Practice relaxation techniques to stay calm and focused during the assessment. Approach each problem with a clear and methodical mindset.

   - **Stay Organized:** Keep track of time and ensure you allocate adequate time to each problem or section of the assessment.

10. **Post-Assessment Reflection**

   - **Evaluate Performance:** After the assessment, reflect on what went well and areas where you faced challenges. Use this reflection to guide future preparation.

   - **Learn and Adapt:** Analyze any mistakes or difficulties encountered and use them as learning opportunities to improve your skills for future assessments.

9.5 Interview Etiquettes and Follow-ups

Mastering interview etiquette and follow-up practices is essential for leaving a positive and lasting impression on potential employers. While technical skills and experience are crucial, the way you conduct yourself during and after the interview can significantly influence the outcome. This section explores the nuances of professional behavior before, during, and after your interview, including punctuality; appropriate dress, effective communication, and respectful interaction.

It also emphasizes the importance of thoughtful follow-up, which can reinforce your interest in the position and demonstrate your professionalism. By adhering to established interview etiquette and executing a strategic follow-up, you not only show respect for the interviewers' time but also strengthen your candidature, setting yourself apart as a well-rounded and considerate applicant.

9.5.1 Interview Etiquette

1. **Research the Company:**
   - **Understand Culture:** Familiarize yourself with the company's values, mission, and recent developments.
   - **Know the Role:** Review the job description and requirements to tailor your responses.

2. **Dress Appropriately:**
   - **Professional Attire:** Choose an outfit that matches the company's dress code, whether it's formal or business casual.
   - **Grooming:** Ensure you are neatly groomed, with attention to personal hygiene.

3. **Arrive on Time:**
   - **Punctuality:** Aim to arrive at least 10-15 minutes early. For virtual interviews, log in a few minutes before the scheduled time.
   - **Plan Ahead:** Account for potential delays by planning your route or checking your technology in advance.

4. **Be Polite and Courteous:**

   - **Respectful Interaction:** Greet everyone you meet with a smile and a firm handshake. Use polite language and address interviewers formally.

   - **Positive Body Language:** Maintain good posture, eye contact, and an attentive demeanor.

5. **Listen Actively:**

   - **Engage Fully:** Pay close attention to questions and instructions. Avoid interrupting and take a moment to think before responding.

   - **Clarify if Needed:** If a question is unclear, ask for clarification rather than guessing.

6. **Communicate Clearly:**

   - **Concise Responses:** Answer questions directly and stay on topic. Avoid rambling or providing overly detailed answers.

   - **Confidence and Honesty:** Speak confidently about your skills and experiences, but be honest about your limitations.

7. **Show Enthusiasm:**

   - **Express Interest:** Demonstrate genuine interest in the role and the company. Show that you are excited about the opportunity.

8. **Be Prepared with Questions:**

   - **Insightful Questions:** Prepare thoughtful questions to ask the interviewer about the role, team, and company culture. This shows your interest and engagement.

9. **Follow the Interviewer's Lead:**

   - **Adapt to Style:** Match the interviewer's tone and pace. If they are formal, respond in kind; if they are more casual, follow their lead but maintain professionalism.

9.5.2 Follow-Up

1. **Send a Thank-You Note:**

   - **Timely Response:** Send a thank-you email within 24 hours of the interview to express appreciation for the opportunity.

     - **Personalized Message:** Mention specific points from the interview and reiterate your enthusiasm for the role.

2. **Reaffirm Interest:**

   - **Express Continued Interest:** Reinforce your interest in the position and highlight how your skills align with the role.

3. **Highlight Key Points:**

   - **Summarize Strengths:** Briefly restate why you are a strong fit for the position based on the discussion during the interview.

4. **Address Any Follow-Up Items:**

   - **Provide Additional Information:** If you were asked to provide additional information or materials, include them in your follow-up communication.

5. **Maintain Professionalism:**

   - **Polite Communication:** Keep all follow-up correspondence professional and courteous. Avoid being pushy or demanding a response.

6. **Be Patient:**

   - **Allow Time:** Understand that hiring decisions can take time. Be patient and avoid sending multiple follow-up emails in a short period.

7. **Prepare for Next Steps:**

   - **Stay Ready:** Be prepared for any additional interviews, assessments, or requests for information that might follow.

CHAPTER 10

Post–offer Considerations

Post-offer consideration is a crucial phase in the professional career decision-making process, occurring after a job offer has been extended but before it is officially accepted. This period is an opportunity for candidates to carefully evaluate the offer, ensuring that it aligns with their career goals, personal values, and lifestyle preferences. During this time, individuals should scrutinize various factors such as salary and benefits, job responsibilities, company culture, and growth opportunities.

It's also important to consider the impact of the job on work-life balance and overall personal satisfaction. By taking a thoughtful approach to this evaluation, candidates can make an informed decision that not only supports their immediate professional needs but also fosters long-term career success and personal fulfillment. This reflective process helps ensure that the chosen role is not just a good fit for the present, but also a meaningful step towards achieving future career aspirations.

10.1 Generic Tasks

Navigating a new job involves a multifaceted approach, where evaluating tasks, negotiating terms, understanding company culture, and balancing personal habits are crucial for long-term success and satisfaction. The initial phase requires a keen assessment of job responsibilities and the offer terms to ensure they align with your career goals and personal needs. Negotiation plays a pivotal role in aligning the offer with your expectations, whether it's adjusting compensation, benefits, or work arrangements.

Concurrently, understanding the company culture helps in seamlessly integrating into the workplace, ensuring that your values and work style align with organizational norms. Achieving a balance between adapting to company expectations and maintaining personal well-being is essential for sustaining productivity and job satisfaction. This comprehensive approach sets the stage for a successful and fulfilling career journey. Here are some fundamental approaches to consider when deciding whether to accept or reject a job offer.

10.1.1 Fresh Graduate Trainees

Planning your first year on the job as a fresh professional graduate trainee is crucial for establishing a strong foundation for your career. This period is not only about applying what you've learned but also about adapting to a professional environment and setting yourself up for future success. Here's a comprehensive guide to help you navigate your first year effectively:

1. **Initial On-boarding and Orientation**
   - **Understand the Company**: Take time to familiarize yourself with the company's mission, values, and structure. Attend orientation sessions and review any provided materials to get a clear picture of the organization.
   - **Complete Required Training**: Engage actively in any mandatory training programs or workshops. These are

designed to equip you with the knowledge and skills needed for your role and the company's systems.

2. **Set Clear Goals and Expectations**

   - **Establish Short-Term Goals**: Define specific objectives for the first 30, 60, and 90 days. These could include learning key processes, building relationships, and understanding your role's responsibilities.

   - **Align with Long-Term Goals**: Set broader goals for your first year that align with your career aspirations. Consider goals related to skill development, project contributions, and potential leadership opportunities.

3. **Build Strong Relationships**

   - **Network with Colleagues**: Take the initiative to introduce yourself to team members, managers, and other departments. Building a professional network can facilitate collaboration and support.

   - **Find a Mentor**: Seek out a mentor or senior colleague who can provide guidance, feedback, and career advice. A mentor can help you navigate the company culture and offer valuable insights.

4. **Understand and Adapt to Company Culture**

   - **Observe and Adapt**: Pay attention to the company's work culture, including communication styles, decision-making processes, and dress codes. Adapt your behavior to fit in while maintaining your personal authenticity.

   - **Participate Actively**: Engage in company events, team-building activities, and informal gatherings to better integrate into the team and understand the company's social dynamics.

5. **Develop and Refine Skills**

   - **Identify Skill Gaps**: Assess your current skill set and identify areas for improvement. Seek opportunities for additional training or self-study to bridge these gaps.

   - **Pursue Continuous Learning**: Take advantage of any available professional development resources, such as workshops, online courses, or certifications, to enhance your skills and knowledge.

6. **Manage Time and Priorities**

   - **Create a Time Management Plan**: Develop a plan to manage your workload effectively. Prioritize tasks based on urgency and importance, and use tools like calendars or task management apps to stay organized.

   - **Set Realistic Deadlines**: Be realistic about what you can accomplish within given deadlines. Communicate any potential delays to your manager promptly.

7. **Seek and Act on Feedback**

   - **Request Regular Feedback**: Schedule regular check-ins with your manager to discuss your performance and seek constructive feedback. Use this feedback to make improvements and align with expectations.

   - **Self-Reflection**: Regularly reflect on your progress and experiences. Identify areas where you've excelled and areas where you could improve, and adjust your approach accordingly.

8. **Demonstrate Initiative and Innovation**

   - **Take Initiative**: Look for opportunities to contribute beyond your standard responsibilities. Volunteer for projects, propose new ideas, and show a proactive attitude towards problem-solving.

- **Be Innovative**: If you identify areas for improvement, propose creative solutions or new approaches. Demonstrating innovation can set you apart and showcase your commitment to the company's success.

9. **Maintain Work-Life Balance**

- **Set Boundaries**: Establish boundaries between work and personal life to prevent burnout. Ensure you allocate time for personal activities and relaxation.

- **Practice Self-Care**: Prioritize your well-being by maintaining healthy habits, managing stress, and seeking support if needed. A balanced approach will help sustain your productivity and job satisfaction.

10. **Prepare for Performance Reviews**

- **Document Achievements**: Keep a record of your accomplishments, positive feedback, and any challenges you've overcome. This documentation will be useful during performance reviews.

- **Set New Goals**: Use performance reviews as an opportunity to set new goals and discuss career development with your manager. Express your interest in taking on new responsibilities or advancing within the organization.

Nut Shell: Following these guidelines, you can effectively navigate your first year as a professional graduate trainee, making a positive impact and laying a strong foundation for your career. This strategic planning and proactive approach will help you adapt to your new role, build valuable relationships, and set the stage for future growth and success.

10.1.2 Experienced Professionals

For an experienced professional transitioning to a new job, the first year is a critical period for acclimating to a new environment while leveraging existing expertise. This phase involves understanding the company's unique culture, processes, and strategic goals, and adapting previous experiences to fit the new role. It's essential to establish credibility quickly by delivering results, building relationships with new colleagues, and aligning with the company's objectives. Balancing the application of prior knowledge with openness to new approaches and feedback will help ensure a smooth transition and set the stage for long-term success in the new position.

1. **Compensation and Benefits**

   - **Salary**: Evaluate whether the offered salary meets your financial needs and is competitive within the industry. Consider your current financial obligations and long-term financial goals.

   - **Benefits**: Review additional benefits such as health insurance, retirement plans (pensions), stock options, and bonuses. Assess how these benefits compare with your current or previous employment.

   - **Perks**: Look into perks like tuition reimbursement, wellness programs, and transportation allowances. These can add significant value to your overall compensation package.

2. **Job Role and Responsibilities**

   - **Role Clarity**: Ensure that you have a clear understanding of the day-to-day responsibilities and expectations associated with the role. Confirm that they align with your career goals and expertise.

- **Growth Opportunities**: Investigate the potential for taking on additional responsibilities or projects that interest you. Evaluate how the role fits into your long-term career path.

3. **Company Culture and Work Environment**

   - **Work Culture**: Research the company's work culture to ensure it aligns with your personal values and work style. This includes the company's approach to collaboration, communication, and inclusivity.

   - **Work Environment**: Consider the physical and social environment of the workplace. Assess aspects such as office layout, remote work options, and team dynamics.

4. **Career Growth and Development**

   - **Professional Development**: Look for opportunities for training, skill development, and career advancement. Check if the company supports continuous learning and offers mentorship programs.

   - **Promotion Pathways**: Understand the typical career trajectory within the company. Ask about potential career paths and the average time frame for promotions.

5. **Location and Commute**

   - **Commute**: Consider the location of the office and the impact on your daily commute. Assess whether it fits into your lifestyle and whether remote work or flexible working hours are options.

   - **Relocation**: If relocation is required, evaluate the associated costs and the impact on your personal life and family.

6. **Work-Life Balance**

   - **Flexibility**: Investigate the company's policies on flexible work hours, remote work, and vacation time. Ensure that the job will allow you to maintain a healthy work-life balance.

   - **Company Policies**: Review the company's policies on work-life balance, including expectations for overtime and availability outside of regular working hours.

7. **Company Stability and Reputation**

   - **Financial Health**: Research the company's financial stability and performance. Look into recent financial reports and news to gauge the company's economic health.

   - **Reputation**: Check the company's reputation in the industry. Read reviews from current and former employees to get insights into their experiences.

8. **Offer Terms**

   - **Contractual Clauses**: Examine the offer letter for any clauses such as non-compete agreements, confidentiality agreements, or mandatory arbitration. Understand the implications of these terms.

   - **Start Date**: Confirm the proposed start date and ensure it aligns with your availability. Discuss any flexibility if needed.

9. **Personal Fit**

   - **Values Alignment**: Reflect on how well the company's values align with your personal beliefs and career aspirations. Consider whether the company's mission and vision resonate with you.

   - **Long-Term Goals**: Assess how this role fits into your long-term career plan. Ensure that accepting the offer will contribute positively to your professional and personal goals.

10. **Negotiation**

- **Identify Areas for Improvement**: Determine which aspects of the offer could be improved, such as salary, benefits, or job responsibilities.

- **Prepare for Discussion**: Prepare a clear and reasonable case for your requests. Be ready to discuss your needs and justify any changes you're seeking.

10.1.3 Way Forward

1. **Thorough Evaluation**: Take time to reflect on all the considerations and how they impact your decision. Create a checklist to systematically review each factor.

2. **Consult with Trusted Advisors**: Discuss the offer with mentors, family, or friends who can provide valuable perspectives and advice.

3. **Communicate with the Employer**: If you have any concerns or require clarification, communicate them to the employer. Be professional and constructive in your discussions.

4. **Make a Decision**: Based on your evaluation, make an informed decision about whether to accept or decline the offer. Ensure that your choice aligns with your career goals and personal well-being.

5. **Formal Acceptance or Decline**: Once you've made your decision, formally accept or decline the offer in writing. If accepting, confirm the details and start date. If declining, do so graciously, maintaining a positive relationship for future opportunities.

Nut Shell: Meticulously considering these factors and following a structured approach, you can make a well-informed decision that sets the stage for a successful and satisfying career move.

10.2 Planning First Year on the Job

Planning your first year on the job is a strategic process that involves setting goals, understanding expectations, and laying the groundwork for long-term success in your new role. This period is crucial for making a positive impression, acclimating to your new work environment, and positioning yourself for future growth. Here's a detailed guide on how to effectively plan your first year:

1. **Understand Company Culture and Expectations**

    - **Observe and Adapt**: Spend time understanding the company's culture, values, and working style. Observe how things are done, from communication norms to decision-making processes. Adapt your approach to fit in seamlessly.

    - **Clarify Expectations**: Meet with your manager to discuss their expectations and key performance indicators (KPIs) for your role. Understand what success looks like in your position and how it will be measured.

2. **Set Clear and Achievable Goals**

    - **Short-Term Goals**: Identify and set specific, achievable goals for the first 30, 60, and 90 days. These might include completing onboarding tasks, meeting key team members, and understanding your role's immediate priorities.

    - **Long-Term Goals**: Develop goals for the first year that align with your role's responsibilities and your career aspirations. These could involve mastering specific skills, leading projects, or contributing to strategic initiatives.

3. **Build Strong Relationships**

    - **Team Integration**: Make an effort to get to know your colleagues and integrate into your team. Participate in team meetings, social events, and collaborative projects to build rapport and trust.

- **Seek Mentorship**: Identify potential mentors within the organization who can provide guidance, feedback, and support as you navigate your new role.

4. **Develop a Learning Plan**

- **Skill Development**: Assess any skills or knowledge gaps and create a plan to address them. This might include formal training, online courses, or self-study.

- **Industry Knowledge**: Stay informed about industry trends and developments that could impact your role. This will help you remain relevant and contribute valuable insights.

5. **Manage Time and Priorities**

- **Time Management**: Develop effective time management strategies to balance your workload and meet deadlines. Prioritize tasks based on their importance and urgency.

- **Project Planning**: For larger projects, break them down into manageable steps with clear milestones and deadlines. Use project management tools if applicable.

6. **Seek Feedback and Reflect**

- **Regular Check-Ins**: Schedule regular check-ins with your manager to discuss your performance, address any challenges, and adjust goals as needed.

- **Self-Reflection**: Periodically reflect on your progress, achievements, and areas for improvement. Use this reflection to adjust your approach and set new goals.

7. **Demonstrate Initiative and Innovation**

- **Proactive Approach**: Take initiative by identifying areas for improvement and proposing solutions. Show enthusiasm for contributing to projects and taking on additional responsibilities.

- **Innovative Ideas**: Share any innovative ideas or suggestions that could benefit your team or the organization. Being proactive in this manner can demonstrate your commitment and value.

8. **Maintain Work-Life Balance**

- **Set Boundaries**: Establish clear boundaries between work and personal life to avoid burnout. Manage your workload effectively and make time for rest and recreation.

- **Self-Care**: Prioritize self-care by maintaining a healthy lifestyle, managing stress, and ensuring you have time for activities you enjoy.

9. **Track and Celebrate Achievements**

- **Document Successes**: Keep a record of your accomplishments, positive feedback, and milestones achieved throughout the year. This documentation will be valuable during performance reviews and future career discussions.

- **Celebrate Milestones**: Recognize and celebrate your achievements, both big and small. Celebrating milestones can boost morale and reinforce your commitment to your goals.

10. **Prepare for Performance Reviews**

- **Review Preparation**: Prepare for performance reviews by gathering evidence of your accomplishments, feedback received, and progress towards goals. Be ready to discuss your achievements and areas for growth.

- **Goal Setting**: Use performance reviews as an opportunity to set new goals and discuss career development opportunities with your manager.

Nut Shell: Focusing on these areas, you can effectively navigate your first year on the job, make a positive impact, and lay a solid foundation for your future career growth. This strategic planning will not only help you succeed in your current role but also position you for continued success and advancement within the organization.

10.3 Probation Period: Dos & Don'ts

Navigating your first year on the job or during the probation period can be pivotal in setting the stage for your long-term success. Here are some key dos and don'ts to help you make a positive impression and establish a solid foundation:

Dos

1. **Do Be Proactive**

   - **Take Initiative**: Show enthusiasm by taking on additional tasks, volunteering for projects, and suggesting improvements. Demonstrating a proactive attitude can highlight your commitment and eagerness to contribute.

   - **Ask Questions**: Don't hesitate to seek clarification on your responsibilities, processes, or company policies. Asking questions shows that you're engaged and willing to learn.

2. **Do Build Relationships**

   - **Network Actively**: Make an effort to get to know your colleagues, supervisors, and other stakeholders. Building positive relationships can facilitate collaboration and create a supportive work environment.

- **Find a Mentor:** Identify a mentor or senior colleague who can provide guidance, feedback, and support. A mentor can help you navigate the company culture and advance your career.

3. **Do Communicate Effectively**

   - **Keep Open Lines:** Maintain clear and regular communication with your manager and team. Provide updates on your progress and be transparent about any challenges you face.

   - **Be Professional:** Communicate professionally in all interactions, whether in meetings, emails, or casual conversations. Effective communication fosters respect and trust.

4. **Do Respect Your Time Well**

   - **Prioritize Tasks:** Use time management techniques to handle your workload efficiently. Prioritize tasks based on deadlines and importance.

   - **Set Goals:** Establish clear short-term and long-term goals. This helps you stay focused and track your progress throughout your probation period.

5. **Do Seek and Act on Feedback**

   - **Request Feedback:** Actively seek feedback from your manager and colleagues. Constructive criticism can provide valuable insights into your performance and areas for improvement.

   - **Implement Suggestions:** Use feedback to make necessary adjustments to your work habits and approach. Showing that you can adapt and improve based on feedback is crucial.

6. **Do Show Reliability and Integrity**

   - **Meet Deadlines:** Ensure you meet deadlines and deliver high-quality work. Reliability is key to building trust and proving your value to the team.

- **Be Honest**: Maintain honesty and transparency in all your dealings. Integrity builds trust and credibility within the organization.

7. **Do Learn and Adapt**

   - **Stay Open-Minded**: Be open to new ideas, processes, and ways of doing things. Flexibility and adaptability are important traits in a dynamic work environment.

   - **Continue Learning**: Invest in learning opportunities, whether through formal training, self-study, or on-the-job experiences. Continuous learning enhances your skills and performance.

Don'ts

1. **Don't Be Overconfident**

   - **Avoid Assumptions**: Don't assume you know everything about the role or the company. Even if you have experience, there may be unique aspects to your new position.

   - **Stay Humble**: While confidence is important, avoid coming across as arrogant. Humility and a willingness to learn are crucial, especially in a new environment.

2. **Don't Neglect Company Culture**

   - **Respect Norms**: Be mindful of and respect the company's culture and values. Ignoring or disregarding cultural norms can create friction and hinder your integration.

   - **Avoid Gossip**: Steer clear of engaging in workplace gossip or negative conversations about colleagues or the company. This can damage relationships and your reputation.

3. **Don't Be Passive**

   - **Avoid Waiting**: Don't wait for tasks or projects to come to you. Take the initiative to seek out opportunities and show your willingness to contribute.

- **Don't Avoid Challenges**: Embrace challenges as opportunities for growth. Avoiding difficult tasks can signal a lack of commitment or resilience.

4. **Don't Ignore Feedback**

   - **Dismiss Criticism**: Avoid dismissing or ignoring constructive feedback. Even if it's challenging to hear, feedback is an important tool for improvement.

   - **Be Defensive**: Don't become defensive when receiving feedback. Listen openly and use it as a chance to enhance your performance.

5. **Don't Overextend Yourself**

   - **Avoid Burnout**: While it's important to show dedication, be mindful of not overworking yourself. Balance is key to maintaining long-term productivity and well-being.

   - **Set Boundaries**: Establish clear boundaries between work and personal life to prevent burnout and maintain a healthy work-life balance.

6. **Don't Skip the Basics**

   - **Neglect Basics**: Avoid skipping fundamental tasks or responsibilities. Even small details matter, and neglecting them can impact your overall performance.

   - **Ignore Policies**: Familiarize yourself with company policies and procedures. Ignoring them can lead to misunderstandings or compliance issues.

7. **Don't Make Hasty Decisions**

   - **Rush into Projects**: Avoid rushing into decisions or projects without proper understanding. Take time to analyze and plan before taking action.

- **Skip the Learning Curve**: Don't rush to take on complex tasks before you're ready. Allow yourself time to learn and adapt gradually.

By adhering to these dos and don'ts, you can navigate your first year on the job or probation period effectively, establishing yourself as a valuable and reliable team member and setting the stage for future career success.

10.4 Balancing Personal Habits with Company Culture

Balancing basic personal habits with company culture is essential for long-term success and satisfaction in your job. Here are some strategies to help you navigate this balance effectively:

1. **Understand and Adapt to Company Culture**

   - **Research and Observe**: Take time to understand the company's culture by observing how employees interact, communicate, and work. Pay attention to unwritten norms and expectations.

   - **Ask Questions**: Don't hesitate to ask colleagues or your manager about cultural norms and expectations. This can provide clarity on how to align your personal habits with the company's culture.

2. **Align Personal Habits with Professional Expectations**

   - **Adapt Where Necessary**: Adjust your personal habits to fit the company's culture where reasonable. For example, if the company has a formal dress code but you prefer casual attire, find a balance that maintains professionalism while reflecting your personal style.

- **Flexibility**: Be flexible in adapting personal routines to fit work expectations. If the company values punctuality, adjust your routine to ensure you arrive on time consistently.

3. **Maintain Your Core Personal Values**

   - **Stay Authentic**: While adapting to the company culture, it's important to remain true to your core personal values. Authenticity builds trust and respect with colleagues.

   - **Personal Integrity**: Ensure that your personal habits reflect your integrity and ethical standards. For instance, if you value transparency and honesty, maintain these principles in all professional interactions.

4. **Set Boundaries**

   - **Work-Life Balance**: Establish clear boundaries between work and personal life. For example, if you value family time, make sure to set boundaries around work hours to preserve this personal time.

   - **Manage Expectations**: Communicate your boundaries respectfully with your team. For instance, if you have specific needs for flexible working hours, discuss these with your manager in advance.

5. **Communicate Effectively**

   - **Open Dialogue**: Engage in open dialogue with your manager and team about any potential conflicts between personal habits and company expectations. Discuss how you can achieve a balance that respects both.

   - **Feedback and Adjustment**: Be open to feedback on how your personal habits might impact your work or team dynamics. Use this feedback to make adjustments while maintaining your personal well-being.

6. **Prioritize Self-Care**

   - **Health and Well-being**: Ensure that personal habits related to health and well-being, such as regular exercise, adequate sleep, and stress management, are maintained. A healthy work-life balance supports overall productivity and job satisfaction.

   - **Mindfulness and Relaxation**: Incorporate practices like mindfulness or relaxation techniques to manage stress and maintain mental well-being. This can help you stay focused and effective in a work environment.

7. **Develop Positive Work Habits**

   - **Professional Etiquette**: Adopt work habits that reflect professionalism and align with company culture, such as punctuality, effective communication, and collaboration.

   - **Continuous Improvement**: Regularly assess and refine your work habits to better align with evolving company culture and expectations while preserving your personal well-being.

8. **Seek Support and Resources**

   - **Utilize Resources**: Take advantage of any company resources or programs designed to support work-life balance, such as employee assistance programs or wellness initiatives.

   - **Find a Support Network**: Build a network of supportive colleagues or mentors who can offer guidance and help you navigate the balance between personal habits and company culture.

9. **Reflect and Adjust**

   - **Regular Reflection**: Periodically reflect on how well your personal habits are balancing with company culture. Identify any areas of conflict or improvement and make necessary adjustments.

- **Adapt Over Time**: Be prepared to adapt as both personal and professional circumstances change. Flexibility in adjusting habits to new roles, teams, or company policies is key to maintaining balance.

10. **Celebrate Your Achievements**

- **Acknowledge Successes**: Recognize and celebrate the successful integration of personal habits with company culture. This can reinforce positive behavior and boost morale.

By carefully balancing personal habits with the demands of company culture, you can create a harmonious work environment that supports both your professional success and personal well-being. This approach not only helps you thrive in your current role but also positions you for long-term career satisfaction and growth.

10.5 Violation of Company Rules

Violations of company rules can be categorized based on whether they are committed knowingly or unknowingly. Here's a detailed breakdown of each category:

10.5.1 Knowingly Violating Company Rules

These violations occur when an individual is aware of the rules or policies but chooses to disregard them. This category includes deliberate actions that intentionally go against company policies and professional ethics.

1. **Ethical Breaches**

   - **Fraud or Misrepresentation**: Deliberately falsifying information, such as financial records or credentials, to gain personal benefit.

   - **Conflict of Interest**: Engaging in activities or relationships that could compromise impartiality or create a personal gain at the expense of the company.

2. **Compliance Violations**

   - **Regulatory Non-Compliance**: Willfully ignoring industry regulations, such as failing to adhere to safety standards or legal requirements.

   - **Data Misuse**: Intentionally using or disclosing confidential or proprietary information without authorization.

3. **Policy Violations**

   - **Unauthorized Access**: Deliberately accessing restricted areas or systems without proper authorization.

   - **Misuse of Company Resources**: Using company resources, such as time, equipment, or funds, for personal gain or activities unrelated to work.

4. **Disciplinary Issues**

   - **Harassment or Discrimination**: Engaging in or condoning behavior that violates company policies on workplace harassment or discrimination despite being aware of the rules.

   - **Substance Abuse**: Using or being under the influence of drugs or alcohol at work, knowing it is against company policy.

10.5.2 *Unknowingly Violating Company Rules*

These violations occur when an individual is unaware of the company rules or policies and unintentionally fails to comply. This category includes actions taken in ignorance or misunderstanding of the rules.

1. **Procedural Errors**
   - **Misunderstanding Policies**: Making mistakes due to lack of awareness or misunderstanding of company policies and procedures, such as incorrect handling of sensitive information.
   - **Errors in Documentation**: Submitting inaccurate or incomplete documentation without realizing it contravenes company standards.

2. **Compliance Lapses**
   - **Unintentional Non-Compliance**: Failing to follow industry regulations or company guidelines due to a lack of knowledge or proper training, such as incorrect safety practices.
   - **Neglecting Training**: Not adhering to best practices or legal requirements because of inadequate training or on-boarding processes.

3. **Policy Missteps**
   - **Unintentional Access**: Accidentally accessing restricted information or areas due to not being fully informed about access controls and restrictions.
   - **Improper Use of Resources**: Misusing company resources in a manner that was not intended, due to a lack of understanding of proper usage policies.

4. **Unintentional Behavioral Issues**
   - **Inadvertent Discrimination**: Engaging in behavior that might be perceived as discriminatory or inappropriate, not

out of intent, but due to ignorance of company policies or cultural norms.

- **Accidental Harassment**: Unknowingly making comments or taking actions that could be interpreted as harassment, due to a lack of awareness of what constitutes inappropriate behavior.

10.5.3 What to do in case of accidental violation?

When company rules are violated accidentally, it is essential to handle the situation promptly and effectively to mitigate any potential consequences and demonstrate a commitment to compliance and integrity. Here's a step-by-step approach to addressing accidental violations:

1. **Acknowledge the Violation**

   - **Recognize the Issue**: Identify and acknowledge that a rule has been violated. Understanding the nature of the breach and the context in which it occurred is crucial.

   - **Take Responsibility**: Accept responsibility for the mistake. Acknowledging the error demonstrates integrity and a willingness to correct the situation.

2. **Report the Violation**

   - **Inform Your Supervisor**: Notify your direct supervisor or manager about the violation as soon as possible. Provide a clear and honest account of what happened.

   - **Follow Reporting Procedures**: Adhere to any formal reporting procedures or protocols established by the company. This might include filling out a report or notifying the compliance department.

3. **Investigate the Cause**

   - **Assess the Situation**: Conduct a thorough assessment to determine how the violation occurred. Identify any gaps in knowledge, training, or processes that contributed to the mistake.

- **Document Findings**: Keep detailed records of the investigation and findings, including any contributing factors and the steps taken to address the issue.

4. **Implement Corrective Actions**

- **Rectify the Issue**: Take immediate steps to correct the violation. This may involve reversing any adverse effects, such as correcting erroneous data or remedying compliance lapses.

- **Adjust Procedures**: If the violation highlights a procedural or training gap, work on revising procedures or updating training materials to prevent similar issues in the future.

5. **Learn and Improve**

- **Reflect on the Mistake**: Reflect on what went wrong and how it can be avoided in the future. Consider personal and organizational improvements.

- **Seek Feedback**: Engage with supervisors or colleagues to get feedback on how to handle similar situations better and learn from the experience.

6. **Communicate Transparently**

- **Update Stakeholders**: If the violation affects other stakeholders (e.g., clients, departments), communicate transparently about what happened and the steps being taken to address it.

- **Provide Assurance**: Reassure stakeholders that measures are being put in place to prevent recurrence and that the issue is being handled responsibly.

7. **Enhance Training and Awareness**

   - **Participate in Training**: Engage in additional training or refresher courses to better understand company policies and compliance requirements.

   - **Promote Awareness**: Advocate for and participate in efforts to increase awareness and understanding of company rules and procedures among team members.

8. **Document and Report Actions**

   - **Keep Records**: Maintain documentation of the violation, investigation, corrective actions, and any communications related to the incident.

   - **Report to Management**: Provide a summary of the incident, actions taken, and outcomes to management or the relevant department for review and record-keeping.

9. **Monitor and Review**

   - **Track Effectiveness**: Monitor the effectiveness of the corrective actions and any changes made to procedures or training. Ensure that the changes are preventing similar violations.

   - **Conduct Regular Reviews**: Regularly review company policies and procedures to ensure they remain relevant and effective in preventing accidental violations.

10. **Foster a Positive Culture**

   - **Encourage Open Communication**: Create an environment where employees feel comfortable reporting mistakes and seeking guidance without fear of undue reprimand.

   - **Support Continuous Improvement**: Promote a culture of continuous improvement, where learning from mistakes and implementing preventive measures are encouraged.

Nut Shell: Following these steps, you can effectively address accidental violations of company rules, demonstrate accountability, and contribute to a culture of compliance and continuous improvement within the organization.

10.5.4　Mitigating Both Types of Violations

A.　For **knowingly** committed violations:

- **Strong Ethical Culture**: Promote a culture of integrity and ethical behavior through clear communication and training.

- **Enforce Policies**: Implement strict enforcement of company rules and disciplinary actions to address deliberate breaches.

B.　For **unknowingly** committed violations:

- **Comprehensive Training**: Provide thorough training and on-boarding to ensure employees are aware of and understand company policies and industry regulations.

- **Clear Communication**: Regularly update and communicate changes in policies and procedures to all employees.

Conclusion

Addressing both types of violations—whether intentional or accidental—companies can foster a more compliant and ethical workplace while supporting employees in understanding and adhering to rules and standards.

10.6　Possible Consequences of Violating Company Rules

Violating company rules and going against professional ethics can have serious and far-reaching consequences, both for the individual involved and the organization. Here are some possible repercussions based on nature of violation:

10.6.1 Lighter Consequences

1. **Disciplinary Actions**

   - **Warnings and Reprimands**: Formal warnings or reprimands may be issued, often including corrective action plans to address minor infractions or initial rule violations.

   - **Suspension**: Temporary suspension from work for more serious breaches, which impacts income and may affect morale but is typically less severe than termination.

2. **Damage to Professional Reputation**

   - **Loss of Trust**: Erosion of trust among colleagues and supervisors, potentially affecting day-to-day interactions and team dynamics but not necessarily causing long-term career damage if addressed.

   - **Internal Company Impact**: Reduction in team morale or minor operational disruptions resulting from the violation. These impacts are often contained within the organization and may be mitigated with corrective actions.

3. **Personal Consequences**

   - **Isolation:** Isolation as a punishment for accidentally violating rules can be counterproductive and may not effectively address the underlying issue.

   - **Stress and Mental Health**: Increased stress or mental strain from dealing with disciplinary actions or ethical issues, which can be managed through support resources and stress management techniques.

10.6.2 Severe Consequences

1. **Termination of Employment**

   - **Immediate Dismissal**: Being fired due to significant rule violations or ethical breaches, leading to immediate loss of income and potentially impacting future employment opportunities.

2. **Legal Consequences**

   - **Lawsuits and Legal Action**: Potential for legal action against you or the company, leading to financial liabilities, legal battles, and substantial legal costs.

   - **Criminal Charges**: In cases of severe ethical breaches, such as fraud or embezzlement, criminal charges can result in fines, imprisonment, and a permanent criminal record.

3. **Damage to Professional Reputation**

   - **Negative Publicity**: High-profile breaches attracting media attention, leading to long-term damage to your personal and professional reputation, which can significantly impact career prospects.

4. **Loss of Professional Licenses or Certifications**

   - **Revocation of Credentials**: For regulated professions, violations can lead to the revocation of licenses or certifications, which are essential for practicing in the field.

5. **Internal Company Impact**

   - **Operational Disruption**: Severe disruptions to business operations or financial losses resulting from the violation, which can have widespread and long-lasting effects on the company's performance and stability.

6. Financial Strain

- **Significant Financial Impact**: Financial hardship from termination or legal fees, affecting personal and family finances substantially.

CHAPTER 11

Long-term Career Development

Long-term career development is a strategic journey that involves intentional planning and ongoing effort to shape your professional trajectory over time. It starts with identifying your career aspirations and setting clear, actionable goals that align with your personal values and ambitions. This process requires a commitment to continuous learning and skill enhancement, which may involve pursuing advanced education, certifications, or specialized training.

Additionally, long-term career development emphasizes the importance of building a robust professional network, seeking mentorship, and gaining diverse experiences to broaden your expertise and adaptability. By regularly assessing your progress and staying attuned to industry trends and emerging opportunities, you can navigate your career path effectively. This proactive approach not only prepares you for advancement and new challenges but also fosters personal satisfaction and resilience in an ever-evolving professional landscape.

11.1 Continuous Learning and Professional Development

Continuous learning and professional development are essential components of a successful and dynamic career. Continuous learning involves the ongoing, self-motivated pursuit of knowledge and skills, enabling professionals to stay current with industry advancements, adapt to new technologies, and foster innovation. It encompasses various methods such as online courses, workshops, and self-study.

Professional development, on the other hand, focuses on structured activities designed to enhance specific competencies and advance career goals. This includes participating in workplace training, obtaining certifications, and seeking mentorship.

Together, continuous learning and professional development ensure that individuals not only keep pace with evolving trends but also strategically position themselves for career growth and excellence. By integrating both approaches, professionals can effectively navigate their career paths, contribute meaningfully to their organizations, and achieve long-term success.

11.1.1 Continuous learning

Continuous learning refers to the ongoing, voluntary, and self-motivated pursuit of knowledge and skills throughout one's career and life. This concept emphasizes the importance of staying informed and adaptable in an ever-evolving professional landscape. Here's a detailed exploration:

1. **Importance and Benefits**
   - **Adaptability**: Continuous learning helps professionals stay current with industry trends, technological advancements, and evolving best practices, making them more adaptable to change.
   - **Competitiveness**: By acquiring new skills and knowledge, individuals enhance their marketability and stay competitive in the job market.

- **Innovation**: Engaging in ongoing learning fosters creativity and innovation, enabling professionals to contribute fresh ideas and solutions to their fields.

2. **Methods and Approaches**

   - **Formal Education**: Pursuing advanced degrees, certifications, or specialized training programs that provide in-depth knowledge and credentials.

   - **Online Courses**: Leveraging platforms like Coursera, edX, or Udemy to access a wide range of courses and tutorials on various subjects.

   - **Workshops and Seminars**: Attending industry conferences, workshops, or seminars to gain insights from experts and network with peers.

   - **Self-Study**: Reading books, articles, and research papers, or engaging in self-directed learning through resources like blogs and podcasts.

3. **Creating a Learning Plan**

   - **Identify Learning Goals**: Set specific, measurable, and relevant learning objectives based on career goals and industry demands.

   - **Allocate Time**: Dedicate regular time slots for learning activities to ensure consistent progress.

   - **Evaluate Progress**: Regularly assess your learning outcomes and adjust your plan as needed to stay aligned with your goals.

4. **Overcoming Challenges**

   - **Time Management**: Balancing learning with work and personal responsibilities can be challenging. Effective time management and prioritization are key.

- **Resource Selection**: Choosing the right resources and opportunities that offer value and relevance to your career can require careful evaluation.

11.1.2 Professional development

Professional development is a structured process aimed at enhancing an individual's skills, competencies, and career growth through targeted activities and experiences. It focuses on advancing one's career trajectory and achieving professional excellence. Here's an in-depth look:

1. **Importance and Benefits**

   - **Career Advancement**: Professional development activities help individuals gain the skills and experience needed for promotions, new roles, or increased responsibilities.

   - **Skill Enhancement**: It provides opportunities to acquire and refine skills that are critical for performing current job functions effectively and preparing for future roles.

   - **Networking**: Engaging in professional development often involves networking with peers, mentors, and industry leaders, which can open doors to new opportunities and collaborations.

2. **Methods and Approaches**

   - **Workplace Training**: Participating in company-sponsored training programs, workshops, or seminars designed to enhance job-specific skills and knowledge.

   - **Mentorship and Coaching**: Seeking guidance from experienced mentors or coaches who can provide personalized advice, feedback, and career guidance.

- **Professional Associations**: Joining industry-related organizations or associations to access resources, attend events, and connect with professionals in your field.

- **Certifications and Licenses**: Obtaining relevant certifications or licenses that validate your expertise and enhance your credibility within your profession.

3. **Creating a Development Plan**

- **Set Career Goals**: Define clear career objectives and identify the skills and experiences needed to achieve them.

- **Select Development Activities**: Choose activities and resources that align with your career goals and address any skill gaps or areas for improvement.

- **Track Progress**: Monitor your development progress and adjust your plan based on feedback, performance evaluations, and evolving career aspirations.

4. **Overcoming Challenges**

- **Budget Constraints**: Professional development opportunities can sometimes be costly. Look for cost-effective options or seek employer sponsorship.

- **Balancing Responsibilities**: Managing professional development alongside current job responsibilities and personal commitments requires careful planning and prioritization.

Conclusion

Continuous learning and professional development are complementary aspects of career growth. Continuous learning focuses on the ongoing acquisition of knowledge and skills, while professional development is more structured and targeted towards achieving career objectives and enhancing job performance. Both are essential for maintaining relevance, advancing in your career, and achieving long-term professional success.

11.2 Certification and Advanced Degrees

Certifications and advanced degrees are pivotal in advancing one's career and enhancing professional expertise. Certifications, often industry-specific, provide a recognized validation of specialized skills and knowledge, demonstrating a commitment to excellence and a readiness to tackle complex challenges within a particular field. They are valuable for gaining credibility, pursuing new opportunities, and staying competitive in the job market.

Advanced degrees, such as a master's or doctoral degree, offer a deeper, more comprehensive understanding of a discipline and can open doors to higher-level positions, increased responsibilities, and specialized roles. Additionally, earning more academic credits through coursework or professional development programs further enriches one's expertise and adaptability. Both certifications and advanced degrees contribute significantly to career advancement by equipping individuals with advanced skills, expanding their knowledge base, and enhancing their professional qualifications.

11.2.1 Certification

Certifications play an important role in personal professional growth by providing formal recognition of specialized skills and expertise. They are valuable tools for individuals seeking to enhance their knowledge, increase their marketability, and advance their careers. Here's an in-depth look at how certifications contribute to professional development:

1. **Enhancing Skill-sets and Knowledge**

    - **Specialization**: Certifications often focus on specific areas within a profession, allowing individuals to develop advanced skills and knowledge in niche fields. For example, a Project Management Professional (PMP) certification deepens expertise in project management principles and practices.

- **Up-to-Date Knowledge**: Many certifications require ongoing education or re-certification, ensuring that professionals stay current with the latest developments, tools, and best practices in their industry.

2. **Improving Career Opportunities**

- **Increased Job Prospects**: Holding relevant certifications can make candidates more attractive to employers by demonstrating their expertise and commitment to the field. This can lead to greater job opportunities and increased job security.

- **Career Advancement**: Certifications can be a prerequisite for promotions or advanced roles within an organization. They signal readiness for higher-level responsibilities and leadership positions.

3. **Boosting Credibility and Professionalism**

- **Industry Recognition**: Certifications from reputable organizations or professional bodies lend credibility and validate an individual's skills and qualifications, enhancing their professional reputation.

- **Demonstrated Commitment**: Obtaining a certification shows a dedication to professional development and a proactive approach to career growth, which can positively influence employer perceptions and peer recognition.

4. **Expanding Professional Network**

- **Industry Connections**: Many certification programs provide access to professional networks, forums, or associations. These connections can be valuable for networking, collaboration, and sharing industry insights.

- **Professional Community**: Engaging with a community of certified professionals can offer support, mentorship, and opportunities for continued learning and growth.

5. **Supporting Personal Development**

- **Confidence Building**: Achieving a certification can boost self-confidence by validating one's skills and competencies. It provides a sense of accomplishment and reinforces personal growth.

- **Goal Setting**: The process of pursuing and earning a certification involves setting and achieving specific goals, which can enhance personal motivation and discipline.

6. **Navigating Industry Changes**

- **Adapting to Trends**: Certifications often address emerging trends, technologies, and practices within an industry. They equip professionals with the tools to adapt to changes and remain relevant in a rapidly evolving job market.

- **Enhancing Competitiveness**: In competitive fields, certifications can distinguish candidates from their peers by showcasing specialized skills and knowledge that are highly valued by employers.

7. **Investment and Cost Considerations**

- **Financial Investment**: While certifications often involve costs related to coursework, exams, and study materials, the potential return on investment includes improved career prospects and higher earning potential.

- **Time Commitment**: Preparing for and obtaining certifications requires a commitment of time and effort. Balancing this with work and personal responsibilities is important for achieving successful outcomes.

Conclusion

Certifications are a powerful tool for personal professional growth, offering specialized knowledge, enhancing career opportunities, and building credibility. They support continuous learning, expand professional networks, and contribute to adapting to industry changes, ultimately helping individuals achieve their career goals and maintain a competitive edge in their field.

11.2.2 Professional Development

Professional development is a vital aspect of personal growth, encompassing a range of activities designed to enhance an individual's skills, knowledge, and career trajectory. It involves a proactive approach to learning and improvement, contributing significantly to both personal satisfaction and professional success. Here's an in-depth look at how professional development fosters personal growth:

1. **Skill Enhancement and Competency Building**

   - **Acquiring New Skills**: Professional development provides opportunities to learn new skills or refine existing ones. Whether through workshops, training programs, or on-the-job experiences, developing competencies in areas like leadership, communication, or technical skills enhances your effectiveness in your current role and prepares you for future responsibilities.

- **Staying Relevant**: Engaging in professional development helps you stay current with industry trends, emerging technologies, and best practices. This continuous learning ensures that your skills remain relevant and valuable in a rapidly evolving job market.

2. **Career Advancement**

   - **Achieving Career Goals**: Professional development activities, such as advanced training or mentorship, can help you set and achieve specific career objectives. By aligning development efforts with your career aspirations, you enhance your potential for promotions, new opportunities, and increased responsibilities.

   - **Expanding Job Opportunities**: Building expertise through professional development can open doors to new roles or career paths that align with your interests and strengths. It increases your marketability and provides a competitive edge in the job market.

3. **Building Professional Credibility**

   - **Certification and Credentials**: Earning certifications or advanced qualifications through professional development validates your skills and expertise, boosting your credibility and reputation within your industry. It demonstrates a commitment to excellence and professional growth.

   - **Reputation and Trust**: Engaging in professional development activities reflects a dedication to your career and a willingness to invest in personal improvement. This commitment can enhance your professional reputation and build trust with colleagues, supervisors, and industry peers.

4. **Enhancing Personal Satisfaction and Confidence**

  - **Sense of Achievement**: Successfully completing professional development programs or acquiring new skills provides a sense of accomplishment and boosts self-confidence. This personal satisfaction can positively impact your overall motivation and enthusiasm for your work.

  - **Personal Growth**: Professional development often involves stepping out of your comfort zone and tackling new challenges. This personal growth fosters resilience, adaptability, and a growth mindset, contributing to overall well-being and career fulfillment.

5. **Networking and Relationship Building**

  - **Connecting with Peers**: Professional development opportunities, such as conferences, seminars, or industry events, facilitate networking with other professionals. Building relationships with peers and industry leaders can provide valuable support, mentorship, and collaboration opportunities.

  - **Mentorship and Guidance**: Engaging with mentors or coaches during professional development can offer personalized guidance, feedback, and career advice. These relationships can play a crucial role in navigating career challenges and making informed decisions.

6. **Improving Job Performance**

  - **Enhanced Capabilities**: By developing new skills and knowledge, you can improve your performance and efficiency in your current role. This increased capability can lead to better job outcomes, increased productivity, and higher job satisfaction.

- **Problem-Solving Abilities**: Professional development often includes training in critical thinking and problem-solving, equipping you with the tools to address complex issues and contribute innovative solutions to your organization.

7. **Adapting to Change**

- **Embracing Innovation**: Professional development helps you stay adaptable and open to change, which is essential in dynamic work environments. Learning about new tools, technologies, or methodologies allows you to effectively navigate and leverage industry changes.

- **Career Resilience**: Developing a diverse skill set through professional development enhances your ability to adjust to shifting job demands and career transitions, ensuring long-term career stability and growth.

Conclusion

Professional development is a cornerstone of personal growth, offering a structured approach to enhancing skills, advancing careers, and building credibility. It fosters personal satisfaction, confidence, and resilience while expanding job opportunities and improving job performance. By investing in professional development, individuals can achieve their career goals, stay relevant in their fields, and contribute meaningfully to their organizations.

11.2.3 Professional Development and Company's Growth

Professional development has a profound impact on a company's growth by enhancing employee capabilities, driving innovation, and fostering a more engaged and productive workforce. Here's a detailed exploration of how professional development contributes to a company's growth:

1. **Increased Employee Competency and Performance**

   - **Enhanced Skills**: Professional development programs equip employees with advanced skills and knowledge, improving their performance and efficiency. Skilled employees are better equipped to handle complex tasks, leading to higher productivity and quality of work.

   - **Improved Problem-Solving**: Training and development help employees develop critical thinking and problem-solving skills, enabling them to address challenges more effectively and contribute innovative solutions.

2. **Boosted Employee Engagement and Retention**

   - **Motivation and Morale**: Investing in employees' professional growth demonstrates a company's commitment to their development, leading to increased job satisfaction and motivation. Engaged employees are more likely to be proactive, contribute positively to the workplace, and remain with the company long-term.

   - **Reduced Turnover**: Companies that offer opportunities for professional development are better positioned to retain top talent. Employees are less likely to seek new job opportunities if they feel their current employer supports their career growth and offers pathways for advancement.

3. **Enhanced Organizational Innovation and Competitiveness**

   - **Fostering Innovation**: Professional development encourages continuous learning and exposure to new ideas and technologies. Employees who engage in ongoing development are more likely to bring fresh perspectives and innovative solutions, driving the company's competitive edge.

- **Adapting to Market Changes**: By staying current with industry trends and advancements, companies can adapt more quickly to market changes. This agility is crucial for maintaining a competitive advantage and responding to evolving customer needs.

4. **Improved Leadership and Management**

   - **Developing Leaders**: Professional development programs often include leadership training, helping to build a pipeline of skilled leaders within the organization. Effective leaders are essential for guiding teams, making strategic decisions, and driving organizational growth.

   - **Better Management Practices**: Enhanced management skills lead to more effective team management, improved project execution, and better decision-making. This contributes to overall organizational efficiency and performance.

5. **Enhanced Company Reputation and Employer Brand**

   - **Attracting Talent**: Companies known for their commitment to employee development are more attractive to potential hires. A strong employer brand that emphasizes growth opportunities can draw high-quality candidates who are looking for supportive and progressive workplaces.

   - **Positive Workplace Culture**: A focus on professional development fosters a positive workplace culture, characterized by continuous learning, collaboration, and mutual support. This culture enhances the company's reputation both internally and externally.

6. **Increased Operational Efficiency**

   - **Streamlined Processes**: Training employees in best practices and new technologies can lead to more efficient processes and workflows. This optimization reduces waste, improves operational efficiency, and enhances overall productivity.

- **Effective Utilization of Resources**: Well-trained employees can make better use of company resources, including technology and tools, leading to cost savings and more effective operations.

7. **Greater Customer Satisfaction**

- **Enhanced Service Quality**: Professional development helps employees improve their skills and knowledge, leading to better customer service and higher-quality products. Satisfied customers are more likely to remain loyal and recommend the company to others.

- **Responsive Customer Support**: Employees who receive ongoing training are better equipped to address customer inquiries and issues promptly and effectively, contributing to a positive customer experience.

8. **Strategic Growth and Expansion**

- **Skill Diversification**: Developing a diverse skill set among employees supports strategic initiatives and business expansion. Employees with varied expertise can contribute to different areas of growth, such as entering new markets or launching new products.

- **Enhanced Strategic Execution**: A well-trained workforce is better prepared to execute strategic plans and initiatives, aligning with the company's long-term growth objectives and achieving business goals.

11.3 Career Opportunities in PSUs and Government

Engineering graduates have a wide array of career opportunities in public sector enterprises, which play a crucial role in national development and infrastructure. These positions often provide job security, competitive salaries, and the chance to contribute to significant projects that benefit society. Here's an overview of the key career opportunities available:

11.3.1 Public Sector Undertakings (PSUs)

India boasts numerous PSUs across various engineering domains, including:

- **Oil and Gas**: Companies like **ONGC** and **GAIL** recruit chemical and mechanical engineers for exploration, production, and refining processes.

- **Power Generation**: Enterprises like **NTPC** and **Power Grid Corporation** seek electrical and mechanical engineers for power plant operations, maintenance, and project management.

- **Telecommunications**: Organizations like **BSNL** and **MTNL** hire telecommunications and electronics engineers for infrastructure development and network management.

11.3.2 Government Research and Development Organizations

Engineering graduates can join institutions like **DRDO, ISRO**, and **CSIR**. Opportunities include:

- **Research Scientists**: Conducting advanced research in fields like aerospace, defense, and materials science.

- **Project Engineers**: Managing projects related to technology development, testing, and implementation.

11.3.3 Civil Services

Engineering graduates can enter civil services through exams like the **UPSC** or **State PSCs**. They can work in roles such as:

- **Indian Engineering Services (IES)**: Handling engineering projects within various government departments, overseeing infrastructure projects, and ensuring compliance with engineering standards.

- **Administrative Roles**: Utilizing technical knowledge to inform policy decisions related to infrastructure and development.

11.3.4 Public Works Departments (PWD)

Engineers can work in PWDs at the state and central levels, focusing on:

- **Infrastructure Development**: Designing and overseeing construction projects, including roads, bridges, and public buildings.
- **Quality Control**: Ensuring that construction materials and practices meet regulatory standards.

11.3.5 State and Central Government Projects

Engineering graduates can engage in various government-funded projects, such as:

- **Smart City Initiatives**: Involvement in planning and implementing modern urban infrastructure solutions.
- **Sustainable Development Projects**: Focusing on renewable energy, waste management, and water resource management.

11.3.6 Educational Institutions

Graduates can pursue careers in teaching and research within government engineering colleges and polytechnics:

- **Lecturers and Professors**: Teaching future engineers and guiding research projects.
- **Curriculum Development**: Designing course content to meet industry standards and technological advancements.

11.3.7 Defense and Security

Organizations like **DRDO, HAL,** and **BHEL** offer opportunities for engineers in:

- **Weapon System Development**: Designing and testing military hardware and systems.

- **Aerospace Engineering**: Working on aircraft and spacecraft design and maintenance.

Skills Required

To excel in these roles, engineering graduates should focus on developing:

- **Technical Proficiency**: A deep understanding of their engineering discipline.

- **Project Management**: Skills in managing timelines, resources, and budgets.

- **Communication**: The ability to convey technical information clearly to non-engineering stakeholders.

- **Problem-Solving**: Strong analytical skills to tackle complex engineering challenges.

Conclusion

The public sector offers a robust landscape for engineering graduates, with numerous pathways to contribute to the country's development and innovation. With the right skills and dedication, graduates can build fulfilling careers that not only enhance their professional growth but also significantly impact society.

11.3.8 Government Jobs

Pursuing a government dnt job in the textile sector in India involves several essential requirements and a specific process. Here's a comprehensive guide:

A. Essential Requirements

1. Educational Qualifications

- A Bachelor's degree in Engineering (B.Tech/B.E.) in relevant fields such as Civil, Mechanical, Electrical, or Electronics. For some positions, a Master's degree may be advantageous.

2. Age Limit

- Generally, candidates must be between 21 and 30 years old for most government jobs, with age relaxations for reserved categories.

3. GATE Exam

- Many PSUs require candidates to have a valid GATE (Graduate Aptitude Test in Engineering) score for recruitment.

4. Competitive Exams

- For IES and civil services, candidates must pass respective entrance exams, which include general studies, engineering-specific subjects, and personal interviews.

5. Technical and Soft Skills

- Strong analytical and problem-solving skills, as well as effective communication and teamwork abilities, are essential.

B. Application Process

1. Research Opportunities

- Keep track of notifications on government job portals, such as UPSC, SSC, and individual PSU websites, to find relevant openings.

2. Prepare Required Documents

- Assemble essential documents, including:
- Resume/CV

- Educational certificates
- Identity proof (e.g., Aadhar card)
- Caste certificate (if applicable)

3. **Application Submission**

   - Apply online or offline as specified in the job notification. Ensure that all information is accurate and complete.

4. **Entrance Exams**

   - Prepare rigorously for entrance exams like GATE or UPSC. Focus on the syllabus, practice previous years' papers, and consider joining coaching classes if needed.

5. **Interviews**

   - Shortlisted candidates will be called for interviews. Prepare by reviewing common interview questions, understanding current trends in engineering, and being ready to discuss past projects.

6. **Medical Examination**

   - Many government positions require a medical examination to ensure candidates meet health standards.

7. **Final Selection**

   - Successful candidates receive an appointment letter detailing their roles, responsibilities, and terms of employment.

Conclusion

Engineering graduates can find diverse and rewarding career opportunities in the government sector. By meeting essential requirements and following a structured application process, they can secure positions that allow them to contribute to the nation's growth and development while enjoying stable and fulfilling careers.

11.4 Work–Life Balance and Personal Well being

Work-life balance and personal well-being are integral components of a fulfilling and sustainable career. Achieving a harmonious equilibrium between professional responsibilities and personal life is essential for maintaining overall health, satisfaction, and productivity. Work-life balance involves effectively managing the demands of one's job while allocating time for personal interests, relationships, and self-care. This balance is typical for preventing burnout, reducing stress, and enhancing job satisfaction.

Personal well-being, encompassing physical, emotional, and mental health, directly influences one's ability to perform effectively at work and enjoy a rich, rewarding life outside of it. By prioritizing both work-life balance and personal well-being, individuals can cultivate a more resilient and motivated mindset, leading to greater success and fulfillment in both their professional and personal spheres.

11.4.1 Work–Life Balance

Work-life balance is the equilibrium between an individual's professional responsibilities and personal life, aiming to ensure that neither aspect overwhelms the other. Achieving a harmonious work-life balance is crucial for maintaining overall health, satisfaction, and productivity. Here's an in-depth exploration of work-life balance and its key components:

1. **Understanding Work-Life Balance**

   - **Definition**: Work-life balance refers to the ability to effectively manage work demands and personal life activities without compromising one's health or well-being. It involves allocating appropriate time and energy to both professional and personal pursuits.

- **Importance:** Striking a balance between work and personal life is essential for preventing burnout, reducing stress, and enhancing overall quality of life. A well-balanced life leads to improved job satisfaction, better relationships, and increased overall happiness.

2. **Strategies for Achieving Work-Life Balance**

   - **Setting Boundaries:** Establishing clear boundaries between work and personal time helps prevent work from encroaching on personal life. This may involve setting specific work hours, avoiding work-related tasks outside of these hours, and clearly communicating these boundaries to colleagues and supervisors.

   - **Time Management:** Effective time management involves prioritizing tasks, setting realistic deadlines, and organizing both work and personal activities. Using tools like planners or digital calendars can help allocate time efficiently and avoid over-committing.

   - **Delegation:** Delegating tasks both at work and home can reduce the workload and free up time for personal activities. Trusting colleagues or family members with responsibilities can lead to a more manageable schedule and reduced stress.

   - **Flexible Work Arrangements:** Exploring flexible work options such as remote work, adjustable hours, or compressed workweeks can help integrate professional and personal needs. Many organizations offer such flexibility to accommodate diverse employee needs and preferences.

3. **Prioritizing Personal Well-Being**

   - **Self-Care:** Incorporating self-care practices such as exercise, proper nutrition, adequate sleep, and relaxation techniques is vital for maintaining physical and mental health. Regular self-care contributes to a higher quality of life and better work performance.

- **Mental Health**: Addressing mental health through mindfulness, stress management, and seeking professional help if needed is crucial. Mental well-being supports resilience and enhances one's ability to handle both work and personal challenges effectively.

- **Quality Time**: Allocating time for personal interests, hobbies, and relationships enriches life outside of work. Engaging in activities that bring joy and fulfillment helps balance work pressures with personal satisfaction.

4. **Creating a Supportive Work Environment**

- **Organizational Culture**: Employers play a significant role in supporting work-life balance by fostering a culture that values employees' personal time and well-being. Implementing policies that promote work-life balance, such as parental leave, vacation time, and wellness programs, contributes to a positive work environment.

- **Communication**: Open communication with supervisors and colleagues about workload, deadlines, and personal needs helps manage expectations and reduce work-related stress. Regular discussions about work-life balance can lead to mutual understanding and support.

5. **Challenges and Solutions**

- **Work Overload**: High workloads and tight deadlines can disrupt work-life balance. Prioritizing tasks, negotiating deadlines, and seeking support when needed can help manage heavy workloads and prevent burnout.

- **Technology and Connectivity**: The constant connectivity facilitated by technology can blur the lines between work and personal life. Setting boundaries around technology use and taking regular breaks from work-related communications can help maintain balance.

- **Personal Commitments**: Balancing work with personal commitments, such as family responsibilities, can be challenging. Effective time management, delegation, and seeking support from family or professional resources can help address these challenges.

6. **Long-Term Benefits**

- **Enhanced Productivity**: A well-balanced life leads to improved focus, creativity, and efficiency at work. Employees who manage work and personal life effectively are often more productive and motivated.

- **Better Relationships**: Maintaining work-life balance allows individuals to invest quality time in relationships with family, friends, and loved ones, leading to stronger connections and greater personal fulfillment.

- **Overall Well-Being**: Achieving a balance between work and personal life supports holistic well-being, contributing to long-term health, happiness, and life satisfaction.

Conclusion

Work-life balance involves managing professional and personal responsibilities in a way that supports overall well-being and satisfaction. By implementing strategies such as setting boundaries, effective time management, and prioritizing self-care, individuals can achieve a harmonious balance that enhances both their career and personal life.

A supportive work environment and addressing challenges proactively further contribute to a successful and fulfilling work-life balance.

11.4.2 Role of Personal Hobbies

Personal hobbies play a significant role in achieving and maintaining a healthy work-life balance by providing a variety of psychological, emotional, and physical benefits. Engaging in hobbies can help individuals manage stress, enhance creativity, and improve overall well-being. Here's an exploration of how personal hobbies contribute to work-life balance:

1. **Stress Relief and Relaxation**

   - **Mental Escape**: Hobbies provide a mental break from work-related stress. Activities like reading, gardening, or painting offer a change of pace and environment, allowing individuals to unwind and recharge.

   - **Reduced Burnout**: Engaging in leisure activities helps mitigate the risk of burnout by providing a necessary diversion from the pressures of work. Regularly scheduled hobby time helps maintain mental health and prevents exhaustion.

2. **Enhanced Creativity and Problem-Solving**

   - **Creative Outlet**: A pursuing creative hobby, such as writing, crafting, or playing a musical instrument, stimulate the brain and fosters innovative thinking. This enhanced creativity can positively impact problem-solving and decision-making skills at work.

   - **Fresh Perspectives**: Engaging in different activities can offer new perspectives and ideas, which can be beneficial for tackling work challenges with a refreshed mindset.

3. **Improved Time Management**

- **Structured Schedule**: Balancing hobbies with work responsibilities necessitates effective time management. Scheduling time for hobbies helps individuals organize their day better and create a more balanced routine.

- **Prioritization Skills**: Allocating time for personal interests encourages individuals to prioritize and manage their time efficiently, ensuring that work and personal life coexist harmoniously.

4. **Boosted Mood and Overall Well-Being**

- **Emotional Satisfaction**: Personal hobbies often provide a sense of accomplishment and joy. Engaging in activities that bring pleasure and satisfaction contributes to a positive mood and overall emotional well-being.

- **Physical Health**: Some hobbies, like hiking, dancing, or sports, involve physical activity, which is beneficial for physical health. Improved physical health can enhance energy levels and resilience, positively influencing work performance.

5. **Strengthened Social Connections**

- **Social Interaction**: Hobbies that involve group activities, such as team sports, book clubs, or community classes, foster social connections and provide opportunities to build relationships outside of work.

- **Support Networks**: Building and maintaining friendships through shared hobbies can offer emotional support and reduce feelings of isolation, contributing to a more balanced and fulfilling personal life.

6. **Increased Motivation and Productivity**

   - **Rejuvenation**: Taking time to engage in hobbies helps rejuvenate and energize individuals. This renewed energy and motivation can translate into increased productivity and focus when returning to work tasks.

   - **Balanced Perspective**: Having interests outside of work helps individuals maintain a balanced perspective, reducing the tendency to overemphasize work-related stress and contributing to a more well-rounded approach to professional challenges.

7. **Enhanced Work Performance**

   - **Skill Development**: Some hobbies can enhance skills that are transferable to the workplace. For instance, hobbies that involve teamwork, strategic thinking, or creativity can positively impact job performance and professional growth.

   - **Work Satisfaction**: A fulfilling hobby can lead to greater satisfaction in one's personal life, which often translates into a more positive attitude and higher satisfaction at work.

8. **Personal Growth and Fulfillment**

   - **Self-Discovery**: Engaging in various hobbies allows individuals to explore their interests and passions, leading to personal growth and self-discovery. This personal fulfillment contributes to a more satisfying and balanced life.

   - **Sense of Accomplishment**: Achieving personal goals through hobbies fosters a sense of accomplishment and boosts self-esteem, which can enhance confidence and overall well-being.

Conclusion

Personal hobbies play a catalytic role in maintaining work-life balance by offering stress relief, enhancing creativity, improving time management, and fostering emotional and physical well-being. They provide valuable opportunities for relaxation, social interaction, and personal growth, which contribute to a more balanced and fulfilling life. By integrating hobbies into their routine, individuals can achieve a healthier balance between their professional responsibilities and personal enjoyment, leading to enhanced overall quality of life.

11.4.3 Personal Well-being

Personal well-being encompasses the overall state of an individual's physical, mental, and emotional health, reflecting their quality of life and ability to handle daily stressors effectively. It involves a holistic approach to living that supports a healthy and balanced life. Here's a detailed exploration of personal well-being and its key components:

1. **Physical Well-being**

   - **Health and Fitness**: Maintaining physical well-being involves engaging in regular exercise, eating a balanced diet, and getting sufficient sleep. Physical activity supports cardiovascular health, muscle strength, and overall vitality, while a nutritious diet provides essential nutrients for bodily functions.

   - **Preventive Care**: Regular health check-ups, vaccinations, and screenings help prevent illness and detect potential health issues early. Taking proactive measures in healthcare contributes to long-term physical well-being.

   - **Stress Management**: Effective stress management techniques, such as relaxation exercises, yoga, or meditation, help mitigate the physical impacts of stress. Managing stress reduces the risk of stress-related health issues like hypertension and chronic fatigue.

2. **Mental Well-being**

   - **Emotional Health**: Mental well-being involves understanding and managing emotions, fostering resilience, and cultivating a positive outlook. Activities such as journaling, mindfulness, and therapy can support emotional health and self-awareness.

   - **Cognitive Function**: Engaging in activities that stimulate cognitive function, such as puzzles, reading, or learning new skills, supports mental acuity and cognitive longevity. Continuous mental stimulation helps maintain sharpness and intellectual growth.

   - **Work-Life Integration**: Balancing work demands with personal life reduces mental strain and supports overall mental health. Effective work-life integration prevents burnout and promotes a healthier mental state.

3. **Emotional Well-being**

   - **Self-Acceptance**: Developing self-acceptance and a positive self-image is crucial for emotional well-being. Embracing one's strengths and weaknesses and setting realistic expectations contributes to a balanced emotional state.

   - **Social Connections**: Building and maintaining meaningful relationships with family, friends, and colleagues fosters emotional support and reduces feelings of isolation. Positive social interactions enhance emotional resilience and satisfaction.

- **Stress and Coping**: Effective coping strategies for dealing with stress, such as seeking social support or engaging in hobbies, are essential for emotional stability. Developing healthy coping mechanisms can mitigate the impact of challenging situations.

4. **Social Well-being**

- **Healthy Relationships**: Nurturing positive relationships and maintaining a supportive social network contribute to a sense of belonging and social fulfillment. Engaging in social activities and fostering connections strengthen interpersonal bonds.

- **Community Involvement**: Participating in community activities or volunteer work enhances social well-being by providing a sense of purpose and contributing to a broader sense of community and belonging.

- **Workplace Environment**: A supportive and inclusive workplace environment fosters social well-being by promoting collaboration, respect, and a positive organizational culture.

5. **Spiritual Well-being**

- **Personal Beliefs and Values**: Spiritual well-being involves aligning one's life with personal beliefs, values, and purpose. Engaging in practices that reflect these values, such as meditation, prayer, or reflection, supports inner peace and fulfillment.

- **Meaning and Purpose**: Finding meaning and purpose in life, whether through personal goals, relationships, or contributions to others, enhances overall spiritual well-being and provides a sense of direction and motivation.

- **Mindfulness and Reflection**: Practices such as mindfulness and self-reflection help individuals connect with their inner selves and cultivate a sense of balance and serenity. These practices support spiritual growth and emotional stability.

6. **Personal Growth and Fulfillment**

   - **Goal Setting and Achievement**: Setting and pursuing personal goals contributes to a sense of accomplishment and fulfillment. Achieving these goals enhances self-esteem and provides motivation for continuous growth and development.

   - **Hobbies and Interests**: Engaging in activities and hobbies that bring joy and satisfaction supports personal well-being by providing opportunities for relaxation, creativity, and self-expression.

   - **Learning and Development**: Pursuing lifelong learning and personal development opportunities fosters growth and adaptability. Learning new skills and exploring new interests contribute to a sense of accomplishment and personal enrichment.

7. **Balancing Responsibilities and Self-Care**

   - **Time Management**: Effective time management helps balance various responsibilities and ensures that personal well-being is not compromised by work or other obligations. Allocating time for self-care, relaxation, and personal interests supports overall health and satisfaction.

   - **Self-Care Practices**: Incorporating regular self-care practices, such as relaxation techniques, hobbies, and time for personal reflection, is essential for maintaining personal well-being. Self-care contributes to physical, mental, and emotional health.

Conclusion

Personal well-being is a comprehensive concept that encompasses physical, mental, emotional, social, and spiritual dimensions. Achieving and maintaining personal well-being involves a balanced approach to health, fostering positive relationships, pursuing personal growth, and aligning life with individual values and goals. By addressing each of these components, individuals can cultivate a fulfilling and resilient life, enhancing their overall quality of life and capacity to handle life's challenges effectively.

11.4.4 Managing Weekend

Managing weekends effectively is essential for achieving a balanced and fulfilling life, as it offers a valuable opportunity to recharge and rejuvenate outside the demands of the workweek. Properly managing this time involves a thoughtful approach to balancing relaxation, personal interests, and social activities, ensuring that weekends serve as a productive break rather than a source of stress.

Whether through pursuing hobbies, spending quality time with family and friends, or engaging in self-care, a well-planned weekend can enhance overall well-being and set a positive tone for the upcoming week. By making intentional choices about how to spend these days, individuals can maximize their downtime, reduce stress, and return to their professional responsibilities feeling refreshed and motivated.

Strategic Approach for Managing Weekend

Managing weekends effectively involves a strategic approach to utilizing the two days away from work to achieve a balance between rest, personal interests, and social engagements. Proper management of weekends can enhance overall well-being, reduce stress, and improve productivity for the upcoming workweek. Here's a detailed exploration of how to manage weekends effectively:

1. **Planning and Prioritization**

   - **Setting Goals**: Begin by identifying what you want to accomplish over the weekend. This might include relaxation, personal projects, social activities, or errands. Setting clear goals helps in prioritizing tasks and ensuring that your weekend is fulfilling and productive.

   - **Creating a Schedule**: Develop a flexible schedule that allocates time for various activities. While spontaneity can be enjoyable, having a general plan helps in balancing different aspects of your weekend, such as leisure, socializing, and chores.

2. **Balancing Relaxation and Productivity**

   - **Rest and Recharge**: Prioritize rest and relaxation to recover from the workweek. Engage in activities that help you unwind, such as reading, taking walks, or simply enjoying quiet time at home. Adequate rest is crucial for maintaining mental and physical health.

   - **Personal Projects**: Use part of the weekend to work on personal projects or hobbies that you're passionate about. This might include creative pursuits, home improvement tasks, or learning new skills. Focusing on personal interests can be both rewarding and energizing.

3. **Social and Family Time**

   - **Quality Time**: Spend meaningful time with family and friends. Plan activities that foster connection and enjoyment, such as meals, outings, or gatherings. Quality time with loved ones strengthens relationships and contributes to overall happiness.

- **Social Engagements**: Participate in social events or community activities that interest you. Whether it's attending a local event, joining a club, or meeting friends, social interactions can enhance your weekend experience and provide a sense of community.

4. **Managing Chores and Responsibilities**

- **Efficient Errands**: Allocate time for running errands and completing household chores. Creating a to-do list for tasks such as grocery shopping, cleaning, or organizing helps in managing responsibilities efficiently without overwhelming your weekend.

- **Delegation and Sharing**: Share household duties or responsibilities with family members to distribute the workload. Effective delegation can help you complete tasks more quickly and free up time for relaxation and enjoyment.

5. **Health and Well-being**

- **Physical Activity**: Incorporate physical exercise into your weekend routine to maintain physical health and boost your mood. Activities like jogging, cycling, or participating in a fitness class can enhance your energy levels and overall well-being.

- **Healthy Eating**: Plan balanced meals and snacks that support your health goals. Weekends offer an opportunity to experiment with new recipes or enjoy leisurely meals, but maintaining a focus on nutritious choices contributes to long-term wellness.

6. **Personal Growth and Learning**

   - **Pursuing Interests**: Dedicate time to personal growth activities such as reading, taking online courses, or engaging in creative endeavors. Investing in self-improvement and learning can be both fulfilling and stimulating.

   - **Setting Personal Goals**: Use weekends to reflect on personal goals and progress. This could involve planning future projects, setting new objectives, or evaluating achievements and areas for improvement.

7. **Creating Boundaries**

   - **Work-Life Separation**: Establish clear boundaries to separate work from personal time. Avoid checking work emails or engaging in work-related tasks during the weekend to fully disengages and enjoys your time off.

   - **Digital De-tox**: Consider limiting screen time and social media use to focus more on offline activities and interactions. Reducing digital distractions can enhance your ability to relax and connect with the present moment.

8. **Flexibility and Adaptability**

   - **Allow for Spontaneity**: While planning is important, allowing some flexibility in your schedule can lead to unexpected joys and spontaneous experiences. Embrace opportunities that arise and adapt your plans as needed.

   - **Adjusting Plans**: Be open to adjusting your weekend plans based on how you're feeling and any unforeseen circumstances. Flexibility helps in managing stress and ensuring that your weekend remains enjoyable and balanced.

9. **Reflection and Adjustment**

- **Evaluating Your Weekend**: Reflect on how your weekend went and what you enjoyed or found challenging. Assessing your experience can help in making adjustments to improve future weekends and enhance your overall balance.

- **Continuous Improvement**: Use insights from your reflections to continuously improve how you manage your weekends. Adjust your approach based on what works best for you in balancing relaxation, productivity, and social engagement.

CHAPTER 12

Real-life Stories v/s Case Studies

Real-life stories and case studies play a pivotal role in shaping the career trajectory of fresh engineering graduates by providing invaluable insights and practical examples from professionals who have navigated similar paths. These narratives offer a window into the diverse challenges, successes, and learning experiences of established engineers, helping new graduates understand the nuances of their chosen field. By examining real-world experiences, graduates can gain a clearer perspective on industry expectations, career progression, and potential opportunities.

Additionally, case studies and personal stories serve as powerful tools for inspiration, offering guidance on strategic career decisions, skill development, and navigating the complexities of the engineering profession. Embracing these resources enables fresh graduates to make informed choices and set a solid foundation for their professional journey.

12.1 Difference between Real-life Story and Case Study

Real-life stories and case studies are both valuable tools for learning and professional development, but they serve different purposes and offer distinct types of insights. Here's a detailed exploration of the differences between these two approaches:

1. **Definition and Focus**

   - **Real-Life Stories**: These are personal narratives or accounts of individuals' experiences, typically focusing on their personal journeys, achievements, challenges, and lessons learned. Real-life stories often highlight individual perspectives and can be inspirational, motivational, or cautionary. They provide a human element to experiences, offering insights into personal growth and career progression.

   - **Case Studies**: These are detailed analyses of specific instances or examples of projects, problems, or scenarios within a particular context. Case studies are more structured and objective, focusing on analyzing complex situations to understand what happened, why it happened, and the outcomes. They often involve a systematic examination of processes, decisions, and results within a professional or academic setting.

2. **Purpose and Use**

   - **Real-Life Stories**: The purpose of real-life stories is often to inspire, motivate, and provide personal insights. They can illustrate how individuals have navigated their careers, overcome obstacles, and achieved success. These stories are used to connect on an emotional level, offer relatable experiences, and provide guidance based on personal experiences.

   - **Case Studies**: The purpose of case studies is to analyze and understand specific instances or problems in detail. They are used to study and learn from particular situations, decisions, and outcomes. Case studies are often employed in educational settings, business analysis, and research to derive lessons, best practices, and insights that can be applied to similar scenarios.

3. **Structure and Detail**

   - **Real-Life Stories**: These are typically more narrative and less structured. They focus on the chronological progression of events and personal reflections. The detail often includes personal anecdotes, emotions, and the broader context of the individual's experiences. Real-life stories may not follow a strict format and can vary in length and depth.

   - **Case Studies**: These are highly structured and follow a specific format. They usually include a detailed background of the situation, an analysis of the problem or challenge, the methods and processes used to address it, and the results or outcomes. Case studies often include data, charts, and a formal analysis, making them more comprehensive and systematic.

4. **Scope and Context**

   - **Real-Life Stories**: The scope is often broader and more personal, focusing on the individual's entire journey or a significant event in their life. The context may include personal, professional, and sometimes social aspects, offering a holistic view of the individual's experiences.

   - **Case Studies**: The scope is more focused and specific to particular projects, problems, or scenarios. The context is usually confined to the particular case being studied, with a focus on understanding the detailed aspects of that specific instance, often within a professional or academic framework.

5. **Learning Outcomes**

   - **Real-Life Stories**: The learning outcomes from real-life stories are often qualitative, including personal inspiration, motivation, and insight into how individual traits and experiences contribute to career success. They offer personal perspectives and emotional connections that can influence attitudes and aspirations.

   - **Case Studies**: The learning outcomes from case studies are typically more analytical and quantitative. They provide concrete lessons, best practices, and actionable insights based on detailed analysis. Case studies help in understanding complex problems, evaluating solutions, and applying these lessons to similar situations.

6. **Presentation and Format**

   - **Real-Life Stories**: These are often presented in a narrative format, such as interviews, biographies, or personal articles. They are more informal and may appear in various media, including books, blogs, or motivational speeches.

   - **Case Studies**: These are usually presented in a formal and structured format, including written reports, academic papers, or business analysis documents. They are often published in journals, case study repositories, or educational materials.

7. **Emotional and Practical Aspects**

   - **Real-Life Stories**: Emphasize the emotional journey and personal experiences of individuals. They provide inspiration and human interest, making them relatable and engaging on a personal level.

   - **Case Studies**: Focus on practical aspects, such as problem-solving techniques, decision-making processes, and outcomes. They provide a more analytical approach, offering practical lessons and insights that can be applied to similar professional scenarios.

Nut Shell: While both real-life stories and case studies offer valuable insights, they differ in their approach and focus. Real-life stories provide personal, inspirational accounts of individual experiences and journeys, whereas case studies offer a detailed, structured analysis of specific situations, problems, and outcomes. Understanding these differences allows fresh engineering graduates and professionals to leverage each tool effectively for personal development and career advancement.

12.2 Importance of Real-life Stories

The importance of real-life stories of professionals in shaping the career trajectory of fresh engineering graduates cannot be overstated. These stories offer practical insights and serve as a powerful resource for new engineers as they embark on their professional journey. Here's an in-depth exploration of why real-life stories are essential:

1. **Providing Practical Insights**

   - **Real-World Experiences**: Real-life stories illustrate how theoretical knowledge is applied in real-world scenarios. They offer concrete examples of problem-solving, project management, and decision-making, bridging the gap between academic learning and practical application.

   - **Understanding Industry Challenges**: Hearing about the challenges and obstacles faced by experienced professionals helps fresh graduates anticipate potential difficulties and prepare strategies to overcome them. This understanding can guide them in navigating their own career path more effectively.

2. **Offering Career Path Guidance**

   - **Diverse Career Paths**: Professionals often have varied career trajectories, including roles in different industries, sectors, or specializations. Real-life stories provide a range of potential career paths and illustrate how different experiences can lead to unique opportunities.

   - **Role Models and Mentorship**: By following the careers of successful engineers, fresh graduates can identify role models and mentors who have achieved what they aspire to. This can provide motivation and a clearer sense of direction for their personal career goals.

3. **Highlighting Skills and Competencies**

   - **Key Skills**: Stories from experienced professionals highlight the specific skills and competencies that have been critical to their success. Understanding which skills are most valued in the industry helps graduates focus on developing those abilities.

   - **Soft Skills**: In addition to technical skills, real-life stories often emphasize the importance of soft skills such as communication, teamwork, and leadership. Graduates can learn how these skills contribute to career advancement and how to cultivate them.

4. **Providing Inspiration and Motivation**

   - **Overcoming Challenges**: Many real-life stories include accounts of overcoming significant challenges and setbacks. These stories can be inspiring and reassuring for fresh graduates, showing that perseverance and resilience are key to career success.

- **Success Stories**: Learning about the achievements of established professionals can motivate new graduates to set ambitious goals and strive for excellence. Success stories serve as evidence that with hard work and dedication, they too can achieve their career aspirations.

5. **Offering Networking Opportunities**

   - **Industry Connections**: Real-life stories often involve networking and building relationships within the industry. Graduates can learn the importance of networking and how to leverage connections for career growth and opportunities.

   - **Professional Communities**: Stories about involvement in professional organizations and communities provide insights into how networking can lead to collaborative projects, career advancement, and ongoing professional development.

6. **Guiding Career Decision-Making**

   - **Informed Decisions**: By understanding the career decisions made by others, fresh graduates can gain insights into which choices might align with their own goals and values. This can help them make more informed decisions about job offers, specializations, and career moves.

   - **Adaptability**: Real-life stories often demonstrate the importance of adaptability and continuous learning. Graduates can learn how professionals have navigated changing industry trends and technological advancements, guiding them in their own career adaptability.

7. **Understanding Industry Expectations**

   - **Workplace Culture**: Stories from professionals provide a glimpse into workplace culture and expectations. Understanding what to expect in terms of work environment, organizational norms, and industry standards helps graduates adjust more smoothly to their new roles.

- **Performance Standards**: Learning about the performance expectations and career progression of others helps graduates understand what is required to excel in their careers and achieve their professional goals.

8. **Learning from Mistakes and Failures**

- **Lessons Learned**: Real-life stories often include accounts of mistakes and failures along with the lessons learned from them. This perspective helps graduates recognize that setbacks are a natural part of the career journey and provides strategies for handling and learning from their own challenges.

- **Avoiding Pitfalls**: Understanding common pitfalls and missteps experienced by others can help fresh graduates avoid making similar mistakes, leading to a more informed and strategic approach to their own careers.

Nut Shell: Real-life stories of professionals are an invaluable resource for fresh engineering graduates. They provide practical insights, career guidance, and inspiration while highlighting key skills, industry expectations, and the realities of the profession. By learning from the experiences of others, new graduates can make informed decisions, set realistic goals, and navigate their career paths with greater confidence and clarity.

12.3 Importance of Case Studies

Case studies are essential tools for fresh engineering graduates as they embark on their professional journey. They provide detailed, real-world examples of engineering projects, problems, and solutions, offering insights into the complexities and dynamics of the industry. Here's an in-depth exploration of the importance of case studies in shaping the career path of new engineering graduates:

1. **Understanding Practical Applications**

   - **Real-World Problems**: Case studies present detailed analyses of real-world engineering challenges, showcasing how theoretical knowledge is applied to solve practical problems. This helps fresh graduates understand how concepts learned in academia are utilized in professional settings.

   - **Problem-Solving Techniques**: By examining the approaches used to address specific issues, graduates gain insights into effective problem-solving techniques and methodologies. This knowledge is crucial for developing the ability to tackle complex problems in their own careers.

2. **Learning from Successes and Failures**

   - **Best Practices**: Case studies often highlight successful projects and the best practices that led to their success. Graduates can learn about effective strategies, innovative solutions, and key factors that contribute to achieving project goals.

   - **Lessons from Failures**: Analyzing cases where projects faced setbacks or failures provides valuable lessons. Understanding what went wrong and how challenges were addressed helps graduates learn how to avoid common pitfalls and manage risks in their own work.

3. **Exposure to Industry Standards and Practices**

   - **Industry Benchmarks**: Case studies offer insights into industry standards, benchmarks, and practices. Graduates can learn about the expectations and norms within different sectors of engineering, helping them align their skills and approaches with industry requirements.

- **Technological Integration**: Many case studies involve the application of cutting-edge technologies and methodologies. Exposure to these innovations helps graduates stay current with industry trends and prepares them to work with advanced tools and techniques.

4. **Developing Critical Thinking and Analytical Skills**

- **Analytical Approach**: Case studies encourage graduates to analyze complex situations, evaluate different solutions, and make informed decisions. This process enhances their critical thinking and analytical skills, which are essential for engineering problem-solving.

- **Decision-Making**: By reviewing how decisions were made in various scenarios, graduates learn to weigh alternatives, consider potential impacts, and make sound judgments in their own projects and roles.

5. **Gaining Insights into Project Management**

- **Project Phases**: Case studies often detail the various phases of project management, including planning, execution, and evaluation. Graduates can learn about effective project management practices and how to handle different stages of a project.

- **Resource Management**: Understanding how resources (time, budget, personnel) were managed in case studies provides insights into efficient resource allocation and management practices. This knowledge is valuable for ensuring successful project outcomes.

6. **Building Domain-Specific Knowledge**

   - **Sector-Specific Insights**: Case studies cover a wide range of engineering sectors, such as civil, mechanical, electrical, and software engineering. Graduates can explore different fields and gain domain-specific knowledge, helping them identify areas of interest and specialization.

   - **Specialized Skills**: In-depth case studies often focus on particular technologies, techniques, or methodologies. Graduates can develop specialized skills and expertise relevant to their chosen field by studying these cases.

7. **Enhancing Communication Skills**

   - **Presentation of Findings**: Many case studies involve detailed reports and presentations. Graduates can learn how to effectively communicate technical information, present findings, and articulate solutions, which are crucial skills in professional settings.

   - **Collaborative Learning**: Analyzing case studies often involves group discussions and collaborative analysis. This experience helps graduates develop teamwork and communication skills, which are essential for working in multidisciplinary teams.

8. **Guiding Career Exploration and Decision-Making**

   - **Career Pathways**: Case studies provide insights into various career pathways and roles within engineering. Graduates can explore different career options and understand the types of projects and responsibilities associated with each role.

   - **Informed Choices**: By examining case studies related to specific industries or roles, graduates can make more informed decisions about their career direction, job opportunities, and areas of interest.

9. **Encouraging Lifelong Learning**

   - **Continuous Improvement**: Case studies often highlight the ongoing nature of learning and improvement in engineering. Graduates are encouraged to adopt a mindset of continuous learning and stay updated with new developments and advancements in their field.

   - **Adaptability**: Exposure to diverse cases fosters adaptability by showing how professionals adapt to changing conditions, technologies, and project requirements. Graduates can apply this adaptability to their own evolving careers.

Nut Shell: Case studies are a crucial resource for fresh engineering graduates as they navigate their career paths. They provide practical insights, enhance problem-solving and analytical skills, and offer exposure to industry practices and project management. By learning from real-world examples, graduates can make informed career decisions, develop specialized knowledge, and build essential skills for their professional journey.

12.4 Success Story v/s Failure Story

Success stories and failure stories both offer valuable lessons and insights, but they do so in different ways. Each type of story provides distinct perspectives and learning opportunities that can significantly impact personal and professional development. Here's a comparative description of success stories versus failure stories:

1. **Definition and Focus**

   - **Success Stories**: These narratives focus on achievements and positive outcomes. They detail how individuals or organizations reached their goals, overcame obstacles, and attained success. Success stories highlight effective strategies, innovative solutions, and triumphant results.

- **Failure Stories**: These narratives concentrate on setbacks and challenges that did not lead to the desired outcomes. They describe situations where goals were not met, problems were encountered, and attempts were unsuccessful. Failure stories emphasize what went wrong, the obstacles faced, and the lessons learned from the experience.

2. **Purpose and Use**

- **Success Stories**: The primary purpose is to inspire and motivate. They demonstrate what can be achieved through perseverance, creativity, and effective strategies. Success stories are used to illustrate best practices, showcase effective methods, and provide role models for achieving similar success.

- **Failure Stories**: The primary purpose is to provide insight and learning opportunities from mistakes. They are used to analyze what went wrong, identify weaknesses, and avoid repeating the same errors. Failure stories offer valuable lessons on risk management, problem-solving, and resilience.

3. **Learning Outcomes**

- **Success Stories**: Learning outcomes often include understanding effective strategies, recognizing successful behaviors, and gaining motivation. They provide examples of how to achieve goals and what contributes to success, which can be emulated in other contexts.

- **Failure Stories**: Learning outcomes focus on understanding what went wrong, how to address similar issues, and how to improve future efforts. They offer practical lessons on handling failures, making adjustments, and developing a more resilient approach to challenges.

4. **Emotional Impact**

- **Success Stories**: Typically evoke positive emotions such as inspiration, satisfaction, and hope. They celebrate achievements and can boost morale and confidence by demonstrating that success is possible.

- **Failure Stories**: Often evoke a mix of emotions, including disappointment, frustration, and empathy. They provide a more nuanced view of challenges, highlighting the emotional toll of setbacks and the resilience required to overcome them.

5. **Presentation and Narrative**

- **Success Stories**: Usually presented with a focus on the journey, including milestones, strategies, and key factors that contributed to success. They often highlight personal or organizational strengths and accomplishments.

- **Failure Stories**: Presented with a focus on the challenges faced, mistakes made, and what was learned from the experience. They provide a detailed account of the difficulties encountered and the corrective actions taken.

6. **Practical Applications**

- **Success Stories**: Serve as benchmarks for what can be achieved. They offer practical examples of successful practices, strategies, and decision-making processes that can be applied to similar situations or projects.

- **Failure Stories**: Provide practical lessons on what to avoid and how to improve. They help identify common pitfalls and offer guidance on risk management, contingency planning, and learning from errors.

7. **Role in Professional Development**

   - **Success Stories**: Play a role in career development by setting examples of what is possible with the right approach. They can guide individuals in setting goals, adopting successful strategies, and aspiring to high achievements.

   - **Failure Stories**: Contribute to professional growth by offering insights into handling adversity and learning from mistakes. They help individuals develop resilience, adaptability, and problem-solving skills.

8. **Impact on Innovation and Improvement**

   - **Success Stories**: Often lead to the replication and scaling of successful strategies and innovations. They inspire individuals and organizations to pursue similar approaches and continue pushing boundaries.

   - **Failure Stories**: Drive innovation and improvement by highlighting areas for growth and learning. They encourage critical thinking, iterative development, and continuous improvement by reflecting on what didn't work and why.

9. **Influence on Organizational Culture**

   - **Success Stories**: Foster a culture of achievement and excellence. They celebrate accomplishments and reinforce positive behaviors and strategies within the organization.

   - **Failure Stories**: Promote a culture of learning and resilience. They encourage openness about mistakes and emphasize the importance of learning from failures and continuously improving.

*Nut Shell: **Success stories and failure stories both offer essential lessons for personal and professional development. Success stories provide inspiration and practical examples of effective strategies and achievements, while failure stories offer insights into overcoming challenges and learning from setbacks. Balancing both types of narratives allows individuals and organizations to gain a well-rounded perspective, drive continuous improvement, and foster a resilient and motivated approach to their goals.***

"Success makes us grow and failure makes us learn"

12.4.1 Lesson Learned and Best Practices

Lessons learned and best practices are two crucial concepts in personal and professional development, and they play a significant role in driving improvement and success. While they are related, they serve distinct purposes and offer different types of guidance. Here's a detailed exploration of both:

A. Lessons Learned

Definition: Lessons learned refer to the knowledge and insights gained from past experiences, particularly from successes and failures. They involve reflecting on what worked well and what didn't, and understanding how those experiences can inform future actions.

Characteristics

- **Reflective Insight**: Lessons learned come from analyzing past experiences, including both positive outcomes and mistakes. They involve a critical examination of what happened, why it happened, and what can be taken away from the experience.

- **Context-Specific**: They are often specific to particular projects, situations, or contexts. The insights gained are applicable to similar future scenarios and help in avoiding repeating the same mistakes.

- **Continuous Improvement**: Lessons learned contribute to continuous improvement by identifying areas for growth and development. They emphasize the importance of reflecting on past actions to enhance future performance.

Application:

- **Problem-Solving**: By understanding past challenges and successes, individuals and organizations can develop better problem-solving strategies and make more informed decisions.

- **Risk Management**: Lessons learned help in identifying potential risks and developing mitigation strategies based on previous experiences.

- **Process Improvement**: They contribute to refining processes and methodologies by incorporating feedback and addressing weaknesses identified in past efforts.

Examples:

- **Project Management**: After completing a project, the team might analyze what went well (e.g., effective communication) and what didn't (e.g., missed deadlines) to improve future project planning and execution.

- **Product Development**: A company might reflect on customer feedback from a product launch to understand which features were well-received and which ones need enhancement.

B. Best Practices

Definition: Best practices refer to the established methods or techniques that have been proven to be the most effective in achieving desired outcomes. They are based on experience, research, and evidence, and are considered optimal approaches for specific tasks or processes.

Characteristics:

- **Proven Effectiveness**: Best practices are typically supported by evidence or success stories demonstrating their effectiveness. They represent the most efficient and reliable ways to achieve results.

- **Standardization**: They are often standardized and adopted widely across industries or organizations to ensure consistency and quality. Best practices provide a benchmark for excellence.

- **Adaptability**: While best practices are generally effective, they should be adapted to fit specific contexts and needs. Flexibility is important to ensure that best practices remain relevant and applicable.

Application:

- **Operational Efficiency**: Implementing best practices helps in optimizing processes and operations, leading to increased efficiency and effectiveness.

- **Quality Assurance**: They contribute to maintaining high standards of quality and consistency in products, services, and processes.

- **Training and Development**: Best practices serve as a foundation for training programs, helping individuals and teams to develop skills and knowledge based on proven methods.

Examples:

- **Customer Service**: Providing timely and personalized responses to customer inquiries is a best practice in customer service that enhances customer satisfaction and loyalty.

- **Software Development**: Agile methodologies, such as Scrum or Kanban, are considered best practices in software development for managing projects efficiently and delivering high-quality products.

C. Comparative Analysis

- **Source of Knowledge**: Lessons learned come from specific past experiences and reflect on what was gained from those experiences. Best practices are derived from a combination of research, evidence, and successful applications, representing optimal approaches.

- **Purpose and Focus**: Lessons learned focus on understanding and improving based on past experiences, while best practices focus on implementing proven methods to achieve desired outcomes.

- **Application**: Lessons learned are used to adapt and refine future approaches based on past insights, whereas best practices provide a standardized approach to achieving success and maintaining high standards.

- **Impact on Improvement**: Lessons learned contribute to continuous improvement by addressing past mistakes and successes, while best practices offer a consistent framework for achieving excellence and operational efficiency.

Nut Shell: *Both lessons learned and best practices are essential for driving growth and success. Lessons learned provide valuable insights from past experiences, helping to refine and improve future actions. Best practices offer proven methods and techniques that ensure consistency, efficiency, and high standards. Together, they enable individuals and organizations to build on past experiences and apply effective strategies for ongoing success and improvement.*

Appendices

Appendix I: Interview Preparation Checklist

Interview preparation is crucial for making a strong impression and improving your chances of success. Here's a comprehensive checklist to help you prepare effectively:

1. **Research the Company**

   - **Company Overview**: Understand the company's mission, values, culture, and recent developments.

   - **Products and Services**: Familiarize yourself with the company's products, services, and key offerings.

   - **Industry Position**: Learn about the company's position in the industry, its competitors, and market trends.

   - **Key Personnel**: Know the names and roles of key executives or team members you might interact with.

2. **Understand the Role**

   - **Job Description**: Review the job description thoroughly to understand the responsibilities, required skills, and qualifications.

- **Required Skills**: Identify the key skills and competencies needed for the role and assess how your experience aligns with them.

- **Potential Challenges**: Consider the challenges or projects you might be involved in and how you can address them.

3. **Prepare Your Answers**

   - **Common Questions**: Prepare responses for common questions, such as:

     - Tell me about yourself.

     - Why do you want to work here?

     - What are your strengths and weaknesses?

     - Describe a challenging situation and how you handled it.

   - **Behavioral Questions**: Use the STAR method (Situation, Task, Action, Result) to prepare for behavioral questions.

   - **Technical Questions**: If applicable, review key technical concepts, tools, or languages relevant to the role.

4. **Prepare Questions for the Interviewer**

   - **Company Culture**: Ask about the company culture, team dynamics, and what makes the company unique.

   - **Role Expectations**: Inquire about the expectations for the role, key projects, and performance metrics.

   - **Growth Opportunities**: Ask about opportunities for professional development, career progression, and learning within the company.

5. **Practice Your Responses**

   - **Mock Interviews**: Conduct mock interviews with a friend, mentor, or career coach to practice your answers and receive feedback.

- **Recording**: Record yourself answering questions to evaluate your tone, body language, and clarity.
- **Feedback**: Seek feedback on your responses and make necessary adjustments.

6. **Review Your Resume**

- **Accuracy**: Ensure your resume is up-to-date and accurately reflects your experience, skills, and achievements.
- **Achievements**: Be ready to discuss specific accomplishments and how they relate to the role you're applying for.
- **Consistency**: Make sure there are no discrepancies between your resume and what you discuss in the interview.

7. **Prepare Your Documents**

- **Copies of Resume**: Bring multiple copies of your resume to the interview.
- **Cover Letter**: If applicable, bring a copy of your cover letter or other application materials.
- **References**: Prepare a list of professional references if requested by the interviewer.

8. **Plan Your Attire**

- **Dress Appropriately**: Choose professional attire that aligns with the company culture and the role you're applying for.
- **Grooming**: Ensure you are well-groomed and presentable.

9. **Logistics and Timing**

- **Interview Details**: Confirm the interview time, date, and location. For virtual interviews, ensure you have the correct link and platform.
- **Travel Arrangements**: If the interview is in person, plan your route and allow extra time for unforeseen delays.

- **Technical Setup**: For virtual interviews, test your internet connection, camera, and microphone.

10. Mental and Physical Preparation

- **Sleep and Nutrition**: Ensure you get a good night's sleep before the interview and eat a nutritious meal.

- **Relaxation Techniques**: Practice relaxation techniques, such as deep breathing or visualization, to manage anxiety and maintain composure.

11. Post-Interview Actions

- **Follow-Up**: Send a thank-you email within 24 hours of the interview, expressing your appreciation for the opportunity and reiterating your interest in the role.

- **Reflection**: Reflect on the interview experience to identify what went well and areas for improvement.

Nut Shell: Following this checklist, you'll be well-prepared to make a strong impression during your interview and increase your chances of securing the job.

Appendix II: Career Development Plan

A **Career Development Plan** is a strategic framework designed to guide individuals in achieving their professional goals and advancing their careers. It serves as a roadmap that outlines the steps necessary to build and enhance one's skills, acquire relevant experience, and reach career aspirations. This plan typically involves setting clear objectives, identifying opportunities for growth, and developing actionable strategies to overcome obstacles.

By providing direction and a structured approach, a Career Development Plan empowers individuals to proactively manage their career trajectory, make informed decisions, and stay aligned with their long-term professional ambitions. Whether for career advancement within an organization or for transitioning to new opportunities, a well-crafted Career Development Plan is essential for sustained success and personal fulfillment in the professional realm.

Here's a four-step process to create an effective Career Development Plan:

1. Self-Assessment

Objective: Understand your current skills, interests, values, and career aspirations.

- **Skills and Strengths**: Identify your existing skills and strengths, including technical competencies, soft skills, and areas of expertise. Reflect on past achievements and performance reviews to gain insights.

- **Interests and Values**: Determine what aspects of work are most engaging and satisfying to you. Consider your personal values and how they align with potential career paths.

- **Career Goals**: Define your short-term and long-term career objectives. Consider what positions or roles you aspire to and what kind of work environment you prefer.

- **Assessment Tools**: Use career assessment tools, personality tests, and skills inventories to gain a clearer understanding of your professional profile.

2. Research and Exploration

Objective: Gather information on career options and opportunities that align with your self-assessment.

- **Industry and Job Market**: Research industries and job roles that align with your skills and interests. Explore current job market trends, demands, and future growth prospects.

- **Educational and Training Requirements**: Identify any additional education, certifications, or training needed to qualify for your desired roles or to advance in your chosen field.

- **Company Research**: Investigate companies or organizations where you might want to work. Look into their culture, values, and career development opportunities.

- **Networking**: Connect with professionals in your field of interest to gain insights, advice, and firsthand experiences. Attend industry events, join professional associations, and use platforms like LinkedIn for networking.

3. Goal Setting and Planning

Objective: Develop a clear and actionable plan to achieve your career goals.

- **Define Objectives**: Set specific, measurable, achievable, relevant, and time-bound (SMART) goals for your career. Break down long-term goals into manageable short-term objectives.

- **Action Steps**: Outline the steps needed to reach each goal. This may include acquiring new skills, gaining relevant experience, or pursuing additional education.

- **Timeline**: Establish a timeline for achieving your goals. Create milestones to track progress and adjust your plan as needed.

- **Resources and Support**: Identify resources and support systems, such as mentors, training programs, or career coaches that can assist you in reaching your goals.

4. Implementation and Evaluation

Objective: Put your plan into action and regularly review your progress to ensure you stay on track.

- **Execute Plan**: Begin taking the necessary actions outlined in your plan. Apply for relevant positions, enroll in courses, or seek out new projects that align with your goals.

- **Monitor Progress**: Regularly review your progress towards your goals. Assess what is working well and what may need adjustment.

- **Adapt and Revise**: Be flexible and willing to adjust your plan based on new opportunities, changes in your interests, or unexpected challenges.

- **Feedback and Reflection**: Seek feedback from mentors, supervisors, or peers. Reflect on your achievements and areas for improvement to continually refine your career development plan.

Nut Shell: Following these four steps—self-assessment, research and exploration, goal setting and planning, and implementation and evaluation—you can create a comprehensive Career Development Plan that guides you towards achieving your professional aspirations and advancing your career effectively.

TEMPLATE

Name: _______________________   Date: ____________

This career development plan template can be used as a tool to guide your thought process and map your progress over a chosen period. Completion of this plan will follow a **4 step process.** Each step will address specific career related questions:

1. What skills do you already possess? (Where are you now?)

2. What do you want for your career? (Where do you want to go?)

3. How might you get there? (What steps do you need to take to get there?)

4. Who can help? (What resources might I use?)

5. You can complete it at your leisure, print and save a copy for your personal use.

1. **Where are you now?**

This process starts with taking a good look at where you are currently at. What are your skills, talents and interests? What are your values – do you like to lead, work with people or alone with data or text? Do you like working face to face with people or prefer independent work? Do you like to work inside or outside? Do you like working to deadlines? Which teams do you like working on, quiet or loud, small or large?

Answering the questions below will assist you in determining your starting point. There are several tools & resources that can assist you with this. Bottom of Form

Question	Notes.
Where am I now in regards to my career?	
What is my view of current situation?	
What have been my experiences to date?	
What do I enjoy most?	
What skills come to me naturally?	
What do I think my strengths/assets are? (Skills, knowledge, talents, interests)?	
What are some things people ask me to help with?	
What do I do well?	
What appeals to me?	
What are my values? (work/life)	
Do I like to lead, work with people as a team or work alone (with data or text)?	
Do I like working face to face with customers or back office work?	
How do I feel when I think about my ideal job (excited, motivated, fear)?	
Is there anything getting in my way of achieving what I want?	

2. **Where do you want to go?**

What you'll do next is:

- Consider your career goals

- Explore your career options.

- Develop concise written statements related to your goals and add them to the table below.

Knowing where you want to go makes the next steps in determining your future career move much easier.

Question	Notes
What does my ideal job look like?	
If I could do any job in the world what might it be and why?	
What are my goals (short/long term)?	
What energizes me?	
Where do I want to be (in 1 yr, in 5 yrs)	
Are there any specific challenges I want to face?	
Why is this important to me?	
What do I want to see/get/do more of?	
What do I want to see/get/do less of?	
What is my preferred balance between work and my personal life?	

Question	Notes
Who else does this affect?	
What normally gets in the way of achieving my goals?	
What kind of work environment suits me best?	
Do I feel I have a calling in life?	

3. How might I get there?

By answering questions 1 & 2, you should now have a clearer idea of what you want & where you want to go. The next step is figuring out how you might get there. What do you need to do? Below are some questions you may consider in deciding what resources may be useful.

Question	Notes
How can I prepare myself and my environment to achieve my goals?	
What resources and tools/resources do I need?	
What steps do I need to take to get from where I am now to where I want to be?	
What new skills, knowledge do I need to possess?	
What new skills do I want to learn?	
What existing skills do I need to develop?	

Question	Notes
How can I commit to achieving my goals?	
What barriers do I need to remove to make this happen?	
How will I know I have been successful?	

4. Who can help (resources)?

Knowing who can assist you and what resources you need to achieve your career goals can greatly assist you in staying focused on your goals.

Question	Notes
What new relationships might I build help me attain my career goals?	
Who do I know who can support me attain my career goals?	
Who have I lost touch with who might be able to support me in my career goals?	
What role can my friends and family take in encouraging me to stay focused?	
What role can my unit head/manager play in supporting my career aspirations?	
What communities of practice currently exist that I can tap into?	

Setting Goals

Now that you have a clearer picture of where you are now and where you want to go, it is now time to set some goals for yourself and create your Career Development Plan – goal summary.

When deciding on your career development goals it is imperative that you set yourself up for success. Using the SMART goal setting process is a good way to achieve this.

SMART

Specific (so you know exactly what you are trying to achieve)

Measurable (so you know when you have achieved it!)

Action-oriented (so you can DO something about it!)

Realistic (so it IS achievable) and

Time-Bound (has a deadline)

Focusing on the Outcome:

1. What is it that you REALLY want to achieve? …
2. What is the SPECIFIC OUTCOME that you are looking for?
3. How will you know you have achieved it?

Personal Career Plan – Goal Summary

Once you have your goals in a SMART format – add them to the Personal Career Plan – Goal Summary below:

Goal	Specific knowledge, skills achieved	How will I achieve the goal?	What resources do I need (people, material etc.)	By when (timeline)	Success criteria – how will I know I have been successful?

"Life without goal is useless".

— Swami Vivekananda

Appendix III: Sample Resume for Fresh Graduate

[Your Name]

[Your Address]

[City, State, ZIP Code]

[Email Address] | [Phone Number] | LinkedIn: [Your LinkedIn URL]

Objective

A passionate and results-oriented [Engineering Discipline] graduate with strong knowledge of [relevant skills, e.g., CAD, MATLAB, programming languages]. Seeking to contribute to innovative projects and further develop my technical and problem-solving skills in a [Job Title] role at [Company Name].

Education

[Degree Name] – [Your Specialization]

[University Name], [City, State]

[Month/Year of Graduation]

CGPA: [Your CGPA, if strong]

Skills

- **Technical Skills**: [List relevant technical skills, such as AutoCAD, SolidWorks, MATLAB, Python, C++, etc.]
- **Software Proficiency**: [Software tools used in engineering work, such as MS Excel, MS Project, etc.]

- **Key Competencies**: Analytical thinking, teamwork, problem-solving, project management

Academic Projects

[Project Title]

[Brief one-line description of the project]

- Key Achievements: [Describe key outcomes or solutions developed]
- Technologies/Tools Used: [List tools or software used]

[Project Title]

[Brief one-line description of the project]

- Key Achievements: [Describe key outcomes or solutions developed]
- Technologies/Tools Used: [List tools or software used]

Internship Experience

Intern, [Company Name]

[City, State] | [Start Date – End Date]

- Assisted in [describe tasks, e.g., research, simulations, designing prototypes].
- Worked on [mention specific tools or systems].
- Gained hands-on experience in [mention key learning points].

Certifications & Training

- **Certification Name**, [Issuing Organization] – [Month/Year]

- **Training Program**: [Course Name], [Institution], [Month/Year]

Extracurricular Activities

- Member of [Engineering Club, University Society, etc.]
- Volunteered in [mention any volunteer work related to engineering, if any]

References

Available upon request.

Sample Resume of Experienced Professional

[Your Name]

[Your Address]

[City, State, ZIP Code]

[Email Address] | [Phone Number] | LinkedIn: [Your LinkedIn URL]

Professional Summary

Accomplished [Your Specialization] Engineer with [X years] of experience in [specific industry or field]. Proven track record in delivering projects on time and within budget, with expertise in [mention areas of expertise, e.g., design engineering, process optimization, project management]. Skilled in utilizing [relevant tools, software] to enhance operations and reduce costs. Seeking to leverage my experience in [mention specific role or task, e.g., leading projects, optimizing processes] in the [Job Title] position at [Company Name].

Professional Experience

[Job Title]

[Company Name], [City, State]

[Start Date] – Present

- Managed [mention key responsibilities, such as designing systems, optimizing processes, project leadership].
- Key Achievements: [Highlight achievements such as cost savings, design improvements, project delivery].

- Led cross-functional teams in [mention key activities or projects].
- Technologies/Tools Used: [List software or technologies used]

[Job Title]

[Previous Company Name], [City, State]

[Start Date] – [End Date]

- Spearheaded [mention specific projects or tasks], resulting in [mention key outcomes].
- Implemented [mention specific techniques or improvements] to [describe impact].
- Collaborated with [mention teams or departments] to achieve [key accomplishments].

Education

[Degree Name] – [Your Specialization]

[University Name], [City, State]

[Month/Year of Graduation]

CGPA: [Your CGPA, if applicable]

Skills

- **Technical Skills**: [List relevant technical skills]
- **Software Proficiency**: [Engineering software or tools like AutoCAD, MATLAB, etc.]
- **Key Competencies**: Leadership, teamwork, project management, analytical thinking

Key Projects

[Project Title]

[Brief one-line description of the project]

- Led [mention specific tasks or responsibility], resulting in [key achievement].
- Technologies/Tools Used: [List tools or software used]

[Project Title]

[Brief one-line description of the project]

- Delivered [mention results or outcomes of the project].
- Technologies/Tools Used: [List tools or software used]

Certifications & Training

- **Certification Name**, [Issuing Organization] – [Month/Year]
- **Professional Development Course**: [Course Name], [Institution], [Month/Year]

Professional Affiliations

- Member of [Professional Organization], [Years Active]
- Participated in [Conferences, Seminars, etc.]

References

Available upon request.

Appendix IV: Covering Letter Templates for Fresh Graduate

[Your Name]

[Your Address]

[City, State, ZIP Code]

[Email Address]

[Phone Number]

[Date]

Hiring Manager's Name

[Company Name]

[Company Address]

[City, State, ZIP Code]

Dear [Hiring Manager's Name],

I am writing to express my interest in the [Job Title] position at [Company Name] as advertised on [where you found the job posting]. As a recent graduate in [Your Degree] from [Your University], I am eager to apply my academic background, technical skills, and passion for engineering to contribute to your innovative projects and technical challenges.

During my academic journey, I gained hands-on experience through various coursework, projects, and internships. I developed a strong foundation in [mention any key skills or software related to the job, e.g., CAD, MATLAB, programming languages, etc.]. Additionally, my final year project on [briefly describe your project] allowed me to apply problem-solving skills and collaborate with team members to achieve practical outcomes.

I am particularly excited about the opportunity to work at [Company Name] because of your commitment to [mention a specific aspect of the company that attracts you, such as innovation, sustainability, or a particular technology they use]. I am confident that my enthusiasm, quick learning ability, and teamwork skills will make a valuable contribution to your team.

I have attached my resume for your consideration. I would welcome the chance to discuss how my academic background and skills align with the needs of your team. Thank you for your time and consideration. I look forward to the possibility of contributing to your company.

Sincerely,

[Your Name]

Covering Letter Templates for Experienced Professional

[Your Name]

[Your Address]

[City, State, ZIP Code]

[Email Address]

[Phone Number]

[Date]

Hiring Manager's Name

[Company Name]

[Company Address]

[City, State, ZIP Code]

Dear [Hiring Manager's Name],

I am writing to apply for the [Job Title] position at [Company Name], as advertised on [where you found the job posting]. With [X] years of experience in [specific engineering field, e.g., mechanical, electrical, civil] engineering, I have honed my skills in [mention key technical skills or expertise], and I am excited to contribute to [Company Name] with my strong background in [specific skill or industry].

In my previous role at [Your Previous Company], I successfully led projects that [briefly mention a major achievement, e.g., reduced production time, increased efficiency, saved costs]. I have experience working with cross-functional teams, utilizing tools such as [mention relevant tools, software, or methodologies], and delivering results under tight deadlines. One notable accomplishment was [highlight a key achievement or project that is relevant to the job you're applying for].

I am particularly impressed with [Company Name]'s focus on [mention something specific about the company's work, goals, or projects]. I believe my experience in [specific area of expertise] and my ability to [mention a relevant skill or strength] align well with the goals of your team.

I have attached my resume for your review. I look forward to the opportunity to discuss how my background, experience, and technical skills can contribute to [Company Name]'s continued success. Thank you for considering my application.

Sincerely,

[Your Name]

About the Author

Dr. D. N. Vyas is a distinguished academic and scholar with a remarkable career in the field of mathematics and engineering education. A Gold Medalist in M. Sc. (Mathematics), Dr. Vyas has been recognized with the prestigious Jawahar Lal Nehru Memorial Fund award for his exceptional academic achievements. He earned his PhD from J. N. Vyas University, Jodhpur, India, where his research contributions have been published in both national and international journals, reflecting his deep expertise and commitment to advancing mathematical knowledge.

Dr. Vyas is a prominent researcher in the field of fractional calculus and its applications, with a particular focus on Dirichlet averages. His research delves into the theoretical underpinnings of fractional calculus, exploring how these advanced mathematical concepts can be applied to solve complex problems in various fields. By bridging the gap between abstract theory and practical applications, his research contributes significantly to advancing the mathematical tools available for tackling real-world challenges.

With over 32 years of experience in teaching engineering graduates and extensive administrative roles, Dr. Vyas has been a pivotal figure in shaping the educational landscape of M. L. V. Textile & Engineering College, Bhilwara. His extensive experience has equipped him with a profound understanding of the academic and professional needs of engineering students.

In addition to his teaching and research contributions, Dr. Vyas is the author of eight popular books in Mathematics and Statistics. These works have served as essential resources for students, showcasing his dedication to fostering a deeper understanding of these critical disciplines.

Dr. Vyas's career reflects a blend of academic excellence, practical experience, and a commitment to education, making him a highly respected figure in his field.

Suraj Kumar Gupta is a young and dynamic scholar in the field of mechanical engineering, holding a degree from the prestigious Indian Institute of Technology (IIT) Delhi. As an Assistant Professor in the Mechanical Engineering Department, Gupta brings a wealth of knowledge and experience to his role, with over five years of dedicated teaching experience. His expertise is particularly notable in the Outcome Based Education (OBE) system, a pedagogical framework designed to enhance educational effectiveness by focusing on measurable outcomes and continuous improvement.

Gupta's teaching interests focus on key areas of Mechanical Engineering, including Computer-Aided Design (CAD), Additive Manufacturing, and Mechanical Design. His expertise in CAD enables students to understand complex design processes and tools crucial for modern engineering. In Mechanical Design, he shares insights into designing effective mechanical systems. Additionally, his emphasis on Additive Manufacturing reflects a forward-thinking approach to cutting-edge fabrication techniques. With proficiency in Finite Element Analysis (FEA), he equips students with skills for analyzing and optimizing mechanical components and systems.

In addition to his teaching and research, Gupta is deeply invested in career guidance, helping students navigate their professional paths. His career guidance efforts include offering advice on career planning, industry trends, and opportunities within the Mechanical Engineering field. By providing mentorship and support, he aims to equip students with the tools and insights needed to make informed decisions about their careers and to achieve their professional goals.

With a keen interest in teaching pedagogy, Gupta is dedicated to developing effective instructional strategies that engage students and foster deep learning. His commitment to the OBE system underscores his drive to ensure that educational practices are aligned with real-world engineering requirements, preparing students for successful careers in the field.

Source: Shiksha

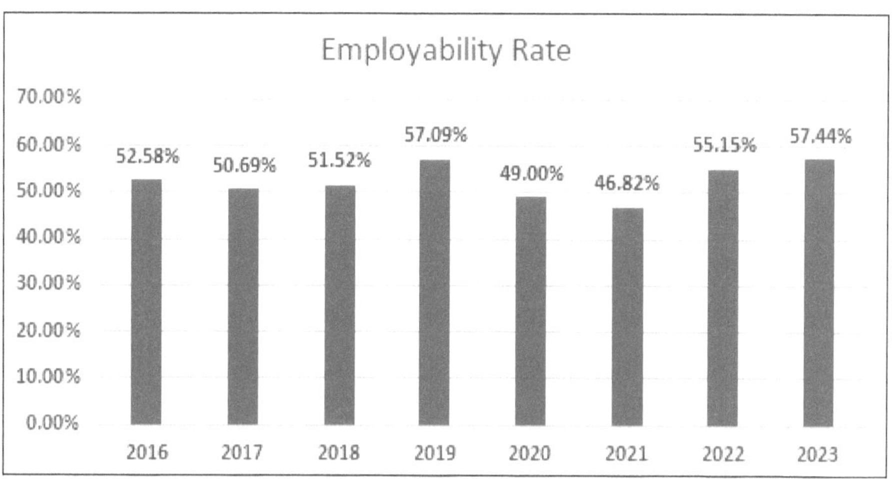

- In 2024, employability among Indian engineering graduates was about 64 percent, an increase from the 57 percent in 2023. The overall employability of the youth in the country was about 52.25 percent in 2024. There has been a significant jump in percentage employability of engineering graduate in 2024 from a consistent rate across last 10 years.

- Nearly 1.5 Million engineering graduates in a variety of disciplines pass out every year through 3300 engineering Institutions across the country.

- A few years ago, a McKinsey report said just a quarter of engineers NSE -2.55 % in India were actually employable. Of late, some other studies put it at less than 20%.

- Recently, a survey by employability assessment firm Aspiring Minds said 95% of Indian engineers can't code.

- Though graduates from India's premiere engineering colleges such as the IITs are still in demand, it is the thousands of other engineering colleges and ITIs that churn out millions of graduates every year whose employability is questionable.

- Prime Minister Narendra Modi's dream project of 'Make in India' is hobbled by lack of employable graduates. The project aspires to increase manufacturing capacity in India and generate 100 million jobs by 2022. That's too difficult with the kind of graduates our engineering colleges churn out.

- India's much-touted demographic dividend, which can help India compete with China in manufacturing in near future, will turn into a burden if employability of graduates does not go up.

- The **jobs sector** is already in stress. If the quality of skilled labour does not improve, **latest technology** that requires updated learning would cause a huge unemployment crisis.

- **Source: www.m.economicstimes.com**